Sociolinguistic Theory

B

Language in Society

GENERAL EDITOR
Peter Trudgill, Professor in the Department of Language and Linguistics, University of Lausanne.

ADVISORY EDITORS
Ralph Fasold, Professor of Linguistics, Georgetown University.
William Labov, Professor of Linguistics, University of Pennsylvania.

Sociolinguistic Theory

Linguistic Variation and its Social Significance

J. K. Chambers
University of Toronto

BLACKWELL
Oxford UK & Cambridge USA

First published 1995

Reprinted 1996 (twice), 1997 (twice)

Blackwell Publishers Inc
350 Main Street
Malden, Massachusetts 02148, USA

Blackwell Publishers Ltd
108 Cowley Road
Oxford OX4 1JF, UK

Library of Congress Cataloging in Publication Data
Chambers, J. K.
Sociolinguistic theory : linguistic variation and its social
significance / J. K. Chambers.
p.   cm. - (Language in society)
Includes bibliographical references and index.
ISBN 0–631–18325–6 — ISBN 0–631–18326–4 (pbk.)
1. Sociolinguistics. I. Title. II. Series : Language in society
(Oxford, England)
P40.C455   1995   94-12848
306.4'4—dc20   CIP

British Library Cataloguing in Publication Data
A CIP catalogue record for this book is available from the British Library

Typeset in 10.5 x 12 pt Ehrhardt
by Graphicraft Typesetters Ltd, Hong Kong
Printed and bound in Great Britain by Athenæum Press Ltd, Gateshead, Tyne & Wear

This book is printed on acid-free paper

For my parents, Connie and Royce,
on their sixty-fifth anniversary

Contents

List of Figures

List of Tables

Series Editor's Preface

During the last thirty years, inspired by the pioneering research of William Labov, work in secular linguistics and variation theory – the most central and theoretically important area of sociolinguistics – has made enormous progress. In particular, it has furthered our understanding of the nature of variation in language, and added numerous insights into the study of linguistic change through empirical studies of language in its social context. Established scholars in this field have always been able to keep in touch with the latest developments through journal papers, notably those in *Language Variation and Change*, and through attendance at conferences, especially the North American *New Ways of Analyzing Variation* series, now in its twenty-third year. It has been a source of some frustration to teachers and students, however, that there has until now been no single book which could be used to introduce beginners to the subject as a whole. This long period of frustration is now over. The present volume distils the most important descriptive and theoretical findings concerning linguistic variation to date from around the world, and synthesizes them into a very exciting whole. Although very accessible to beginning students, this book is no simple, uncritical rehearsal of the work of others. Professor Chambers is himself one of the foremost scholars in the world in the field of variation studies and, in addition to considerable amounts of data from his own studies, he provides here highly original and insightful interpretations, suggestions and proposals that all interested researchers will be concerned to take note of. In particular, his discussion in the final chapter of the origins and functions of linguistic variation is one of the most challenging and exciting pieces of work ever to emerge from the field of sociolinguistics. Linguistic variation theory has, in these pages, truly come of age.

Peter Trudgill

Preface

Data without generalization is just gossip.

Robert Pirsig (1991: 55)

The correlation of dependent linguistic variables with independent social variables, the subject matter of this book, has been the heart of sociolinguistics since its inception more than three decades ago. By a strange quirk, there has never before been a book-length appraisal of the way we have treated that covariation – about our terms of reference, our strengths and omissions, our results. Or perhaps it is not so strange. Sociolinguistics is young even compared to the other social sciences, and our emphasis, quite properly, has been on amassing case studies, refining our methods, seeking new evidence, testing recent results, and defining our boundaries.

The general books about sociolinguistics, apart from Trudgill's non-technical introduction (1983a), have been mainly textbooks (for instance, Fasold 1990, Holmes 1992, Wardhaugh 1992) and they have followed a tradition of unknown origin whereby covariation gets allotted exactly one chapter, the same as diglossia, ethnography and ethnomethodology, dialect geography, and any number of other topics. Instead of the heart of the matter, covariation has been treated as one appendage among many.

It is a situation that, as a lecturer in courses using those books, I frequently deplored. As an author, I must say that I have come to revel in it. Some of the finest accomplishments in modern linguistics have come from the study of covariation, and in writing this first critical synthesis of it I had all of them to choose from. I would like to think that the most striking, most enlightening, most crucial research of the three decades (and beyond) has found its proper place in the pages of this book. Of course there is already too much of it for one person to know, too much for one synthesis of manageable length. Failing thoroughness in that sense I have tried to attain it in another, by identifying key issues and marshalling the best research I knew about on each of them.

I have tried to make the material in this book accessible to readers who know no more than the rudiments of linguistic analysis. The book's obvious classroom use is in a second-level course after a general introduction along the lines of the textbooks mentioned above, but it could also be used at the first level if the instructor preferred a concentration on linguistic variation. Perhaps there it would need to be used judiciously. I have not avoided controversies when they arise either in sociolinguistics or in linguistic theory and history. The book was not written solely for students, and I hope it will find some readers curious about the intricate interrelationships of language and society.

More than once it came to my mind while writing the book that the lecture hall and the students who filled it have served me well. My own researches have taken me into the middle of several issues and forced me to sort out their critical dimensions. Those issues and some of my own contributions to them are represented in this book. But there is so much else, and it was my lecture notes and seminar hand-outs that gave me a semi-draft, a chronicle of my orientation on many issues. In my urban dialectology seminar at the University of Toronto, the students' research projects stretched my mind as well as my interests. After several students had stretched me in the same direction I sometimes began to think that I was not only keeping up but running ahead. The breadth of this book is partly thanks to those students.

I am also pleased to thank Philip Carpenter, Paul Kerswill, William Labov and Peter Trudgill for their comments on drafts of some chapters. Alison Truefitt, the copy editor, made the style consistent and often made my meaning clearer. Gloria Cernivivo provided a cheerful conduit for the cover art.

In my reading for this book I came upon Haver C. Currie's "Projection of socio-linguistics" (1952), the very first article to speak of "sociolinguistics" by that name. The article has not aged very well (for reasons discussed in 1.2.2.1), but I could not help but admire Currie's optimism that the newly named field would thrive. He wrote (1952: 28):

> The present purpose is to suggest, by the citing of selected and salient studies, that social functions and significations of speech factors offer a prolific field for research. It is the intention in this connection to project, partly by means of identification, a field that may well be given the attentions of consciously directed research. This field is here designated *socio-linguistics*. Attention will be called to certain relevant research done or under way. Possibilities for further socio-linguistic research are, in fact, beyond estimation.

Currie guessed right about the possibilities, even in the absence of any genuine examples of how sociolinguistics would work. It took a few years more for the studies to begin accumulating, but he rightly described their potential as "beyond estimation."

Of course we are still learning, in Weinreich, Labov and Herzog's resonant phrase (1968: 100), "to see language . . . as an object possessing orderly heterogeneity." Looking at language that way is, as I show in §1.3 below, a revolutionary departure from the venerable traditions of language study. This book should make it abundantly clear – not only from the accomplishments it describes but also from the number of open questions, questionable answers, and unasked questions that remain – that the possibilities for sociolinguistic research, no less now than in 1952, are beyond estimation.

Jack Chambers
Toronto, Canada

Acknowledgements

The author and publishers wish to thank the following for permission to use copyright material: Edward Arnold (Publishers) Ltd for adapted figure 2.11 and table 2.11 from Ellen Douglas-Cowie, 'Linguistic code-switching in a Northern Irish village: Social interaction and social ambition'; figure 4.2 from Euan Reid, 'Social and stylistic variation in the speech of children: some evidence from Edinburgh'; and figure 3.7 from James and Lesley Milroy, 'Belfast: change and variation in an urban vernacular' in Peter Trudgill, ed., *Sociolinguistic Patterns in British English*, 1978; John Benjamins Publishing Company for adapted figure 4.5 from David Sankoff et al., 'Montreal French: language, class and idealogy' in Ralph Fasold and Deborah Schiffrin, eds., *Language Change and Variation*, 1989; figure 2.3 from Henrietta Hung, 'Comparative sociolinguistics of (aw)-Fronting' in Sandra Clarke, ed., *Focus on Canadian English*, 1993; and figure 4.9 from Peter Trudgill, 'Norwich revisited; recent linguistic changes in an English urban dialect' in *English World-Wide*, 9:33–49, 1988; Blackwell Publishers for adapted table 4.2 from Peter Trudgill, *Dialects in Contact*, 1986; tables 5.1, 5.2 from Peter Trudgill, *On Dialect: Social and Geographic Factors*, 1983; table 4.1 from Suzanne Romaine, *The Language of Children and Adolescents*, 1984; and figure 1.1 from Ronald Wardhaugh, *An Introduction to Sociolinguistics*, 2nd ed., 1992; Bernard Blishen for adapted table 2.2 from *Canadian Society: Sociological Perspectives*, 1971; Cambridge University Press for adapted figures 2.1, 3.1 and table 2.3 from Peter Trudgill, *The Social Differentiation of English in Norwich*, 1974; figure 3.2 from Barbara M. Horvath, *Variation in Australian English: The Sociolects of Sydney*, 1985; figure 4.1 from Hede Helfrich, 'Age markers in speech' in Scherer and Giles, eds., *Social Markers in Speech*, 1979; figure 4.4 from Penelope Eckert, 'Adolescent social structure and the spread of linguistic change,' *Language in Society*, 17, 1988; table 3.3 from Abu-Haider, 'Are Iraqi women more prestige concious than men? Sex differention in Baghdadi Arabic,' *Language in Society*, 18, 1989; figure 2.7 from Walter F. Edwards, 'Sociolinguistic behavior in a Detroit inner city black neighborhood,' *Language in Society*, 21, 1992; and figure 2.6 and tables 2.6, 2.9 from Jenny Cheshire, *Variation in an English Dialect: A Sociolinguistic Study*, 1982; Center for Applied Linguistics for adapted figures 3.3, 3.4, 3.5, 3.6 and table 3.1 from Walter A. Wolfram, *A Sociolinguistic Description of Detroit Negro Speech*, 1969; Sandra Clarke for adapted table 2.5 from 'Dialect mixing and linguistic variation in a non-overtly stratified society,' *Variation in Language*, NWAV-XV at Stanford, eds., Denning et al., 1987; Georgetown University Press for adapted table 4.5 from Gillian Sankoff and Pierette Thibault, 'Above and Beyond Phonology in Variable Rules' in Charles-James, N. Bailey and Roger W. Shuy, eds., *New Ways of Analyzing Variation in English*, 1973; figure 2.10 from Crawford Feagin, *Variation and Change in Alabama English*, 1979; and figure 4.10 from Henrietta Cedergren, 'The spread of language change: verifying inferences of linguistics diffusion' in P. H. Lowenberg, ed., *Language Spread and Language Policy: Issues, Implications and Case Studies*, Georgetown University Round Table on Languages and Linguistics, 1987; Niloofar Haeri for adapted figure 3.8 from 'Male/female differences in speech: an alternative interpretation,' in *Variation in Language*, NWAV-XV at Stanford, ed. Denning et al., Stanford; Heinle and Heinle Publishers for adapted table 3.2 from Patricia C. Nichols, 'Linguistic options and choices for Black women in the rural South,' in Thorne et al., eds., *Language, Gender and Society*, 1983; Paul Kerswill for adapted figure 2.2 from Paul Kerswill and Ann Williams, 'Some principles of dialect contact: evidence from the New Town of Milton Keynes,' *Working Papers*, 1992, Occasional Papers in General and Applied Linguistics, Department of Linguistic Science, University of Reading; Linguistic Society of America for adapted figure 4.3 from J. K. Chambers, 'Dialect acquisition,' *Language*, 68, 1992; University of Pennsylvania Press for adapted table 2.10 from William Labov, *Language in the Inner City: Studies in the Black English Vernacular*, 1972; Christine Zeller for adapted figure 4.8 from 'The investigation of a sound change in progress: /ae/ to /e/ in Midwestern American English,' presented at NWAV-XXII University of Ottawa.

Every effort has been made to trace all the copyright holders, but if any have been inadvertently overlooked the publishers well be pleased to make the necessary arrangement at the first opportunity.

1

Correlations

It is precisely because language is as strictly socialized a type of behavior as anything else in culture and yet betrays in its outlines such regularities as only the natural scientist is in the habit of formulating, that linguistics is of strategic importance for the methodology of social science. Behind the apparent lawlessness of social phenomena there is a regularity of configuration and tendency which is just as real as the regularity of physical processes in a mechanical world ... Language is primarily a cultural or social product and must be understood as such ... It is peculiarly important that linguists, who are often accused, and accused justly, of failure to look beyond the pretty patterns of their subject matter, should become aware of what their science may mean for the interpretation of human conduct in general.

Edward Sapir (1929)

This book is about language variation and its social significance. By now, the research literature on this topic, from the first breakthroughs more than 30 years ago to the most recent refinements, amount to a formidable accumulation. They include, by any reasonable yardstick, some of the most incisive discoveries in the long history of humanity's inquiries into the structure and function of language. My purpose is to make a critical synthesis of as much of that research, great and small, as I can handle within the covers of one book.

Looked at that way, my topic perhaps looks grand. But there is a sense in which it is narrow. The social significance of language variation is only one aspect of the discipline of sociolinguistics, broadly conceived. I will be dealing only with what might be called urban dialectology, that is, with accent or dialect as an emblem of an individual's class, sex, age, ethnicity, ambition, or some other social attribute. When we consider the enormous number of uses that language serves in our daily interactions with other people, its social significance does really not cover much of the territory. In §1.1 below, I sketch the various social uses of language in order to put into a larger perspective the area to be covered in detail in this book.

The rest of this chapter is also devoted to providing perspectives on the analyses that follow. In §1.2, I explore the main theoretical construct of sociolinguistics, the linguistic variable, and look at its historical development, methodological premises, and theoretical basis. In §1.3 I compare and contrast categorical theories, especially Chomskyan linguistics, with sociolinguistics, a variationist theory, emphasizing the essential difference between them.

1.1   The Domain of Sociolinguistics

Sociolinguistics, as the study of the social uses of language, encompasses a multitude of possible inquiries. Ordinarily, we simply take for granted the numerous ways we use language in our social interactions because they are so deeply embedded in our daily affairs. It is sometimes hard for people to understand that a brief telephone conversation could possibly be of interest as an object of serious linguistic study. It is also hard for them to understand how much we reveal about ourselves – our backgrounds, our predilections, our characters – in the simplest verbal exchange.

One common conceit used by authors trying to get people to take a fresh look at mundane activities is to ask them to put themselves in the place of an extraterrestrial visitor who would view all of our customs and actions, even the most trivial-seeming, as fresh, fascinating and exotic. How would this Martian (or whatever) view our linguistic interactions? How many sub-systems would a social scientist E. T. tease out of the levels of interaction in a single speech event?

In reality, we do not need to indulge in flights of fancy about extraterrestrials. All that is really needed is a degree of objectivity – the willingness to step back and reflect upon the multitude of inferences individuals make when they are engaged in a conversation. The best kind of conversational exchange for reflecting upon is one in which the information is almost exclusively linguistic, as when you overhear a conversation between strangers sitting behind you in a bus or when you receive a telephone call from a total stranger. On those occasions, you begin the exchange with the minimum of knowledge and presupposition. And yet, after hearing only a few sentences, you find yourself in possession of a great deal of information of various kinds about people whom you have never seen.

The kinds of inferences you tacitly make fit roughly into five general categories. In the following sections I call them personal, stylistic, social, sociocultural and sociological.

1.1.1   Personal characteristics

One level of information is **personal**. You immediately make observations about the *voice quality* of the individuals you are listening to. Is the voice high-pitched or low? Nasal or open? Does the pitch move up and down the scale or is it relatively monotonal? Does the speaker lisp?

Like all the other linguistic observations we make, even those at much more sophisticated levels, these take place spontaneously, with very little consciousness on our part. And they are very often accompanied by spontaneous judgements, partly culture-driven and partly experience-driven. One obvious one is that monotonal speech is monotonous. Indeed, those two words – monotonal and monotonous – are etymologically almost identical as adjectives derived (by different Latinate suffixes -*al* and -*ous*) from a complex noun meaning "one tone."

Also at the personal level are inferences about the *speaking ability* of the individuals you are listening to. Is their speech fluent or hesitant? Is it articulate or vague? These are among the simplest, most superficial observations we make but, even at this level, the observations interact to give strong (though not necessarily accurate) impressions of character. A speaker who is fluent but vague will seem to us to be evasive, perhaps deceitful, and one who is articulate but hesitant will seem pensive and thoughtful. And there are of course many other possible judgements at this level. Is the person's vocabulary current and slang-inflected or ornate and careful?

Johnstone (1991) shows that even in circumstances in which people are expected – actually required – to adopt a linguistically neutral, self-effacing manner, they cannot resist revealing their personal styles. She studied interviewers in the Texas Telephone Poll, a standardized, state-wide survey in which the interviewers speak to individuals whose numbers are dialed at random and lead them through a series of questions for which both the order and the wording is fixed. Even though the interviewers are trained and their interviews are supervised, they "make changes in the scripted introduction and add unscripted answer-acknowledgements and commentary throughout the interviews, the effect of which is to point up their identities as individuals rather than merely fillers of the interviewer role" (1991: 557). Anyone who has answered one of these seemingly interminable polls is well aware that the hints of personality revealed by the interviewer are among the few incentives to complete it, and Johnstone sees that as the interviewers' main motivation in cajoling the respondent to stick with it.

Johnstone also notes, as have other discourse analysts, that conversation is always a kind of personal expression, a form of verbal art less self-conscious than story-telling or joking but nevertheless a performance in its own right. This comes through very clearly in certain circumstances, as

Tannen (1984) shows in her analysis of Thanksgiving dinner conversation or Johnstone (1990) shows in her analysis of autobiographical interviews. But in analyzing telephone pollsters, Johnstone demonstrates that people are "performing talk" even when the situation inveighs against it.

Observations like these at the personal linguistic level have attracted relatively little serious linguistic study. Traditionally, they were considered too idiosyncratic or individualistic for framing hypotheses about language in general. With the insurgence of studies of the social use of language, including sociolinguistics (as discussed in §1.3 below), research into personal characteristics has increased.

Still, it is probably true that most personal linguistic characteristics offer little of interest to sociolinguists. If some aspect of a person's voice quality comes to be thought of as pathological, as are some kinds of lisp or stuttering, that person might be referred to a speech therapist, and speech therapists naturally classify the kinds of conditions referred to them in order to develop treatments for them, but their studies are outside the domain of sociolinguistics. By the same token, if some aspect of the person's speaking ability is deemed an impediment for cosmetic or occupational reasons, that person might seek the help of an elocutionist in hopes of learning how to speak more "attractively" (whatever that might mean) or more conventionally. The elocutionists' manual of speaking aids is irrelevant to sociolinguistics, except perhaps in the way that a manual of etiquette might be of interest in sociology, as an indicator of the social values attached to particular mannerisms at a particular time.

Observations about personal speech characteristics could perhaps be better integrated into sociolinguistic research than they are. Sapir (1927) made an attempt at considering speech as a "personality trait" but his fascinating study has not inspired productive research by others. One avenue that would surely be interesting and possibly productive would be studying how (if at all) personal speech characteristics differ from society to society or, conversely, how they remain constant across social and cultural boundaries. It would also be of considerable sociolinguistic interest to discover how consistently these varied personal characteristics are used by listeners to form judgements about the speakers. For the time being, however, considerations like these are at the fringe of socioliguistic research.

1.1.2   Linguistic styles

Another level of observation is **stylistic**. Here again listeners are capable of considerable discrimination, spontaneously and almost instantaneously, concerning the degree of familiarity between the participants in a conversation, their relative ages and ranks, the function of their conversation, and many other aspects. The main determinant is the speech styles they are using. The range of possibilities encompasses, on the one hand, the casualness of utterly familiar, long-time friends who share a wealth of common experience and, on the other hand, the formality of unequal participants who have no common ground but are forced to interact for some reason or other – perhaps one is hiring the other to mow the lawn, or instructing the other to serve the tea – with numerous possibilities in between.

Observations about speech styles fall squarely into the domain of sociolinguistics. Stylistic differences have a simple social correlate, viz., formality tends to increase in direct proportion to the number of social differences between the participants. The most relevant social factors are the topic of the next heading (§1.1.3), but for now it is enough to know that age is one of them, and to think of the effect that age differences often impose upon a discussion. Imagine a conversation between two women from the same neighborhood who unexpectedly meet in the waiting room of a dentist's office; imagine first that both women were, say, 30; and then imagine the difference in the conversation if one was 30 and the other 70.

The sociolinguistic relevance comes about because our ability to judge the formality of a conversation is largely determined by linguistic cues. Casual conversations tend to be more rapid, with more syntactic ellipses and contractions, and more phonological assimilations and coalescences. Highly formal conversations can also be very rapid if a participant is very nervous, but in that instance the syntax is usually stilted and somewhat breathless and the phonology articulated unnaturally. In English, one stereotype of hyper-formality is the pronunciation of the indefinite article "a", which is ordinarily pronounced [ə], as hyper-correct [eɪ]. There is also a middle ground between casual style and formal style, typically found in linguistic interactions between peers, that is, people who share many social characteristics, called careful style.

Clearly, if the relative formality of a conversation can cause speakers to adjust their phonology and other aspects of dialect and accent, then style is an independent variable that affects the dependent speech variables. The importance of style was recognized in what is perhaps the very first attempt at modern sociolinguistics, when Fischer (1958: 49) noted that the choice of the suffix [ɪn] for [ɪŋ] in participles like *walkin'*, *talkin'* and *thinkin'* in the speech of Boston schoolchildren "changed from an almost exclusive use of *-ing* in the [testing] situation to a predominance of *-in* in the informal interviews." (Fischer's study is discussed further in §§2.9.2.1 and 3.2.1.)

Style was firmly established as an independent variable, as were so many other factors, when Labov made it an integral part of his interview protocols in his ground-breaking survey of New York City (1966: 90–135 and passim). Labov asked his subjects to talk about topics such as street games and life-threatening experiences. He also asked them to read passages of connected prose and lists of words into the tape recorder.

These tasks elicit a range of styles from the speakers. The essential difference between speech styles is the amount of self-monitoring people do when they are speaking. When people are asked to read lists of words they obviously concentrate on their pronunciation almost completely, especially when the reading is being recorded by someone who is admittedly studying language. The care and attention is even greater than usual if the words are arranged as minimal pairs – "cot" and "caught", or "poor" and "pour", or (from Labov's list) "God" and "guard" (see §1.2.2.6).

The reading of connected prose is also highly monitored – so much so that most people are well aware of sounding different when they read – but the requirement of maintaining coherence when reading a passage aloud deflects some attention away from speech and on to the content of the passage.

In a free discussion, the content becomes even more important. Though self-monitoring is normal as an interviewee frames answers to the interviewer's questions, it must obviously be less than when reading a passage because the content of the answer must be foremost.

The unmonitored style – casual speech – is the one that sociolinguists want most to study, and it is the one that cannot be elicited by any foolproof devices. After the interviews have been going on for several minutes, the subjects become accustomed to the recording apparatus and more relaxed with the interviewer. When they are asked to tell the interviewer about near-fatal car accidents or fires in the toaster or other events that involved them, they are likely to get caught up in the recollected urgency of the situation and forget their self-consciousness. As interviewers, we can work at developing good rapport in the course of the interview, and at finding some topic that will touch a nerve. Apart from that, the best prospect of eliciting casual speech comes about when some intimate third person interrupts the interview, by telephone or in person, while the recording is taking place. (The elicitation of a range of styles is further exemplified in the summary of Labov's New York interview protocol in the next section.)

Elicitation of a range of styles is routinely included in sociolinguistic interviews. In the discussion of results throughout this book, style is often included as an independent variable. I refer to the styles in the conventional way by using self-explanatory terms: word list (WL) style is elicited by the reading of a list of words; the more self-conscious variant elicited by arranging the words based on their phonological similarities is called, simply, minimal pairs (MP); reading passage (RP) style is elicited by recording a prepared text; interview style (IS) is the free discussion of topics with perhaps some direction by the interviewer; and casual style (CS) is the unmonitored natural vernacular.

Throughout the book, style is an important independent variable but it is never the focal point. (For a thorough discussion of sociolinguistic style, see

Bell 1984.) The focal point in this book will be social variables of the type to which we now turn.

1.1.3 Social characteristics

Whenever we speak we reveal not only some personal qualities and a certain sensitivity to the contextual style but also a whole configuration of characteristics that we by and large share with everyone who resembles us socially. Usually without any conscious effort on our part, we embody in our speech, as in our dress, manners, and material possessions, the hallmarks of our social background. Our speech, from this perspective, is emblematic in the same sense as is the car we drive or the way we habitually dress for work but, obviously, our speech is much less manipulable, much harder to control consciously, and for that reason much more revealing.

The **social class** to which we belong imposes some norms of behavior on us and reinforces them by the strength of the example of the people with whom we associate most closely. The sub-elements of social class include education, occupation and type of housing, all of which play a role in determining the people with whom we will have daily contacts and more permanent relationships. They tend to be similar to those of our parents, so that the class trappings that most adults surround themselves with are to some degree an updated replication of those they grew up with. In all of this, of course, there is some latitude and, in relatively free societies, some mobility. The effects of social class on speech are the subject of chapter 2.

The other major social factors that exert a tacit but partly irrepressible effect on our behavior, including the way we speak, are **sex** and **age**. Their effects on our speech are the subjects of chapter 3 and chapter 4, respectively.

In modern industrial societies, these three social characteristics – class, sex and age – are the primary determinants of social roles. They are, of course, enormously complex, subsuming a host of social factors. The chapters on the primary characteristics break them down into their molecular elements in so far as those elements have a demonstrable effect on the way people speak.

For social class, the essential distinction separates non-manual and manual workers (§2.1). The effect of occupational mobility blurs the class lines not only socially but also linguistically (§2.4). In close-knit social clusters of the kind often (but not exclusively) found in manual workers' communities, the degree to which individuals are integrated into their local networks may affect their uses of regional markers (§2.6). Even with class distinctions and network pressures impinging upon the individual, linguistic behavior is by no means rigidly defined but can vary within certain limits (§2.9).

For sex, the essential distinction separates sex roles, which are biological, and gender roles, which are sociological (§3.1). In various communities, men and women divide the linguistic labor in different ways, with demonstrable consequences in their use of the local dialect (§§3.3, 3.5). In many other communities, including some of the best-studied ones, the roles of men and women are not fundamentally different with respect to language use, and in those instances there are still found typical differences in female – male use of sociolinguistic markers requiring explanation (§3.4).

For age, the relative ease with which listeners can estimate speakers' ages within a few years appears to be a function of non-idiosyncratic voice quality changes that are a function of normal aging (§4.1). Of much greater social significance is the acquisition of sociolectal features beginning in infancy (§4.2), as a normal development along with basic linguistic competence. Individuals in complex modern societies pass through at least three stages that have significant linguistic consequences, from the formation of a local peer group in childhood (§4.3) through the dense networks of adolescence (§4.4) to the settling into a style of life in early adulthood (§4.5). Linguistic differences between groups of people that differ from one another only in age can signal either a regular, maturational change (§4.6.1) or, more likely, a linguistic change in progress in the community (§4.6.2).

The correlations between these independent variables and speech is complex, sometimes dauntingly so, and endlessly interesting.

Our speech also – inevitably – reifies some less pressing but nevertheless important realities, which, for want of a ready set of terms for the broad categories, I will call sociocultural and sociological factors.

1.1.4 *Sociocultural factors*

To some extent, the very topics we talk about are culturally determined, and to a greater extent the way in which we talk about them is too.

This is obviously true of phatic communion, the repertoire of speech events we use when we greet people, pass the time in brief encounters at bus stops or waiting rooms, and take our leave of them. Consider, as an example, the conversation-ender, "Have a nice day." It has a peculiarly American ring to it because it came into use in the United States and started spreading outward from there as recently as the 1970s. Outside of the United States, its use is occasionally unselfconscious, a sign that the users have either lost track of its foreignness altogether or have adopted it as a stylish Americanism. But at least as often its use outside of the United States is imbued with a sense of parody, and its users are well aware not only of its foreignness but also as a stereotype of jaunty, hail-fellow American tourists.

Culture-laden interactions abound, and usually their verbal component is less important than the non-verbal. For instance, for Canadians and Americans in Budapest, it takes some time to adjust to fact that shop-keepers will sell them their wares in silence and then end the transaction by placing their change on the counter, not in their hand. It no doubt takes Eastern Europeans at least as long to come to grips with the fact that shop-keepers in Toronto and Chicago make small talk and maintain eye contact with their customers.

Similarly, almost all people who are not native New Yorkers are likely to feel they are being insulted and shouted at by taxi and bus drivers or waiters when they visit that city. Partly this is the result of a cultural difference, what Tannen identified as the New York conversational style, which favors "cooperative overlap – i.e. speakers who like a lot of talk going on in casual conversation, much of which occurs at the same time that others are speaking" (Tannen 1987: 581). To outsiders, it seems as if they are being constantly interrupted and shouted down. The rules governing speech acts, though not encoded anywhere (except by ethnographers), are understood thoroughly by natives and often misunderstood by outsiders.

Less obvious sociocultural influences are found in the use of conversational implicatures. In some middle-class settings, it is permissible to request an action by asking a question that is, taken literally, highly indirect. "Do you find it cold in here?" literally invites one's assent or denial, though it might in a polite gathering in most cultures lead to a discussion of the weight of one's cardigan or the unseasonal June weather. In certain English-speaking social circles a perfectly polite response to the question would be for the host to rise and stoke the fire or close the window.

Numerous discourse rules differ subtly from culture to culture, such as the conventions for maintaining the conversational topic, ways of assuming a turn as speaker, the intimacy of disclosures, and the amount of overlapping or interrupting. (For an overview of discourse analysis, see Wardhaugh 1985.)

1.1.5 Sociological factors

Language also functions sociologically in various ways as an accoutrement of the social structure. This is especially clear in the conventionalized use of address forms. Linguistically it is irrelevant whether someone addresses someone else as "Mr Jones" or as "Sam", or whether someone chooses the pronoun *to* or *shomā* "you" in a Persian-speaking community (or Spanish *tu* or *Usted*, Italian *tu* or *Lei*, Ukrainian *ty* or *vy*, Greek *esi* or *esis*). Sociologically, it can make an enormous difference, if the distinction obligatorily marks the social ranks of the participants.

Also largely sociological is the importance of particular languages as "codes" in multilingual societies. Co-existent languages are never sociologically equal, though of course they are linguistically equal. In Haiti, it is important to know when to use French and when to use Creole in order to gain and maintain status in the diglossic society. In the bilingual belt of Canada, it is important to know when to use French and when to use English and, more subtly, when to mix the codes (Poplack 1988). In all bilingual regions, there are times when it is appropriate to code-switch and times when it is inappropriate or incongruous. Native speakers understand the unwritten rules for diglossia and for code-switching because they are integral elements of the value system of their societies.

Just as the most idiosyncratic personal factors in our speech are outside the domain of sociolinguistics, so at the sociological end of the continuum the topics tail off into linguistically extrinsic matters. Purely ideological issues that impinge upon language planning in multinational administrations belong properly to political science, and debates about linguistically equivalent but sociologically distinct spelling reforms may touch educationists, politicians, and sociologists. In these areas, the linguist as linguist will have little or nothing to offer, whatever the linguist as teacher, politician or citizen may think.

1.1.6 Sociolinguistics and the sociology of language

The preceding outline of the various ways in which social structure and linguistic structure come together is intended to cover the field in the broadest possible terms. Figure 1.1 provides a kind of summation. Studies of the various aspects – personal, stylistic, social, sociocultural and sociological – are subsumed by either sociolinguistics or the sociology of language, depending upon the purposes of the research. The distinction is largely a matter of emphasis, as the definitions in the figure indicate, and the area of overlap at the boundary of the two aspects is considerable.

The domain of sociolinguistics deals centrally with stylistic and social aspects and also takes in some personal and some sociocultural aspects. The subject matter of this book concentrates, as I have already said, on the core area: linguistic variation and its social significance. Each of the three chapters following this one concentrates on one of the three major social correlates of linguistic variation – class, sex, and age – along with the web of related social factors that each of them entails. The final chapter steps back and considers the purposes of linguistic variation in general, and the reasons for its perpetuation.

As necessary background for the synthesis of the major results of sociolinguistic research that follow, the rest of this chapter reviews the essentials

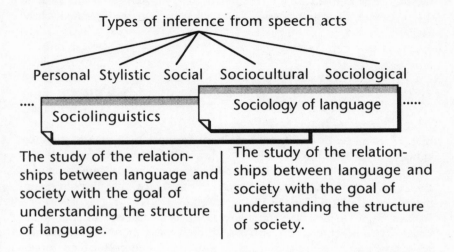

Types of inference from speech acts

Personal Stylistic Social Sociocultural Sociological

.... Sociolinguistics   Sociology of language .....

| The study of the relationships between language and society with the goal of understanding the structure of language. | The study of the relationships between language and society with the goal of understanding the structure of society. |

Figure 1.1 The complex role of language in society, and the division into overlapping domains of sociolinguistics and the sociology of language (definitions based on Wardhaugh 1992: 13 and references therein)

of data-analysis and data-presentation that underlie those results. Methods of data-gathering will not be reviewed here. For that, see Labov (1975, 1984a), Chambers and Trudgill (1980: chapters 4–6), L. Milroy (1987), and Poplack (1989).

Sociolinguists are sometimes accused of giving more space to their methods than to their results. That will certainly not be true of this book. Still, it seems prudent to allot some space to analytical matters because they contextualize the results as nothing else can.

The methodological matters that are dealt with in the following sections arise incidentally and (I hope) unavoidably as adjuncts of the main theme. In the rest of this chapter, I provide a theoretical perspective on linguistic variation. I will show that the admission of the variable as a structural unit in linguistic analysis – the topic of §1.2, immediately below – represents a breakthrough of considerable magnitude in linguistic theory – the topic of §1.3. These theoretical considerations may be less well understood even by experienced sociolinguists than they perhaps should be. They are, at any rate, almost never discussed by them. One reason for the relative paucity of discussion may simply be that the social science content of sociolinguistics has overshadowed its theoretical implications. Where research in more formal branches of linguistics has little or no content apart from its theoretical implications, sociolinguists have had to face empirical matters of enormous complexity as well. Those empirical matters dominate this book as they do the discipline, but for the rest of this chapter they are relegated to the background.

1.2   The Variable as a Structural Unit

In 1885, Schuchardt (1972: 48) noted that "the pronunciation of the individual is never free from variations." A few decades later, Sapir (1921: 147) wrote, "Everyone knows that language is variable." Though linguistic variation may be obvious, no linguists analyzed it systematically until the inception of sociolinguistics in the 1960s.

Even Sapir, in practice, was unprepared to incorporate insights about variability into his linguistic analysis. While he was more willing than his contemporaries – or, for that matter, most of his predecessors and successors – to recognize variation, he did it mainly by acknowledging and discussing the loose ends of a particular analysis. It was his awareness of these loose ends that led to his epigrammatic conclusion: "Unfortunately or luckily, no language is tyrannically consistent. All grammars leak."

Sapir's persistent allusions to the fact of variation in language, though it was never more than an addendum in his work, were not considered commendable by some of his immediate successors. Thus Joos (1957: 25) summarized Sapir's contribution by saying, "We welcome the insights of his genius, which allowed no scrap of evidence to escape at least subconscious weighing; where it is possible to check up, we normally find him right; thus we may seem captious when we point out that he also said many things which are essentially uncheckable ('invulnerable') and not science." Joos's view of science as behaviorist and anti-mentalist, which he held in common with most of his contemporaries, perhaps forestalled any significant influence from "the insights of [Sapir's] genius." Though Sapir was respected and emulated as a practicing linguist, he inspired no movement devoted to accounting for variability within linguistic theory.

Instead, the generation that came after Sapir adopted a very strong form of what I will call the axiom of categoricity, the simplifying assumption that data for linguistic analysis must be regularized to eliminate real-world variability. (The axiom of categoricity is discussed in greater detail in §1.3.2 below.)

Among many statements that characterize the axiom, one by Joos stands out as the most pellucid. "We must make our 'linguistics' a kind of mathematics within which inconsistency is by definition impossible," Joos said (1950: 701–2), and he offered this elaboration:

Ordinary mathematical techniques fall mostly into two classes, the continuous (e.g. the infinitesimal calculus) and the discrete or discontinuous (e.g. finite group theory). Now it will turn out that the mathematics called "linguistics" belongs to the second class. It does not even make any compromise with continuity as statistics does, or infinite-group theory. Linguistics is a quantum mechanics in the most extreme sense. All continuities, all possibilities of infinitesimal gradation, are shoved outside of linguistics in one direction or the other.

As we shall see in the next section, Chomsky influentially perpetuated the axiom of categoricity for the next generation.

1.2.1 *Coexistent systems and free variation*

Of course the fact that variation exists in language remains as obvious as Schuchardt and Sapir said it is, regardless of the axiom that rules it out. People use the lexical item *car* on one occasion and *automobile* on another, pronounce the participle *walking* sometimes and *walkin'* other times, and ask the technician to *back up the disk* on their computer one day and to *back the disk up* the next. These mundane examples – lexical, phonological and syntactic as illustrated, but pronunciation and morphological examples also abound – represent dozens of others like them. They are perhaps easy to ignore because linguistically they make no difference: the sentences mean the same thing no matter which variant is used.

When variants attracted the attention of linguists at all, they were generally regarded either as belonging to different co-existent linguistic systems or as unpredictably free substitutes. The notion of co-existent systems, explicated most influentially by Fries and Pike (1949), held that speakers maintained separate phonologies (and also, by inference, separate grammars) that gave them access to more than one code, thus allowing them or perhaps causing them to switch from one to the other. The notion of free variation, widely subscribed to but, as far as I can discover, never discussed or examined critically, held that the variants were merely random fluctuations.

The idea of co-existent systems carries certain implications that must have made it seem dubious from the beginning. It implies, for instance, that speakers should maintain one phonology consistently until the circumstances arise that trigger the second system. Mixing elements from the two systems, that is, varying between the two, should not, in principle, take place as long as the conditions surrounding the speech event remain unchanged. Access to the second system, because it is in some sense separate from the first, should not be momentary or sporadic. Variants, as constituents of separate systems, should not co-occur.

Yet all these things are known to happen in casual conversations. Speakers do mix variants of the same variable in the same discourse, indeed in the same sentence. Subsequent chapters will describe numerous variables in which large groups of people – class cohorts, or age or sex cohorts – maintain similar proportions of variant-mixing in similar circumstances. Rather than the co-existence of linguistic systems, their behavior appears to provide evidence for a single system in which variants co-exist (also see Weinreich, Labov and Herzog 1968: 159–65).

The idea of free variation carries a strong implication as well. If the variants are truly free, that is, if the occurrence of one variant or another is arbitrary, then it must follow *a fortiori* that the variants cannot be predicted by any factor. Yet the most casual observations of speech show that its variants are associated with social factors. Discussions of free variation routinely included observations that "free" variants like *automobile* were used in advertisements because the word had a dignity lacking in its counterpart *car*. In other words, the variants were predictable, at least probabilistically, and not free in any meaningful sense of the word.

One of the first systematic studies of variation, by Fischer (1958), set out to discover "the determinants of the selection of the variants" *-in'* and *-ing* in participles as used by Boston schoolchildren. Fischer sought and found those determinants in correlations with the social class, the sex, and other independent variables (also see §§2.9.2.1, 3.2.1.2). Fischer (1958: 47–8) concluded: "'Free variation' is of course a label, not an explanation. It does not tell us where the variants came from nor why the speakers use them in differing proportions, but is rather a way of excluding such questions from the scope of immediate inquiry."

1.2.2   The socioliguistic enterprise

Soon after Fischer's study, questions about the frequency and the source of linguistic variants became important to a few linguists. The next important step was to gather evidence of variability on a large scale and demonstrate that its occurrence in the speech community was systematic, patterned, and orderly.

The very act of gathering and analyzing variable data would in itself constitute proof that such data was manageable. One of the premises in support of the axiom of categoricity, as Joos suggests above, was that abstracting linguistic data from the vagaries of the real world was necessary in order to make it coherent and manageable. Demonstrating the falseness of this premise would in itself show that categoricity is not an axiom one must accept in order to undertake linguistic analysis but merely a postulate that one may or may not wish to make.

1.2.2.1 Precursors Several theoreticians were aware that categoricity was a postulate rather than an axiom, long before the analysis of variability was successfully demonstrated. (See, for example, the citations from Bolinger, Gleason and Chomsky in the next section.) Nevertheless, the fact that the axiom had been adopted in virtually all linguistic research prior to sociolinguistics, all the way back to classical Greece (§5.5) and including traditional dialectology and anthropological linguistics, must have given it an aura of necessity.

The genesis of the sociolinguistic enterprise required a systematic survey of real speech in its social context. The term itself, or at least the near-homograph *socio-linguistics*, was coined before any research of the kind that came to be called sociolinguistic was attempted. Haver C. Currie (1952), a poet and philosopher, noted that linguists' definitions of language conventionally included a clause about its social function but actual research usually ignored any consideration of it. Currie lauded Mencken's popular book, *The American Language* (1919), noting that Mencken "pleases Americans in general by pointing out that they have a national language of their own with respectable regional variants," and that "the American middle class has for thirty years rewarded him by buying every copy of his book that his publishers would print" (1952: 46). In Mencken's popularity Currie saw the impetus for a chauvinist extension of linguistics, which he calls "a field for quite conscious study here called *socio-linguistics*," for "the consideration of the social significance of English as spoken in the United States" (1952: 47).

Currie's proposal was not pursued immediately but the term he coined later came into general use, even against opposition. Twenty years later, Labov (1972: xiii) said, "I have resisted the term *sociolinguistics* for many years, since it implies that there can be a successful linguistic theory or practice which is not social." Indeed there can be if Chomskyan linguistics is successful, but it was not that consideration so much as the universal attachment of the term to Labov's work by others that broke his resistance. A few years later, Chambers and Trudgill (1980: 205) complained that the term *sociolinguistics* had become "perhaps too general to be meaningful" and proposed some alternatives, to no avail. By now, there is no hope of detaching the term from the discipline, and, it must be admitted, no good reason.

By the time sociolinguistics came into being a little more than a decade later, virtually no one remembered that Currie had coined the term. It was Labov's exemplary work in the Lower East Side of New York City that inspired other linguists to head into the streets with notepads in their hands and tape recorders over their shoulders.

The New York survey was not the first sociolinguistic study. That honor may also belong to Labov, for his work in Martha's Vineyard in 1962 (Labov 1963; also §2.7.1 below), though a slightly looser definition would give it to Fischer (1958), whose research prefigured most of the essential components of sociolinguistics. An even looser definition would credit Louis Gauchat (1905), whose dialect study of the French vernacular in the town of Charmey, Switzerland, broke the conventions of traditional dialectology by correlating linguistic variability with the sex and age of the individual informants, prefiguring at least sociolinguistic network studies (§2.6 below, including discussion of Gauchat's work in §2.6.3). But Labov's New York survey was so enormously influential that it is indisputably the fountainhead.

1.2.2.2 Labov's New York survey   There are by now literally dozens of analyses in the literature that I could choose as prototypes in order to demonstrate how the analysis of variable data proceeds and what its correlations with independent variables reveals. The one I will use here as the case study is one of the very first analyses published by Labov, based on data from his New York survey.

The choice of this particular analysis, besides serving an expository purpose at this point, is also meaningful for other reasons. The article in which it appeared was called "The linguistic variable as a structural unit" (Labov 1966a), the source of my section title. This particular article was obscurely published and seems to have been all but forgotten. Most of Labov's articles have been anthologized – Labov 1972 and 1972a are self-anthologies – but this one never has been. For me, it was his single most influential article. When I came upon it about ten years after it was published it deflected my attention decisively away from theoretical syntax and the other kinds of research I was involved in and on to urban dialectology.[1]

In it, Labov explains that he undertook a study of the social stratification of English in New York City well aware that his predecessors had come to the conclusion that New York was the site of massive free variation. One of them, Hubbell (1950), said, "The pronunciation of a very large number of New Yorkers exhibits a pattern . . . that might most accurately be described as the complete absence of any pattern. Such speakers sometimes pronounce /r/ before a consonant or a pause and sometimes omit it, in a thoroughly haphazard pattern."

When Hubbell undertook his New York study, dialect research in urban areas had been almost completely ignored because of the widespread apprehension that accents in densely populated places with mobile populations would be capricious, vacillating and disparate. Hubbell's conclusion about "the absence of any pattern" accorded perfectly with the expectations of the day. With hindsight, of course, it seems a bizarre conclusion. The essential premise of all linguistic research is that language is systematic. If it is not, there is nothing more to be said. Linguistics cannot exist. Yet Hubbell's conclusion sounded no alarms.

1.2.2.3 Linguistic variables Against this background, Labov set out to discover not only when individual speakers pronounced /r/ but also what factors might govern its occurrence. Besides /r/, he isolated four other features known to vary in the city. In order to symbolize the variables graphically, he used parentheses: (r) means "variable r". The parentheses are intended as equivalents to slashes for phoneme /r/ and square brackets for phone [ɹ] but they indicate a level of analysis that is neither phonemic nor phonetic.

In order for something to be a linguistic variable, it must occur in variant forms. Variable (r) has two variants: [ɹ] and Ø. Another of Labov's variables, (eh), the vowel in words such as *bad, ask, dance,* and *laugh,* has six variants: [ɪe], [ɛe], [æ], [æ:], [a:] and [ɑ:].[2] This variable plots the raising and tensing of standard /æ/ from the low front position. The essential pattern of variation is somewhat obscured by the inclusion of the two back variants, which are rare and, in the case of [ɑ:], aberrant in New York City speech.

Like the phonemes /r/ and /æ/, the variables (r) and (eh) represent abstract linguistic entities. Just as phonemes are actualized as one or more allophones, so variables are actualized as one or another of the variants. Unlike the allophones of phonemes, the variants of variables such as (r) and (eh) are not always predictable by phonological, morphological, or any other kind of linguistic conditioning. Allophones *must* occur when their linguistic conditioning factors are present; for instance, in English, voiceless stops must occur as aspirates in syllable-initial position. Variants may have a tendency to occur when certain linguistic factors are present in the environment; for instance, the higher variants of (eh), [ɪe] and [ɛe], may occur more frequently before alveolar nasals, as in *Ann, candy* and *dandruff,* than before bilabial nasals, as in *Sam, ramble* and *ambulance,* but they do not occur invariably before alveolar nasals and they do sometimes occur before bilabial nasals.

1.2.2.4 Independent variables The occurrence of one or another of the variants may thus correlate with some linguistic factor in the environment, but as a probability rather than a necessity. Non-linguistic factors may also be found to correlate. One of these is style, as already noted in §1.1 above. A particular variant may tend to occur more often in casual interchanges than in formal ones, or vice versa. Various social factors may also exert an influence. Certain variants may be associated with working-class speech more than middle-class, with adolescents more than their parents, with men more than women, or some other social category.

Correlating linguistic variation as the dependent variable with independent variables such as linguistic environment, style or social categories is the primary empirical task of sociolinguistics. From recordings of the speech of a sample of individuals, transcriptions of the variants by which variables get realized can be counted and quantified. If the variable has two variants, as (r) does, the quantification can be made simply in terms of percentages. If it has more variants, as (eh) does, the variants must be counted proportionally.

By a convention established by Trudgill (1974), the basic variant in the set of variants is the one that occurs in standard speech: thus, [ɹ] rather than Ø for (r), and [æ] rather than [ɪe] or [ɛe] for (eh). This means, in the case of a percentage calculation as for (r), that the individual's score will be indicated by the percentage of Ø variants among the total of all variants (all [ɹ] + Ø). The number, whether a percentage or a proportion, is called the weighted index score, or, quite commonly, the index. (For details about the calculation of weighted index scores, see Chambers and Trudgill 1980: 61–4; for other methods of quantifying linguistic variables, see, for example, Cedergren and Sankoff 1974, D. Sankoff 1985, and Horvath and Sankoff 1987.)

Beyond this primary empirical task lies the problem of interpretation. What is the relative significance of, say, age and style if both are involved in the variation? How do favoring linguistic factors and disfavoring social factors interact? What is the social significance of the linguistic variation?

1.2.2.5 Speech in the community   Starting with a stratified random sample of New York's Lower East Side, Labov selected his subjects from a sub-set of the adult native speakers who had not moved for two years. He sought representatives of all ethnic groups, age levels, and social classes. Various problems in getting access to individuals affected the sample's randomness in the end but in any case left him with a large, well distributed judgement sample, the kind of sample that has proved most judicious in sociolinguistic research. (On sampling, see §2.1 below.)

Labov and his associate interviewer Michael Kac then set about interviewing 157 adults and, as opportunities arose, added interviews with 58 of their children. The interview protocol, as has become standard procedure, involved discussions of various topics broken up by set tasks such as the reading of a minimal pair list (MP style), an isolated word list (WL), and a reading passage (RP). The purpose, as already discussed above (§1.1.2), was to elicit a variety of styles from the subjects, based on the amount of self-monitoring they were doing. The bulk of the recorded interviews consisted of relatively careful but free-flowing speech as the subjects responded to various topics introduced by the interviewer. This register is known as interview style (IS).

Of course the style most desired for sociolinguistic purposes is completely unmonitored, and that is the very style that is hardest to elicit in the presence of an interviewer and recording equipment. This fundamental problem of sociolinguistic research was dubbed by Labov the "observer's paradox" (1970: 32) and stated thus: "the aim of linguistic research in the community must be to find out how people talk when they are not being systematically observed; yet we can only obtain this data by systematic observation." The observer's paradox is the sociolinguistic counterpart of the general problem in social sciences known as the Hawthorne effect (as pointed out by Murray 1985): "the behavior of any given experiment's subjects is changed just because the subjects perceive themselves as participants in the experiment."

Of the topics used by Labov (1966: 143–9), the most successful in making the subjects forget the unnaturalness of the situation were the recollection of street games and of life-threatening situations. Most reliable in eliciting truly casual speech were fortuitous interruptions by family members and friends while the tape recorder was turned on.

1.2.2.6 One subject, Susan Salto   When the interviews were transcribed and analyzed, Labov correlated the linguistic variables with the social and stylistic variables. One individual, Susan Salto, a 37-year-old third-generation New Yorker, showed striking variation in her use of Ø for (r) in the two polar styles. When she was reading the list of minimal pairs such as *god* and *guard*, which in New York speech are realized as [gɔːd] 'god' and either [gɔɹd], [gɔːˈd] or [gɔːd] 'guard', she invariably distinguished all pairs that could possibly differ by r-fulness of one of the variants. For the pair just cited, she read [gɔːd] for 'god' and [gɔɹd] for 'guard'. In other words, in the most self-conscious style, she scored zero because she had no instances of the variant Ø in the set of MP tokens. By contrast, in her most casual speech, as in her breathless account of a life-threatening incident (for instance) and fortuitously when she chatted with a friend on the telephone part-way through the interview, she used the Ø variant 98 percent of the time. Her style-shifting thus covers almost the whole gamut – zero to 98 percent.

In the absence of further information, nothing about Susan Salto's responses with respect to the (r) variable is incompatible with the hypothesis of free variation. The differences in her use of [ɹ] or Ø could be merely random. Obviously the plausibility of randomness seems somewhat suspicious because the percentages are so extreme, and because they are not evenly distributed throughout her speech but each is associated with a different linguistic context.

When Labov took a further step and examined her responses in the other contextual styles, he got the results shown in table 1.1. Now the plausibility of randomness as an explanation of her behavior becomes totally unrealistic. What we notice in table 1.1 is a systematic gradation in the use of variants

Table 1.1 Susan Salto's (r) index in five styles, from most formal to least formal (from Labov 1966a)

Style	(r) index
MP	00
WL	39
RP	42
IS	74
CS	98

from style to style. In the styles between the two polar ones, her use of the (r) variants alters in a regular way. For the word list it is 39, a considerable leap from zero in the minimal pairs, and for the reading passage (RP) it is similar, 42; in the conversational styles, there is another considerable leap to 74 in interview style (IS) and then nearly categorical use in the casual style (CS). These results are consistent with a hypothesis that Susan Salto uses more non-standard variants as her speech style becomes more casual. The corollary is that she uses more standard variants as she monitors her speech more attentively.

In terms of phonological structure, we might attempt to analyze Susan Salto's responses by saying that she has a phoneme /r/ with allophones [ɹ] and Ø, but there is no way of capturing the probabilistic occurrence of one or the other allophone. Or we might posit a generative process by which underlying /r/ gets realized as Ø sometimes. Since the variants are not linguistically conditioned, there is no way to make these generalizations explicit unless we incorporate non-linguistic conditions into the structural statements and probabilities into the application. But these are impossible in a phonological theory that includes the axiom of categoricity. Apparently the linguistic description of Susan Salto's behavior belongs to a different level.

1.2.2.7 All subjects in three social classes For all we know from the evidence presented so far, it remains a possibility that Susan Salto's behavior is idiosyncratic. If so, the stylistic correlation is merely personal – an interesting fact about Susan Salto but not generally revealing. Labov showed that this is not so by agglomerating the data from the entire sample. Table 1.2, which categorizes the subjects according to their social classes, shows that Susan Salto is one of many speakers whose more formal speech includes more instances of the standard variant [ɹ]. Indeed, according to the table, her behavior conforms to everyone else in her speech community. For all

Table 1.2 (r) indices for three social classes in five styles in New York City (from Labov 1966a)

	Class		
Style	LC	WC	MC
MP	50.5	45	30
WL	76.5	65	44.5
RP	85.5	79	71
IS	89.5	87.5	75
CS	97.5	96	87.5

three social classes, whether lower class (LC), working class (WC), or middle class (MC), the (r) indices increase as the formality decreases, that is, as one reads down the columns in table 1.2.

Equally important, table 1.2 shows that the speech community is stratified linguistically with respect to social class. That is, all social classes use more instances of the non-standard variant Ø in their more casual styles, but the proportions differ depending upon the class. The lower class (LC) has higher percentages in all styles than either the working class (WC) or the middle class (MC). Similarly, there is a gap between the percentages of the WC and the MC. Each of the three social groups uses the (r) variants in proportionately different ways, although all of them use them in stylistically similar ways. The Ø variant is more characteristic of the LC than of the other two classes because it is more frequent in their speech in all styles.

Results such as these, now replicated hundreds of times in dozens of disparate social circumstances, demonstrate beyond any doubt that linguistic variation is not free but is patterned. The patterns have social significance, as revealed by the significant correlations of the frequency of linguistic variants, the dependent variable, with independent variables such as style and social class. Above all, the patterns show that data can be gathered, analyzed and interpreted without requiring regularization, that is, without invoking the axiom of categoricity. Even the rudimentary correlations in this straightforward example show that the result is not chaotic – indeed far from it. It is meaningful, and revealing of the way in which language encodes social relations.

It represents, moreover, a theoretical breakthrough of considerable magnitude, an aspect that has seldom been recognized. The sociolinguistic enterprise, realized so auspiciously in Labov's New York survey, is one of the most significant departures from the conventions of language study in history (as discussed in §1.3).

1.2.3   Figures and tables

Before going on to an elaboration of the theoretical significance of the
sociolinguistic enterprise in the next section, it is worthwhile pausing a
moment here and considering the way we have presented the data in table
1.2.

Because sociolinguistic correlations are usually quantitative, like those in
table 1.2, it often takes readers a few minutes of study to discover the
meaning of the data. If the correlations were qualitative rather than quantitative, this would not be so. For instance, if one social group always used
Ø where another social group always used [ɹ], then it would be obvious at
a glance how they differed from one another linguistically. But actual sociolinguistic variation is much more subtle. Social groups typically differ by
the proportions of particular variants they use in particular circumstances.
Hence it is necessary to look closely at a matrix of numbers like table 1.2 in
order to discover its trends: in this instance, that the numbers in the rows
decrease from left to right, that is, from lower to higher social groups, and
that the numbers also increase from top to bottom in the columns, that is,
from more formal to less formal styles, and, further, that these trends are
consistent in all rows and columns.

As with all quantitative disciplines, sociolinguistics also uses graphic
representations of data. Table 1.2 can be graphically represented as figure
1.2. The chapters that follow use both tables and figures, occasionally together but usually one or the other, depending upon what is being discussed. All in all, figures will be used more often than tables, especially for
complex data. The reason for this is that figures usually require somewhat
less effort for the reader to comprehend than tables. This is undoubtedly so
once readers are used to their formal conventions.

Although figures and tables may differ in comprehensibility, it is important to understand that they must have exactly the same content. Figure 1.2
contains exactly the same information as table 1.2, and not an iota more
or less. Every cell of the matrix in table 1.2 can be located in the graph of
figure 1.2, and so can every label on its rows and columns. They are, we say,
notationally equivalent. By that, we mean that their form (or notation) is
different, but their content (or meaning) is exactly the same. For every table
it must be possible to construct an equivalent graph, and for every graph it
must be possible to construct an equivalent table.

Figure 1.2 is a typical sociolinguistic figure as far as its form goes, though
(as we will see) it is a bit unusual in its content in one respect. It is a line
graph, with the (r) index scores – the dependent variable – represented
along the ordinate (also called the Y-axis or the value axis) from zero at
the base, and the five styles along the abscissa (or X-axis, or series axis).

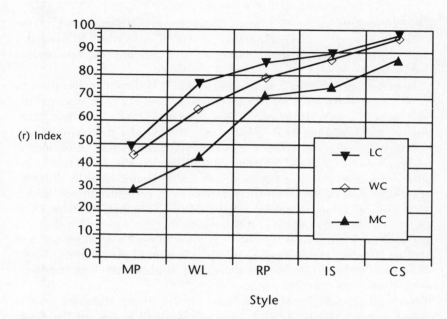

Figure 1.2. Social and stylistic stratification of (r) for three social classes in five styles in New York City (based on Labov 1996a)

Because there are two independent variables in the data and it is only possible to represent one (at a time) on the abscissa, the second one, social class, is represented graphically by the symbols ▼, ◇, and ▲, and identified in the legend. This much is standard graphing procedure for any discipline.

If we look at figure 1.2 for the evidence of the stratification we already observed in table 1.2, it is immediately evident in the way the lines move across the graph separately. The fact that there are gaps between the lines means that each social group occupies its own stratum. Also more obvious in the graph is the near convergence of the two lower social groups in the least formal styles, IS and CS. At this point, the convergence threatens the stratification as the two groups nearly merge. Looking back at table 1.2, we can see that the indices at these points are 87.5 and 89.5 for IS, and 96 and 97.5 for CS.

An important convention that is peculiar to sociolinguistics is that the variants are always counted in such a way that the one that belongs to the standard accent is zero (as in §1.2.2.4 above). Once this convention is understood, it makes the "reading" of graphs very straightforward. In the case of New York (r) taking the variant [ɪ] to be standard and the other variant, Ø, to be non-standard, the index scores are calculated by determining the percentage of Ø in the total. For instance, the MC speakers used variant Ø in the MP style 30 percent of the time: 3 out of 10 times, or 48 out of 160, or something proportional.

The central purpose of making the calculation this way is to fix the archetypical standard accent at zero or, in graphic terms, along the abscissa. When you look at a sociolinguistic graph, then, you know that the abscissa represents categorically standard speech. You also know that the distance of the lines from the abscissa indicates their degree of non-standardness.

It is in this respect that figure 1.2 is slightly unusual. We usually expect the MC to approximate the standard. In numerous graphs later in this book, the MC will be found on a line only slightly above the abscissa. This is not so in figure 1.2. Instead, the MC ranges from 30 percentage points to 87.5 above the abscissa. The reason for the considerable gap is that Labov's survey took place at a time of great changes in New York City speech. In the 1930s and 40s, for reasons not fully understood, the distinctive urban vernacular of New York became the subject of jokes. People everywhere could imitate stereotyped New York speech, in phrases such as *de sawng-boids on toity-toid street* "the songbirds on Thirty-Third Street". Features that had formerly been distinctive, regionally prestigious indicators of New York City speech were suddenly subjected to criticism and derision. The stigmatized features in the phrase above include [t] and [d] for [θ] and [ð] in "third" and "the", the long, very rounded vowel [ɔːˀ] in "song", the diphthong [ʌɪ] for [ɚ] in "bird", "thirty" and "third", and, of course, the r-lessness of those same three words. All these features showed signs of modifying toward standard American English in the 1940s, and at the time of Labov's survey in 1963 a feature like (r) was occurring as [ɪ] quite often in more self-conscious styles but still was heard as Ø more often in the other styles.

It is not altogether clear that my decision to calculate the variants on the assumption that [ɪ] is standard is really correct. Certainly the direction of style-shifting by Labov's subjects indicates that they consider [ɪ] more prestigious, since that is the variant they use when monitoring their speech most closely. But Ø had been standard a generation or so earlier. The transition from one dominant variant to the other was so balanced that either one of them could have been chosen.

Apart from this irregularity, the dependent variable (r) has well-defined attributes. It varies systematically with two independent variables. As style becomes more casual, the Ø variant becomes more frequent for all speakers in the community. As one goes down the social class hierarchy, the Ø variant becomes more frequent in all styles. (Obviously, these statements could as readily be rewritten as their converses, in terms of the [ɹ] variant in more formal styles and up the social hierarchy.)

These correlations are crucial. Socially significant linguistic variation requires correlation: the dependent (linguistic) variable must change when some independent variable changes. It also requires that the change be orderly: the dependent variable must stratify the subjects in ways that are socially or stylistically coherent. Labov's New York survey demonstrated more convincingly than anything that came before it that linguistic variation correlates with social factors, and that it is not only amenable to analysis but also linguistically interesting and socially revealing.

1.3   Variation and the Tradition of Categoricity

The variable as a structural unit represents a momentous innovation in linguistics. Hitherto, all linguistic units – phones, phonemes, morphemes, phrases, clauses – had been invariant, discrete, and qualitative. The variable is none of these. Instead, it is variant, continuous, and quantitative (Labov 1966a). It is variant in the sense that it is realized differently on different occasions. It is continuous in the sense that certain variants, such as the vowel gradations for (eh) above, take on social significance depending upon their phonetic distance from the standard variant, or, as with the variants for (r), their phonetic differentness from the standard variant. It is quantitative in the sense that its significance is not determined merely by the presence or absence of its variants but by their relative frequency.

1.3.1   Langue *and* parole

The variable can only exist in a theory that abandons the axiom of categoricity. Until the inception of modern sociolinguistics, all major linguistic theories adopted the axiom of categoricity. The domain of linguistic investigation was taken to be, in Saussure's celebrated dichotomy, *langue*, the grammatical system, rather than *parole*, the social uses of language (1916: 9–15). The reason is precisely because *langue* is removed from the turbulence in which *parole* exists, the quotidian flux, or in Sapir's terms (1929: 166) "the apparent lawlessness of social phenomena." *Langue* is homogeneous, Saussure says, whereas *parole* is heterogeneous. Furthermore, *langue* can be studied in the absence of a community of speakers.

This last point leads to what Labov (1972: 185–6) calls the "Saussurean Paradox," whereby the data from a single informant, usually the linguist relying on his or her own intuitions, are all that are needed to study the communal *langue*, but in order to study the individualistic *parole* one must study language in the community.

Distinctions similar to *langue* and *parole* can be found both before and after Saussure. Humboldt (1836: 129) observed: "Language comprehends in fact two contrasting properties: namely, it is divided up into an infinity as the sole language in one and the same nation; and at the same time these many variants are united into one language having a definite character." The two properties presumably underlie Humboldt's distinction between language as "an *ergon*, that is a mere means of exchange for purposes of communication," and as "an *energeia* which reconstitutes human experience ideally" (Basilius 1952: 98).

Saussure's distinction is paralleled closely by Chomsky's equally well-known distinction between competence, "the speaker-hearer's knowledge of his language", and performance, "the actual use of language in concrete situations" (1965: 4).

1.3.2   The axiom of categoricity

The decision that the proper domain of linguistics should be homogeneous *langue* rather than heterogeneous *parole* – or the united *energeia* rather than the variable *ergon*, or the speaker–hearer's knowledge rather than actual use – aroused very little debate historically. Given the central fact of variability in language, the only way to study linguistic competence will be by approaching language at some remove from its real-life performance. Therefore the object of study, langue–energeia–competence, must be abstracted from its real-world contexts.

The basis for this abstraction is, of course, the axiom of categoricity. Chomsky, with the kind of clarity that sets him apart from all other linguists, is the author of what is probably the most explicit, and certainly the best known, statement of the axiom of categoricity (1965: 3):

> Linguistic theory is concerned primarily with an ideal speaker–listener, in a completely homogeneous speech–community, who knows its language perfectly and is unaffected by such grammatically irrelevant conditions as memory limitations, distractions, shifts of attention and interest, and errors (random or characteristic) in applying his knowledge of the language in actual performance.

Even though this idealization underlies virtually all linguistic research before sociolinguistics – including Bloomfieldian structuralism[3] and other schools whose practitioners dissociated themselves from the Chomskyan enterprise – it attracted considerable criticism.

Its basic contention is simply to point out that linguists in this tradition take as their data what Labov once called, in a memorable phrase, "normative edited texts": sentences or pronunciations based on the linguist's intuitions recollected in tranquility, or based on an informant's intuitions, recollected under the linguist's direction.

Chomsky's statement makes the removal from reality glaringly obvious. The non-social world it depicts irked some linguists, including some who were unwittingly working in it. Their objections to the passage were so persistent that Chomsky felt enjoined to respond several years later (1980: 24–5), pointing out that he had intended the statement as "an innocent and uncontroversial statement of an idealization." Innocent it is but not, as it turned out, uncontroversial. In discussing the various objections to the statement, Chomsky makes the following points:

> Exactly what is the source of objection? Obviously it cannot be that real speech communities are not homogeneous. That is as obvious as it is irrelevant. Nor can the objection be that this idealization necessarily impedes the study of matters that do not fall within it, say, linguistic variation or what Putnam calls "the social division of linguistic labor". On the contrary, what is implicitly claimed by someone who adopts the idealization is that these further questions are properly studied within a framework that makes use of the results obtained by inquiring into the idealization. If the idealization does make it possible to unearth real and significant properties of the language faculty, this conclusion would seem to be justified, indeed inescapable.

Chomsky is right, of course. The accomplishments of linguistics carried out under the "idealization" – the axiom of categoricity – are not really disputable, especially those under Chomsky's leadership. Labov (1972: 186) concurs: "The science of *parole* never developed [prior to sociolinguistics], but this approach to the science of *langue* has been extremely successful over the past half-century."

1.3.3 Saussure and the mainstream

Linguistics has been dominated by sub-fields that incorporate the axiom of categoricity from the beginning so that, not surprisingly, even our terminology reflects it.

Sub-fields that do *not* adopt the axiom are relatively new and have morphologically complex names: sociolinguistics, some areas of psycholinguistics, instrumental phonetics, discourse analysis, dialectometry, and the like.[4]

But what do we call the sub-fields that *do* adopt it? Apart from syntax, morphology and phonology, which are not unique identifiers since all of those structural levels are also studied in sociolinguistics and elsewhere, what do we call the kind of linguistics practiced by Chomsky, Bresnan, Selkirk, Prince, and so many others?

Various names have been tried, but none has stuck. "Theoretical linguistics" has the virtue of indicating that its findings illuminate only its own internal relationships, without direct reference to "external" contingents such as society, psychology, cognition, development, and so on. But the epithet "theoretical" is well established in the physical sciences in opposition to the "applied" sub-fields, which have as their mandate the testing of the theorecticians' hypotheses – a relationship that does not hold, and probably never will, in linguistics. "Descriptive linguistics" was the structuralist term (as we shall see below in the references to Gleason, §1.3.5) but it is now avoided, perhaps because it connotes a non-technical framework.[5] "Formal linguistics" had currency a few years ago, when generativists concentrated on writing explicit rules, but it seems otiose now that they no longer do. Lass (1976: 213–20) argued persuasively for the term "metaphysical linguistics," offering methodological and philosophical reasons, but as far as I know the name was never used by anyone else despite its merits.[6]

In the end, it becomes clear that linguistics with the axiom of categoricity has been known simply as "Linguistics." This is exactly what Saussure intended. He said, "One might if really necessary apply the term linguistics to each of the two disciplines, and speak of a linguistics of speaking [*parole*], but that science must not be confused with linguistics proper, whose sole object is language [*langue*]" (1916: 19–20).

In our time, linguistics (unmarked by a modifier or hyphenated prefix) is Chomskyan linguistics in the broadest sense, and before that it was Bloomfieldian linguistics in America and the dominant structuralist schools elsewhere. The unmarked term has thus referred to the traditions that perpetuate Saussure's science of *langue*. That was inevitable a few decades ago, and no one questioned it. Now, however, the alternative linguistics, the science of *parole*, has come into existence and has forged a tradition in its own right.

1.3.4   Linguistics without categoricity

Chomsky's critics complained about the lack of realism in his 1965 statement about the ideal speaker-listener in a homogeneous speech community, but most of them unwittingly adopted the same idealization in their own work. There were very few contemporary proposals for a program of linguistic research *without* the idealization.

One of the clearest came from Bolinger (1961: 10) four years before Chomsky's statement of the axiom:

From the standpoint of what has become traditional in American linguistics, the question is not whether there are such things as continuous phenomena in parts of human behavior that lie close to linguistics – many would grant that there are – but whether such phenomena should be regarded as the object of linguistic study. It comes down more to a scheme of priorities than to a denial of possible ultimate importance: a higher value, for the present, is placed on phenomena that lend themselves to an all-or-none analysis.

Bolinger's interests lay primarily in phonetic gradience rather than in variability but his contention that categorical (all-or-none) linguistics was a matter of priority rather than necessity was borne out a few years later when sociolinguistics came into being.

Saussure, in contrast to Bolinger, appeared to harbor no hopes at all for a science of *parole*. "As soon as we give language [*langue*] first place among the facts of speech," he says (1916: 9), "we introduce a natural order into a mass that lends itself to no other classification."

Chomsky, in contrast to both Saussure who held out no hope for studying *parole* and Bolinger who believed that *parole* could be studied if linguists thought it as interesting as *langue*, felt that there was an ordered relationship between the two in which the study of *langue* was necessarily the precursor of the study of *parole*. In other words, he maintains that any "theory of performance" will necessarily be dependent upon a theory of competence. "Performance models," he says, must "incorporate generative grammars of specific kinds," or at least incorporate "assumptions about underlying competence" (1965: 10; similarly, 1980: 24–8).

There is a sense in which his claim appears to me to be true, and another sense in which it seems quite false. On the one hand, it is true, I think, that any worthwhile non-categorical theory such as a theory of linguistic variation must incorporate – or at least must be consistent with and must not contradict – the general properties of linguistic competence that have emerged with wonderful clarity in the Chomskyan paradigm. By "general properties" I mean language as a mental faculty, species-specific and innately predetermined, which when stimulated by social experience creates a grammar by setting parameters on universal principles that may in some instances be structure-dependent and thus independent of non-linguistic cognitive principles.

On the other hand, it is certainly not true – and Chomsky may even agree with this in view of the way categorical linguistics has developed since 1965 when he first stated the idealization – that variation theory must incorporate or in any other way take account of the specific postulates of categorical grammar. That is to say, variation theory need not incorporate notions like – to cite just a few – the affix shift transformation (Chomsky 1957: 39–42), the Katz-Postal principle (Chomsky 1965: 132), the specified-subject condition (Chomsky 1973), the root clause filter (Chomsky and Lasnik 1977: 486), or the antecedent trace chain (Chomsky 1988: 116–17).[7] These postulates gather dust with dozens of others in the generativist scrapyard that is surely one of the most bizarre and tragicomic residues of any intellectual tradition. Any ancillary theory that adopted those elaborate postulates, such as a theory of performance dependent upon Chomsky's theory of competence, would necessarily share their evanescence.

The reason that these postulates come and go so quickly is presumably a measure of the gulf between the axiom of categoricity as presently formulated and empirical reality. As Naro (1980: 159) puts it, "the construction of the sort of elaborate formal theories achieved in the generative school requires many clear-cut decisions on very esoteric sentence types. This is possible because data collection is so easy for this school, and the data sources are malleable enough to conform to the theorist's wildest desires." With no branch of applied linguistics to test and balance its postulates, as in physics, theoretical linguistics is destined to continue proliferating postulates with few effective constraints.

It does not seem to me to be paradoxical for sociolinguistic theory to avoid specific proposals of theoretical linguistics while embracing its general conception. On the one hand, a theory that presupposed an opposed view of the language faculty, contrary to the general (and essentially immutable) Chomskyan view, would be basically flawed. On the other hand, the root clause filter and all the other trappings are in no way integral to Chomsky's view of the language faculty. Luckily, categorical theory and variation theory are separate enough that they need only share the general view of the language faculty. That shared view marks their common ground as linguistic theories. Beyond that, they have their own domains and ways of proceeding.

1.3.5 Categorical theory and variation theory

The essential separability of these two approaches to linguistic research does not seem to be widely understood. In the earliest proposals for variable rules, Labov and others clearly conceived of them as a refinement of the optional rules in contemporary generative theory (Labov 1972a: 93–5; Wolfram and Fasold 1974: 99–100). Cedergren and Sankoff (1974: 352) declared, "The full importance of variable rules can be appreciated only from a certain paradigmatic viewpoint, one which constitutes a slight but distinct shift from generative theory." They then went on to enumerate the need for generative theory to, first, broaden its notion of competence by including variability, and, second, use actual speech samples as data rather than intuitions. But those changes, far from slight, would amount to generative theory giving up the axiom of categoricity. That, as we have seen, would move the domain of study away from langue–energeia–competence.

The axiom of categoricity is not an accidental property of categorical linguistics but an essential one. Over the years, as rules have been discarded by categorical linguists in favor of notationally different generalizations variously called filters, templates and principles, so variable rules have ceased to be discussed in variationist linguistics (Fasold 1991, Wolfram 1991). However, the statistical program underlying variable rules (Cedergren and Sankoff 1974, Rousseau and Sankoff 1978, Rand and Sankoff 1990) did not disappear along with the notion of "rule." Instead, it remains as one of a set of statistical procedures available to researchers for correlating dependent and independent variables.

The fundamental difference between variationist and categorical theories was surprisingly well understood and astutely explained by Gleason (1961: 391–2), in what was the standard introductory textbook in linguistics from its first edition in 1955 until the 1970s. In a chapter called "Variation in Speech," Gleason outlined how the "descriptive linguist" goes about assembling a "narrowed corpus" by "restricting his attention as far as possible to utterances produced by one speaker under a single set of circumstances." In the terms of reference we have been using in this chapter, Gleason is describing the effort of a categorical linguist in thinking up data or eliciting it from a native speaker.

He then goes on to contrast that methodology with "another quite valid, but basically very different, approach" which could be put into practice. This approach would take an unregularized corpus and study the variants in it "by seeking correlations with non-linguistic factors, commonly the speaker and the circumstances." He continues: "Obviously, the results are predestined to be fundamentally different from those which the descriptive linguist will attain, since the variation under examination is precisely that which the descriptivist will attempt to eliminate."

Again, in our terms, he is suggesting that a linguist might gather data by, say, recording a conversation and then analyzing the usage of the participants by looking at how the variants in their speech are determined by social conditions.

"Here is the basis for a second type of linguistic science," he says. "Since most workers have restricted their attention to single aspects of the problem, we lack a general term for the discipline as a whole." The general term, a few years later, came to be "sociolinguistics," and its methods took shape very much along the lines that Gleason described. Although he never tried to apply those methods himself, he understood their singularity, their fundamental differentness from the mainstream tradition in linguistics, more clearly than many who did.

To the best of my knowledge, Gleason's chapter, despite the wide distribution of the book it appeared in, was not a direct influence on the new discipline. Neither was Currie's equally programmatic proposal that coined the word sociolinguistics. Both predated the actual practice, and Gleason's outline was remarkably prescient. Both were "in the air" when Labov laid the groundwork for discovering patterns where his predecessors had found only noise.

1.3.6   *Categoricity in other disciplines*

Around the same time that Labov put into practice this second type of linguistic science dispensing with the axiom of categoricity, researchers in other disciplines were doing exactly the same thing.

The axiom of categoricity is not, of course, unique to linguistics. Mathematics is probably its most celebrated host. It was once known as the "perfect science" simply because it admitted no exceptions, was perfectly explicit, and was never stuck for an answer. That is no longer so. Since mid-century several branches have begun inquiring into the mathematical properties of variability. Fuzzy set theory studies the considerable implications if an object is a member of a set not categorically but partially, to some intermediate degree (Zadeh 1965). Many-valued logic computes multi-dimensional truth tables based on values part-way between "true" and "false" (Rescher 1969). Physicists are tracking the geometry of behavior without such protective idealizations as non-friction and non-gravity in an emerging field called "nonlinear dynamics" (Abraham and Shaw 1992). Scientists interested in the mathematical properties of such diverse natural phenomena as cloud shapes, spider webs, and hurricanes are working out a new branch of mathematics called "chaos" (Stewart 1990).

If branches of mathematics can give up the axiom of categoricity, then so can branches of other disciplines, and many have, including philosophy, psychology, geography and statistics as well as linguistics. Looked at from this general perspective, the variationist movement is surely one of the most significant in the intellectual history of our time.

What is under investigation in many of these disciplines is the idea of categories themselves (Taylor 1989). What happens if we give up the idealization that categories are intensionally defined and have sharp boundaries? Observations of real-world phenomena show that, in fact, most categories have odd or variable members and fuzzy or indefinite borders. The real revelation of contemporary intellectual history has been the discovery that the variability is explicable and the fuzziness has form. In other words, once we stop filtering real-world phenomena through the axiom of categoricity it begins to look as if the idealization was unnecessary. It was a convenient fiction, erected in order to simplify reality in hopes of making data manageable and analyzable. It is being abandoned by researchers in numerous disciplines after many centuries of dominance, perhaps because we now have better tools – laser beams, microcircuitry, fibroptic scanners, acoustic microscopes, silicon chips – for managing and analyzing data.[8]

One of the more lucid general inquiries into categoricity and variability was made by William James (1911), who distinguished "percepts," the apprehension of reality, from "concepts," the idealization of reality. "There must always be a discrepancy between concepts and reality," he said (1911: 365), "because the former are static and discontinuous, and the latter are dynamic and flowing." Although James, like his contemporary Saussure, probably did not foresee that scholars might one day study percepts directly, he, unlike Saussure, recognized their primacy (1911: 96):

> The deeper features of reality are found only in perceptual experience. Here alone do we acquaint ourselves with continuity, or the immersion of one thing in another, here alone with self, with substance, with qualities, with activity in its various modes, with time, with cause, with changes, with novelty, with tendency, and with freedom.

James's rhetoric seems to me to capture something of the much more modern spirit that underlies work in chaos theory and in fuzzy semantics and in language variation.

Once the axiom of categoricity has been abandoned, one of the filters separating the "features of reality" from their investigators is removed. The attraction of studying the universe without the protective shield of the axiom of categoricity is counterbalanced, predictably, by the recalcitrance of the data it yields. As the statistician Moroney (1957: 5) says, "Life and nature may be simple enough to the Almighty who designed them and keeps them going, but to the human mind there is presented an unending stream of problems that cannot be given a clear-cut answer of the type $p = 1$ or $p = 0$." The answers 1 and 0 are of course categorical, and if the problems we confront have answers that belong in the interval between 1 and 0, then we have an unbounded set of possibilities. The challenges of observing, analyzing and understanding percepts are imposing. Facing those challenges is a relatively recent development in the natural and social sciences.

Sociolinguistics has met those challenges in interesting, sometimes exciting, ways. The rest of this book presents observations, analyses and interpretations made in the core area of sociolinguistics, the study of the social significance of linguistic variation.

2

Class, Network, and Mobility

The earliest records of our species point to group organizations – the primitive horde, nomadic tribes, settlements, communities, cities, nations. As these groups progressed in numbers, wealth and intelligence, they subdivided into specialized groups – social classes, religious sects, learned societies, and professional or craft unions. Is this complication or articulation of society in itself a symptom of progress? I do not think it can be described as such in so far as it is merely a quantitative change. . . . If the individual is a unit in a corporate mass, his life will be limited, dull, and mechanical. If the individual is a unit on his own, with space and potentiality for separate action, then he may be more subject to accident and chance, but at least he can expand and express himself. He can develop – in the only real meaning of the word – in consciousness of strength, vitality, and joy.

Herbert Read (1940)

All societies are characterized by inequalities in the distribution of wealth, privilege, and opportunity. And in all societies, people who have very similar wealth, privileges and opportunities usually have very similar recreations, attitudes and values, thus further distinguishing themselves from the social groups above and below them.

In just societies, as people go about their mundane activities, these inequalities are so innocuous that they usually go unnoticed. We seldom take the time to reflect on the fact that the people with more or fewer privileges than us are not necessarily endowed with greater or less intelligence, strength, or competence. We accept the fact that there is, in other words, an element of arbitrariness in the social inequalities. Indeed, it is this very arbitrariness that makes those inequalities acceptable, for as soon as it becomes clear that they are not arbitrary but systematic – that the underprivileged belong to one sex or one race or one ethnic group or any other identifiable element in the society – then the social system must undergo reform. The most powerful group must be persuaded to reform the social contract in order to increase the arbitrariness of the allocation of privilege, and if they refuse, as they might be inclined to do if doing so would leave them and their offspring vulnerable, then revolution becomes necessary.

Revolution is relatively rare but reformation is constant, in as much as it is the motivating force for amendments to legislation, lobbying by special interest groups for new legislation, quadrennial elections of legislators, and other aspects of the political process. It is only when the political processes are curtailed by some form of oligarchy or rendered useless by some form of fraud that revolution becomes necessary.

The social theorist, Karl Marx (1818–83), postulated revolution as the inevitable destiny of all industrial societies. Time has proven him wrong, of course, but for reasons he could not possibly have anticipated. For one thing, Marx could not have imagined the extent to which the working class, the proletariat that he assumed would be the revolutionaries, would become involved in the political process of reformation in all the first world nations. Their involvement came about partly through the labor movement that Marx's theorizing inspired. The proletariat, far from the despised, unenfranchised majority of Marx's day, became a political juggernaut, with political candidates and parties as well as lobbyists and spokespeople representing their interests as vociferously and effectively as most other constituencies.

For another thing, Marx could not imagine the extent to which the new world societies such as Australia, Canada, New Zealand and especially the United States would become the prototypes for industrial societies in the twentieth century. Economically, the new world societies had the accidental advantage of embracing industrialization later, after the Industrial Revolution was well established in the European nations. (This advantage also fell to Japan and some other old nations which industrialized belatedly.) Where the old world nations were freighted with nineteenth-century technology and plants, the new world nations were less encumbered and could more readily accommodate assembly lines, distribution networks, specialization, automation, and other advances of the post-Industrial Revolution.

Socially, the old world nations were also freighted with rigidities of class inherited as vestiges of feudalism. The new world nations, preoccupied at first with clearing their land and pushing back their frontiers, had too few amenities to support an aristocracy and too few people to support many ranks. The egalitarianism of the pioneers soon gave way to classes, all right, but with more fluid boundaries. They permitted occupational mobility to an unprecedented degree, and with it, social mobility unimaginable to Marx and his contemporaries.

Wherever these two social forces, social mobility and political enfranchisement, disseminated across political boundaries, they robbed Marxism of its apocalypse. In the twentieth century, political tension has been generated less by the distribution of wealth, as Marx claimed, than by the distribution of opportunity. The basic political poles, known generically as conservative and liberal, have remained much the same since the Enlightenment. By whatever names, they encompass those who would preserve the status quo and, with it, their own privileges, and those who would extend it, putting those privileges within reach of more people. The poles persist hardily, and the most uncompromising advocates of one or the other are as antithetical as ever. Their perennial contentions are surely no less fierce than they ever were. But between the poles there are vastly more of the citizenry than ever before. The proportion of politically informed, issue-conscious voters is surely greater, and the proportion of unenfranchised, alienated ciphers is surely less.

Our consideration in this chapter of the linguistic consequences of the ways we affiliate ourselves with other members of our society will lead us into three major areas. The first is class (§§2.1–2.5), the stratification of society on the basis of occupational, educational and economic similarities. In the industrialized nations, social class is the most linguistically marked aspect of our social being. Our closest social ties, of course, are more local, in what are called networks (§§2.6–2.8). The extent to which we participate in the activities of our families, neighborhoods, clubs, and other local entities – or distance ourselves from them – also has linguistic consequences. But no matter how prototypical we might be in our social class or how integrated we might be in our local networks, we still retain our individuality. That too has linguistic consequences, and in the final section (2.9) we will look at some individuals who, for better or worse, stand linguistically apart from their peers.

2.1   Social Class and Sociolinguistic Sampling

The notion of social class is inherently fuzzy, especially compared to the other two major social partitions, age and sex. Those two are relatively cut and dried in the sense that an individual is either, say, 48 years old or some other age, and either female or male. Of course, the social *significance* of age and sex is not altogether well defined. With regard to age, societies differ in deciding when a person ceases to be suckled as an infant, or takes on adult responsibilities, or retires from active duties as provider. Similarly, with regard to sex, societies can differ considerably in the extent to which sex differences, which are biologically determined, are allowed to define gender roles, which are socially determined (as discussed in detail in chapter 3).

Table 2.1 Social class divisions with general occupational correlates

MIDDLE	Upper (UMC)	Owners, directors, people with inherited wealth
CLASS	Middle (MMC)	Professionals, executive managers
(MC)	Lower (LMC)	Semi-professionals, lower managers
WORKING	Upper (UWC)	Clerks, skilled manual workers
CLASS	Middle (MWC)	Semi-skilled manual workers
(WC)	Lower (LWC)	Unskilled labourers, seasonal workers

2.1.1 Blue collar and white collar

The major social division in industrialized nations is between people who earn their livings by working with their hands and those who earn them by pencil-work and services. By a historical accident, the manual workers have become known as the "working class" (as if the others were not working) and the non-manual workers as the "middle class." The "upper class," consisting of people with inherited wealth and privileges, is so inconsequential – nonexistent outside of Europe and Asia, and dwindling rapidly there – that it will not be considered here.

A host of social differences normally follow these class lines: non-manual workers usually have more years of schooling, often work at supervising manual workers or other support staff, and earn more money.

Although class is fuzzy, it is usually fairly easy to judge whether an individual is middle-class or working-class. Informally, in America and elsewhere, this difference is talked about in conventional, non-controversial, everyday terms as "white collar workers" and "blue collar workers." Though these terms are intended to express the major class division, they err in at least one respect, as we will see above in table 2.1. The metaphors about collar colors instantiate a couple of sociological facts about the concept of class: first, social classes are perceived primarily as a function of occupation, hence the conventional workplace attire of white-shirt-and-tie or open-necked blue denim; and, second, one's class is also expressed by certain non-essential traits such as style of dress (going well beyond traditional workclothes) and also manners, recreation, entertainment, and tastes in the broadest sense.

In complicated industrial societies, divisions into middle class and working class are too gross to be very meaningful except for the most general discussions. Usually we need to make further distinctions, partitioning these two major groups into upper, middle, and lower sub-groups. Here the distinctions grow cloudy. For many individuals, it is possible to argue for their inclusion in either the middle or lower categories, or the middle and upper. Leaving aside individuals, however, we could probably find a fairly widespread consensus about the way occupational groups tie into these finer social class distinctions. Table 2.1 lists the general occupational groups that correlate with the class levels. At this level of generality, one would not expect any serious arguments over the lists.

It is worth noting in passing that the terms white collar and blue collar fit this schema imperfectly. Although for the most part they coincide with middle class and working class, the clerical workers listed in the UWC in table 2.1, comprising appliance salespeople in department stores, check-out tellers in supermarkets, mail couriers in corporations, and other non-supervisory indoor workers, are literally white collar rather than blue in their attire, though their occupational status puts them in the UWC with blue collar plumbers, electricians and cabinet makers. Less obviously but no less salient, those blue collar plumbers, electricians, cabinet makers, and so on, who rise through the ranks to take on duties as supervisors and over-seers are generally LMC, though their attire may not be different from the workers in their crews.

Thinking about particular individuals instead of large groups makes an effective reminder that class is a continuum rather than a set of discrete ranks. In any society, very few individuals match one another exactly with respect to occupation, education, income, tastes, and the other trappings that might be taken as measures of class. Social class, like all fuzzy categories, is better defined for prototypical members than for peripheral ones. In other words, it is easier to categorize individuals in the middle of a category than those near the boundary between two classes.

2.1.2   *Judgement samples*

Sociolinguists (and sociologists) often rely on their intuitions in assigning social classes to individuals in the sample population in their studies. Doing so is a short cut – a way of avoiding the digression required in making a specific index, gathering information ancillary to the main study, and determining the rank of each individual in the group. Generally, it is a short cut that can be taken only when the sociolinguist is dealing with a restricted sample in a well-defined setting. For instance, the Milroys felt no need to work out a class index for the individuals in their survey of three Belfast neighborhoods (Milroy and Milroy 1978, L. Milroy 1980; the study is reviewed in some detail in §3.3.2 below). All three neighborhoods were well-defined sociologically, having been established in the Industrial Revolution to provide modest housing for the workers in the factories they surrounded, with a highly stable occupancy that usually went back one or more generations. Their subjects could only be WC because no one else lived there.

Similarly, in a survey I conducted on a MC sample in Canada, I chose my subjects from a neighborhood known as North Toronto with emphasis on the condition that the younger subjects must be lifelong residents and the older ones residents there at least since childhood. (The results of this research are reviewed briefly in §2.5.4.) The neighborhood is homogeneously MC, and well established as such. It has never been anything else. The particular linguistic variable I was investigating was not restricted to residents of North Toronto but was known from casual observations to be general in Toronto and much further afield. I purposely chose the subjects from one neighborhood and extrapolated their linguistic behavior to other MC people. (The alternative, of course, would be to choose subjects from numerous neighborhoods, determine their social status, and directly investigate their linguistic similarities.) Linguistically, my study focused on differences in the speech of young and old Torontonians. Besides the adult speakers, there were two younger groups, 12-year-olds and 22-year-olds. At these ages, education is often incomplete and occupation, income and other class markers are not yet established. By selecting subjects whose social class was well defined, I avoided having to determine it.

Choosing subjects from predetermined social classes or, for that matter, by any other predetermined social criterion constitutes a judgement sample. Selecting people from one or more well-defined neighborhoods, as the Milroys and I did, carries few risks, especially for investigators who know the regions intimately. Feagin (1979: 25–26), for a study of speech of a town in northeastern Alabama, exploited her knowledge as "a native of the town, with local relatives and other contacts" to select a much more complex judgement sample, involving urban and rural teenagers and elders, both male and female, in two classes she calls "upper class" and "working class."

2.1.3   Random samples

Usually a large, complex sample, especially if it has a high degree of randomness, as in an urban setting in which the neighborhoods are not preselected, requires some kind of indexing procedure in order to cluster the subjects into appropriate social groups, as discussed in the next section. It is important to note that, technically, sociolinguistic samples have varying degrees of randomness. Truly random samples of the type used in opinion polls, marketing research, and other social surveys have proven to be both unmanageable and unnecessary in sociolinguistic research. Although Labov took his New York sample as a random selection from the lists of a sociological survey called the Mobilization for Youth Program (1966: 157), numerous commentators have noted that the final sample was not random but a partly random sub-set.

Labov himself (1966: 180) discussed the discrepancy between the Mobilization for Youth sample and his own, and justified the difference in terms of the kind of information elicited in their survey and his own:

> If the type of behavior which was being studied was similar to most forms of behavior that are investigated by social survey, the value of the study could be measured by how far it [the sample] fell short of the MFY standards. However, linguistic behavior is far more general and compelling than many social attitudes or survey responses. The primary data being gathered . . . are not subject to the informant's control in the way that answers on voting choices would be.

This distinction is so fundamental as to make an abyss between the sampling methods of sociolinguistic surveys and the type of sociological survey represented by opinion polls.

Another problem with using a truly random sample in sociolinguistic studies is the practical impossibility of carrying out fine-grained linguistic analysis on a large sample. Obviously, the task of analyzing dozens or often hundreds of linguistic variants for each subject poses an analytic task of a different magnitude from opinion polls and the other surveys for which random samples were originally devised. As Gillian Sankoff (1974: 22–3) points out:

> A speech community sample need not include the large number of individuals usually required for other kinds of behavioral surveys. If people within a speech community indeed understand each other with a high degree of efficiency, this tends to place a limit on the extent of possible variation, and imposes a regularity (necessary for effective communication) not found to the same extent in other kinds of social behavior. The literature as well as our own experience would suggest that, even for quite complex speech communities, samples of more than about 150 individuals tend to be redundant, bringing increasing data handling problems with diminishing analytical returns.

The New York Mobilization for Youth Program listed 340 subjects in its sample but Labov interviewed only 88 of them. Applying Labov's methodology, Shuy, Wolfram and Riley (1968) interviewed 702 subjects for the Detroit Dialect Study but the principal sociolinguistic analysis that came out of it (Wolfram 1969) analyzed results from 36 speakers.

Both the New York and the Detroit surveys were attempts at adapting sociological sampling to a much more exacting task than it was designed for.

Since then, sociolinguists have generally chosen subjects on the basis of predetermined social characteristics, that is, judgement samples. In this respect, sociolinguistics is no different from most other social sciences that make use of field research. The social anthropologist Mead long ago noted (1953: 645–6) that the "validity" of a sample

> depends not so much upon the number of cases as upon the proper specification of the informant, so that he or she can be accurately placed, in terms of a very large number of variables – age, sex, order of birth, family background, life experience, temperamental tendencies . . . , political and religious position, exact situational relationship to the investigator, configurational relationship to every other informant, and so forth. Within this extensive degree of specification, each informant is studied as a perfect example, an organic representation of his complete cultural experience.

Critiques of sociolinguistic sampling that presume it should be more like opinion poll sampling – for instance, bald statements such as "a judgment sample is obviously less adequate than a random sample" (Wardhaugh 1992: 153) – are simply naïve.

Because sociolinguistics developed later than most of the social sciences, its particular sampling requirements took some time to be recognized. Only recently has the consensus become clear. Milroy (1987: 28), in her review of sociolinguistic sampling, concluded, "Certainly, in view of the problems associated with strict representative sampling, it may be more realistic for researchers conducting, for example, an urban dialect survey, to judgement sample *on the basis of specifiable and defensible principles* than to aim for true representativeness." Similarly, Davis (1990: 11) reviewed the failed attempts at randomizing the New York and Detroit samples and concluded: "What we are left with, then, is the fact that classic random sampling is, for all practical purposes, not really feasible for us: instead, our efforts should be spent in eliminating destructive bias."

2.2 Indexing Social Class

Intuitions about the class membership of individuals are reliable only under the most favourable conditions, when one is judging prototypical individuals rather than fringe members, or is intimately familiar with the community, or is dealing with homogeneous neighborhoods, and so on. Under ordinary conditions, it is necessary to devise a set of criteria for ranking individuals in order to discover the status groups they belong to.

Table 2.2 Socioeconomic index for 40 Canadian occupations (from Blishen 1971: 499–504)

Occupation	Index	Occupation	Index
Lawyers and notaries	75.41	Firemen, policemen, watchmen	35.80
Biological scientists	73.22	Baggagemen, transport	34.85
Osteopaths and chiropractors	70.25	Logging foremen	34.61
Advertising managers	66.05	Switchmen and signalmen	33.76
Authors, editors, journalists	64.23	Boiler-makers and platers	32.93
Credit managers	60.81	Bus drivers	31.86
Clergymen and priests	59.20	Crushers, millers – chemical	31.12
Social welfare workers	55.62	Labourers, primary metal industries	30.68
Artists commercial	54.06	Waiters	30.47
Teachers and instructors	52.07	Taxi drivers and chauffeurs	30.07
Funeral directors and embalmers	49.47	Attendants, recreation/ amusement	29.92
Batch and continuous still operators	47.60	Fruit, vegetable canners and packers	29.60
Foremen, paper and allied industries	45.36	Truck drivers	29.31
Interior decorators window-dressers	44.37	Launderers and dry cleaners	28.93
Mechanics and repairmen, aircraft	42.76	Woodworking occupations, n.e.s.	28.56
Electricians and wiremen	40.68	Janitors and cleaners, building	28.22
Engineering officers, ships	39.86	Shoemakers and repairers in shops	27.87
Pressmen, printing	39.49	Carders, combers, fibre-preparers	27.37
General foremen, construction	37.90	Weavers	26.77
Sales clerks	37.14	Trappers and hunters	25.36

2.2.1 Socioeconomic indices

Sociologists have long been engaged in devising such indices. Insofar as their methods exploit and objectify the criteria which underlie our intuitions, they provide the most useful guidelines for coming to grips with the concept of social class.

Table 2.2 lists a representative sample of occupations with their "socioeconomic index" scores. Although this sample comes from the calculations for Canada (Blishen 1971), both the method of deriving them and the actual indices are very similar to those for other industrialized nations. (In fact, the correlations are .94 with the United States, .90 with Japan, .89 with New

Zealand, .85 with Great Britain, and .74 with Germany [Blishen 1971: 504].) The indices were derived by, first, assigning each occupation a score for "social standing" based on the relative ranks assigned them by a random sample of Canadians, and then adding in proportionate scores for income and for educational level based on individuals in those occupations in the census. Table 2.2 randomly lists 40 occupations of the 320 ranked by choosing every seventh, eighth or ninth one in the complete list. Although the index appears to be stated in terms of occupations, it is important to note that the index score for each occupation incorporates income and education data as well. As we noted above and will demonstrate in §2.2.3 below, occupation is the touchstone of social class membership.

The sociological principle incorporated into the calculation above was stated by the sociologist Otis Dudley Duncan as follows: "If we characterize an occupation according to the prevailing levels of education and income of its incumbents, we are not only estimating its 'social status' and its 'economic status', we are also describing one of its major 'causes' and one of its major 'effects.' It would not be surprising if an occupation's 'prestige' turned out to be closely related to one or both of these factors" (quoted by Blishen 1971, 498).

The practice of deriving socioeconomic indices by combining occupational status with *means* for income and education is an abstraction. In reality, individuals with the same occupations can vary to some extent in the other aspects. With respect to education, for instance, some journalists come into their profession after taking postgraduate degrees and others by working their way up from obituary writing. With respect to income, lawyers can make large incomes by devoting their attentions to corporate clients or relatively modest ones devoting themselves to social issues. Though these individuals have the same occupation, in each case one would fall above the mean of the socioeconomic index for his profession and the other below it. The socioeconomic index characterizes neither of them individually.

2.2.2   Subject indices

When a sociolinguistic (or other) survey includes too few individuals from any one category to make the socioeconomic indices useful, the interviewer can elicit appropriate information from each subject to calculate an index score. Questions related to independent variables (age, mother tongue, residences, etc.) make a useful opening for any interview. These questions can readily include aspects of socioeconomic status (occupation, education, income, etc.), and then combine them according to some scheme.

Labov (1966: 170–74, 211–20) used a three-component index for his New York City subjects. Based on information about occupation, education and family income, he placed individuals on a ten-point scale (0–9) with each factor weighted equally. His scale partitioned the subjects as follows:

0–2   lower class
3–5   working class
6–8   lower middle class
9   upper middle class

In analyses with social class as the independent variable, Labov clustered his speakers inconsistently: for example, he presented the class stratification of (dh) (p. 244) in terms of groups 0, 1, 2, 3, 4, 5, 6, 7–8 and 9; of /ʌy/ (p. 340) in terms of groups 0–1, 2–3, 4–5, 6–8 and 9; of (oh) (p. 306) in terms of groups 0–2, 3–5, 6–8 and 9; and other combinations also occur. This kind of fluidity, clustering speakers indexed at 2, for instance, sometimes with those below them (0, 1) and sometimes with those above them (3) as well as standing independently as a sub-group (opposed to both 1 and 3) probably over-represents the gradation of the class continuum.

Trudgill (1974: chapter 3), modeling his approach partly on English sociologists, used a six-component index in which each component had scores ranging from 0–5. The six components are occupation, father's occupation, income, education, locality (of residence), and housing type. The criteria and their associated weights for each component are listed in table 2.3.

In determining his subjects' scores, Trudgill had to devise and apply several rules to ensure consistency. For their occupations, married women and widows were rated on their husbands' occupations because occupational limitations on women might otherwise skew the scale. However, working women whose occupational status exceeded their husband's were counted on their own. Students and unmarried women were counted by their fathers' occupations, so that for these groups the father's occupations were added in twice (under both I and II). Similarly, for income, women and students were ranked as for occupation. For education, students over 15 who had not taken external examinations (called O-levels and A-levels at the time of Trudgill's survey, equivalent to secondary school completion examinations and university entrance examinations, respectively) were allotted a score of 3. The localities were ranked subjectively by Trudgill, a native of the city; "council estates" are housing areas subsidized by the local governments for lower-income families. The type of housing has three sub-components, ownership, age of house, and type; a "flat" is an apartment, a "terrace" a house attached to other houses in a row; "semi-detached" is a house adjoined to its neighbor on one side. These sub-components would have to be adapted outside of England, and even there some of them are likely to be as antiquated now as the salary and wage scales shown in III.

From this index, the range of possible scores is 0–30. The actual range

Table 2.3 The six components in Trudgill's socioeconomic index for Norwich with their relative weights (1974: chapter 3)

I occupation and II father's occupation

a	professional workers	5
b	employers, managers	4
c	other non-manual workers	3
d	foremen, skilled, self-emp.	2
e	semi-skilled, agricultural	1
f	unskilled	0

III income

annual	over	£2,000	5
		£1,000–1,999	4
	under £999		3
weekly	over	£20	3
		£15–19	2
		£10–14	1
	under £9		0

IV education

a	some university, college	5
b	A-level or equivalent	4
c	O-level, CSE, or equivalent	3
d	terminal age 15 or over	2
e	terminal age 14	1
f	terminal age 13 or under	0

V locality

a	Eaton (excluding council estates)	5
b	Thorpe	4
c	S. Lakenham, Eaton counc.	3
d	Central Lakenham	2
e	Hellesdon	1
f	Westwick	0

VI housing

	council rented			privately rented			owner occupied		
	T/F	S-D	D	T/F	S-D	D	T/F	S-D	D
pre-1914	0	0	1	0	1	2	1	2	3
pre-1939	0	1	2	1	2	3	2	3	4
post-War	1	2	3	2	3	4	3	4	5

T = terrace; F = flat; S-D = semi-detached; D = detached

for Trudgill's subjects was 3–26. Based on the subjects' use of a particular grammatical variable, which, as we shall see in the next section, often mark social groups more rigidly than phonological variables, Trudgill assigned his subjects to social classes as follows:

MMC	over 19
LMC	15–18
UWC	11–14
MWC	7–10
LWC	3–6

In the analysis of the phonological variables with social class as the independent variable, as in the representation of Norwich (a:) cited in §2.3.3 below, these clusters were maintained in all cases.

2.2.3   The primacy of occupation as a determinant of class

Just as sociology provided the model for the first attempts at random sampling in sociolinguistics, so it also provided the model for elaborate social class indices of the type used by Labov and Trudgill.

Random sampling, as we saw in §2.1.3, proved to be unmanageable for the intensive structural analysis required by sociolinguists in their subject interviews. The use of random sampling has consequently declined. Similarly, the use of elaborate class indices has declined since the early studies. Partly this is the result of alternative, micro-level indices of social status such as the network scales described below in §2.6. But it is also partly the result of the realization, through experience and practice, that multidimensional indices are much more complicated than is necessary in sociolinguistics.

Whereas sampling methods have attracted a fair amount of discussion among sociolinguists, socioeconomic indexing has attracted much less. One of the few substantial discussions is by Macaulay (1976), based on the results of his sociolinguistic study of Glasgow.

Macaulay relied solely on occupation as a class indicator. His Glaswegian subjects fell into four occupational groups based on the Registrar General's classification, a categorized index for Great Britain calculated in a manner similar to the one for Canada discussed above (§2.2.1). He refined the classification as indicated in the following list by subdividing the group II subjects – roughly UWC in the terms we have used above – according to manual and non-manual occupations, so that his categories were these (1976: 174):

class I	professional and managerial
class IIa	white-collar, intermediate non-manual
class IIb	skilled manual
class III	semi-skilled and unskilled manual

It is worth noting in passing that these groups correspond in a straightforward way to the categories listed above in table 2.1, such that I = MMC, IIa, IIb = UWC, and III = MWC, LWC. Macaulay's subdivision of the UWC is based on his intuition that the occupational use of language by clerks and sales assistants might make a sociolinguistic difference between them and the plumbers and cabinet-makers who share their social status but not their need to talk in their jobs. Macaulay's intuition, as we will see later (§4.6.1.2) when we describe one of his results, proved insightful. It is also the intuition that underlies the concept of the *marché linguistique* or "talk market" in §4.5.

Macaulay's reliance on occupation alone as a class indicator turned out to be sufficient. His results showed a fine and regular correlation for all the phonological variables with class distinctions based solely on occupation (1976: 175–7). Their consistency makes a cogent demonstration of the systematic nature of sociolinguistic variation. Equally striking, when Macaulay separated the members of his occupational groups and ranked the individual subjects by their linguistic indices, the regularity of the correlation was even finer; "there is," he says (1976: 178), "not a single individual out of place according to the order predicted on the basis of occupation alone."

The Glasgow sample thus offers empirical support for simplifying class as an independent variable in sociolinguistic studies by using occupation as the sole indicator. It is, as all social scientists concede, the best single indicator. It may be, Macaulay's results suggest, the only one necessary when we are dealing with robustly embedded social markers such as linguistic variables. Against that, Macaulay (1976: 183–4) points out that its particular applicability here may be the result of conditions peculiar to the Glasgow survey rather than any general conditions. For one thing, his sample was made up of mature, settled adults whose occupations were largely fixed for the rest of their working lives, without any 20- to 30-year-olds whose occupations, and with them their styles of life, linguistic or otherwise, were still developing. For another thing, Glasgow's stagnant economy for almost five decades imposed some limits on occupational and social mobility within the city and may have made linguistic class markers more sharply defined. Under different circumstances, the correlations may not have been as convincing.

The correlation of dependent linguistic variables with occupation alone and with complex class indicators must obviously be tested in other cities. If it proved generally valid, the prospect of relying largely (if not exclusively) on occupation as an indicator in sociolinguistic studies would be an interesting and very welcome result. When several class indicators are used, each one increases the fuzziness of the individual index for reasons discussed above; the fuzzier the scores – or, in other words, the less discrete the class continuum – the vaguer the correlations. Using occupation alone would thus have a salutary practical effect.

It would also have an interesting theoretical implication because it would provide further evidence of the clarity with which linguistic variation actuates social differences. In this respect, the subject matter of sociolinguistics differs considerably from the other social sciences, especially what Bolinger (1980: 127) calls "the softest of the soft sciences, sociology and its branches."

Macaulay (1976: 187) went so far as to propose that sociologists and other social scientists might be able to capitalize on the sociolinguistic clarity:

> The highly systematic nature of linguistic variation, which has been demonstrated again and again . . . , could probably provide social scientists with much more reliable information about social stratification than is usually available and provide it quickly and easily once the basic pattern had been determined. . . . A sociolinguist, working in conjunction with a sociological

survey in a community where the pattern of linguistic variation had been mapped out, could provide independent evidence of social–class membership which would complement other easily obtainable data such as occupation.

This proposal has not been followed up. In fact, one of the most conspicuous theoretical gaps after more than thirty years of sociolinguistic research is the lack of a bridge between the sociolinguists and other social scientists. Attempts at constructing such a bridge – by, for instance, Fishman (1970) or Williams (1992), to cite two of the more serious ones – have brought little satisfaction to either side.

One reason is almost certainly the fundamental differences in the two enterprises. In sociolinguistics but not in sociology, random sampling is virtually unmanageable because of the analytic depth, and social stratification is often crystal clear because of systematic subconscious symbolization. These may be more than just methodological and analytic differences. They may instead result from epistemological differences so profound that they defy integration at any level accessible by the social sciences as they are presently conceived.

2.3   Class Markers

Social classes constitute barriers to communication every bit as real as mountain ranges or rivers. Even in very fluid societies, where the social classes are breachable by ambitious individuals, most people carry on their meaningful interactions with people who are similar to them materially, occupationally and recreationally. Individuals who do ascend the social scale, jumping up a class or two from their parents, most often entrench themselves in their new class as far as possible rather than attempting to maintain relations in two classes. Various stereotypes are associated with upward mobility: people who rise might be classed, depending upon who is judging them, as people who put on airs or who forget their roots, as "Liza Doolittles" or "Beverly Hillbillies," or as *nouveau riche*. These stereotypes suggest the discomfort that can be involved in breaching social barriers, and to some extent they may function as mild deterrents or vague social pressures to keep people "in their place."

2.3.1   Spreading the news in Westerntown

In a classic sociological study, Bogart (1950–1) demonstrated that the class system blocks channels of communication even when what is being communicated is a local event in a small, apparently close-knit community.

In Westerntown, an American prairie town of 25,000, a 17-year-old high school student won an invitation to fly to New York as the guest of the New York Philharmonic, where she would attend concerts, meet celebrities, and be interviewed by Deems Taylor at the intermission of the Philharmonic's Sunday radio broadcast. In 1949, it was an event of great moment in the town, reported in the local newspaper and talked about in all kinds of meeting places. One person, identified as a "civic leader," said:

> The impact was terrific! Something like that coming to a local girl was just terrific. . . . We all just went hog wild. . . . I think definitely that everyone was listening [to the Philharmonic broadcast] that Sunday. Of course, we all listen to the music on Sunday. You know, everyone does. But, I'm certain that people were listening especially hard that day.

Three weeks after the event, Bogart and his associates undertook systematic inquiries among the townspeople in order to assess the impact of the event upon them. Upon interviewing 68 people personally and 200 others by telephone, they found no difference in the knowledge of the event or the ability to recall its details by people of different ages or between men and women. In other words, neither age nor sex differences posed a barrier to knowledge of the event. There was, however, "a sharp cleavage along social class lines." Among the lower class, defined as those with less than high school education, only 27 percent knew about the event compared to 77 percent of the best educated group. The discrepancy could not be explained as the result of direct personal contact with the winner or her family, because people from other neighborhoods, including those who did not know the family at all, were as well informed as the immediate neighbors, if they were in the same social class.

The Westerntown case study took place in circumstances that must surely have favored the widest possible diffusion of news: a popular teenaged member of a respected family in a small town receives a glamorous, big-city honor with national publicity. Yet even in these circumstances the diffusion was significantly restricted when it came to crossing the line from the middle-class citizens to the working-class citizens. In larger urban centres with working-class and middle-class neighborhoods less proximate, the line must be even more palpable. In modern industrial societies, it is probably never impermeable, but penetrating it clearly requires some initiative and perhaps considerable resolve.

Partly by choice and partly by chance, then, the social classes are not in constant or close contact. Their segregation allows differences to take root. In their speech as in other attributes, these differences may come about in the first place unwittingly, simply because one group is unaware of changes taking hold in the other group. Once established, the differences may take on status as emblems or markers of a particular class.

2.3.2   Boston "short o̱"

The fact that the social classes all belong to the same community explains why many linguistic differences are quantitative rather than qualitative, marked not by their presence or absence in the speech of the other group but by their relative frequency. The feature itself may be a distinctive characteristic of the speech of the community at large. For instance, one of the stereotypes of Boston speech is known as "short o," the low back slightly rounded vowel [ɒ]. Laferriere (1979) shows that it occurs at all levels of Boston society, regardless of the ethnicity, age or educational level of the speakers. However, she also shows that it is a variant in the Boston speech, competing with the standard North American variant [o], so that Bostonians sometimes say [fóriy] 'forty' and other times [fɒ́riy], or sometimes say [ʃoˀt] 'short' and other times [ʃɒˀt]. In a sense, it is part of a Bostonian's identity to say [fɒ́riy] and [ʃɒˀt] sometimes, but those Bostonians who say it most frequently, and with little regard to the formality of the occasion, are the least educated Bostonians, that is, members of the lower classes.

The fact that [ɒ] occurs in these words in the speech of an urban North American is an indicator to many listeners that the speaker is from Boston. Within Boston, it is its high frequency and especially its use in formal contexts that makes it a marker of Boston working–class speech.

2.3.3   Norwich (aː)

In Norwich, Trudgill (1974: 97–9) found a variable that marked the social classes by the degree of vowel fronting. Variable (aː) indicates the vowel in words such as *after*, *path* and *cart*. The prestige dialect RP and most MC southern England accents have a back unrounded vowel, [ɑː], in these words. In Norwich, in addition to the back unrounded vowel, these words sometimes occur with front vowels: either [ä:], a low central vowel, or [a:], the low front open vowel.

Figure 2.1 shows the class distribution of these vowel variants. Although the Norwich classes are stratified for this variable, the class gradation is sharpest between the WC and MC groups. There is no overlap at all between them, so that even in the most casual styles the MC does not reach the index of the UWC in its most formal style. The index scores from about 90 to 120 serve as a divider between the main social divisions. Norwich WC accents, with scores always above 120 for this variable, typically have the [ä:] or [a:] variants. The MMC has the back variant [ɑ:] most of the time, with some fronting in casual styles. The mild style-shifting, indicated by

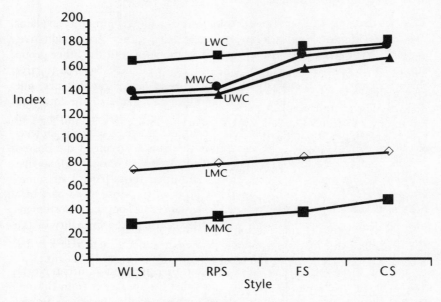

Figure 2.1 Norwich (a:) as a class marker, showing a large gap between the MC and WC groups and little style-shifting (after Trudgill 1974: 98)

the gentle incline of the lines of figure 2.1 from left to right, points out that this vowel difference is a stable, relatively unremarked class marker.

2.3.4 Grammatical variables

The two preceding examples are phonological variables. Grammatical variables tend to mark social stratification more sharply so that it is probably safe to say that most grammatical variables function as class markers. WC dialects in English include numerous grammatical variables that are almost never found in MC dialects. These include leveled past tense forms such as *seen* and *come* in *I seen the accident last Tuesday* and *John come home yesterday* (discussed in some detail in §5.6.3.1); genitive reflexives such as *hisself* and *theirselves* in sentences like *John seen hisself in the mirror*; double negatives such as *We weren't interested in nothing to eat*; and the stigmatized negative form of *be* and auxiliary *have* in sentences like *We ain't interested* and *We ain't bought any*. (The class stratification of two grammatical variables in Detroit BEV – Black English Vernacular – is discussed in §3.3.1.) Variables such as these are widespread and persistent in English WC dialects but occur very infrequently, if at all, in English MC dialects.

2.3.5   *Montreal* que-*deletion*

The same holds in other languages, probably universally. A well-studied grammatical variable in French, *que*-deletion, is widespread in French WC dialects. The complementizer *que* is obligatory in standard MC French, but not in other dialects. The following sentence, from Cedergren and Sankoff (1974: 347), was recorded without the parenthesized complementizer in the survey of Montreal French:

Au début je pense   (que) ça a été plutôt un snobisme
At the start I think (that) it was   rather a   fad

The probability of deleting the complementizer *que* depends crucially upon the preceding and following phonological environments, a correlation that historically provided one of the most important test cases for quantitative analytic methods (discussed in G. Sankoff 1974 and Bickerton 1973, as well as Cedergren and D. Sankoff 1974).

Generally, however, the most significant correlation for the use of *que*-deletion is not its phonological conditioning but its social conditioning. It occurs frequently in the speech of WC Montrealers and infrequently in the speech of MC Montrealers. In WC speech, *que* is deleted 37.32 percent of the time regardless of phonology, style, or any other factor, whereas in MC speech it is deleted only 11.2 percent of the time. The figures are even more dramatic when we compare the WC men, who delete it 55.72 percent of the time, with the professional men, who delete it only 6.19 percent of the time (based on Cedergren and Sankoff 1974: table 5, 348).

In other words, *que*-deletion occurs with decreasing frequency in the speech of people higher on the social scale. In that respect it is a class marker, as are most grammatical variables.

2.4   The Effects of Mobility

2.4.1   *Caste and class*

Sociologists routinely begin their discussions of social class by distinguishing caste systems from class systems. Caste systems are societies based on hereditary occupational groups, in which individuals automatically and inexorably become members of the occupational group they were born into (Littlejohn 1972: chapter 4). The best studied caste system is the Hindu of India, with ranks rigidly ordered starting from Brahmins (priests), Kshatriya (military commanders), Vaisya (scribes), Sudra (labourers), to Untouchables (menial workers or beggars).

Although caste systems may at first appear exotic to people raised in class systems, when they are stripped of their cultural excrescences, such as the Sanskrit caste names in the Hindu example, they take on a more familiar look. In fact, they resolve into hierarchical social organizations in which the distribution of wealth, privilege and opportunity is not only unequal, as it also is in class systems, but where those inequalities are fixed and permanent. In the fixedness of the inequalities, they resemble the feudal system of Medieval Europe with its impenetrable gulf between seigneurs and serfs, or the plantation system of eighteenth-century Virginia and Jamaica with its unbreachable social abyss between masters and slaves (Calvert 1982).

Rather than separate types of social organization, class systems and caste systems appear to be poles on a continuum. (This social similarity presumably accounts for certain general sociolinguistic similarities shared by caste societies and class societies, discussed in §3.5.3 below.) They share the essential characteristic of an unequal distribution of material and personal goods. They differ in that in a class system people who by birth and circumstance start out as members of one rank can ascend (or descend) to another rank. In other words, the essential difference is mobility. A caste system is a class system with no social or occupational mobility.

2.4.2 Comparative mobility

Not all class systems are equally mobile by any means. For instance, class membership in Victorian England was rigidly defined, with little opportunity for WC offspring to gain access to higher education or white collar employment, whereas in the contemporary United States it is highly fluid, with scholarships for underprivileged achievers and "equal opportunity" legislation for enhancing their employment prospects. At the beginning I mentioned the political significance of social mobility as a counter-measure to non-arbitrary social inequalities in modern industrialized nations. This idea, traceable from the Magna Carta of 1215 to the US Declaration of Independence of 1776 among many other bellwethers, has gained political clout in the industrialized nations since the time of Marx, perhaps partly due to the impact of his political theories. It is probably safe to say that in developed nations the opportunity for people to alter their social status is, for the first time in history, presumed to be an inalienable right.

Sociologically, class mobility has attracted research on a macro-scale.

Ganzeboom, Luijkx and Tremain (1989) have devised a mobility index that weighs statistics made available in government documents for international comparisons. Their results show, not surprisingly, that there are significant between-country differences in mobility patterns, and, rather disquietingly, that inequality in mobility is generally increasing at the present time. Given the central importance of social mobility as a channel for individual fulfilment in stratified communities of all sizes, micro-level studies ought to become a burgeoning field of inquiry as sociologists, political scientists, and others seek an understanding of the sociopolitical correlates than enhance it.

2.4.3 Mobility in language variation

The sociolinguistic consequences of greater or lesser social mobility have attracted very little research, presumably because the crucial hypotheses could only be generated by a comparative study of two (or more) diametrically different societies. The differences would furthermore have to be long-standing and well defined. It should follow that class dialects in highly mobile societies have fewer absolute class markers (as discussed immediately above in §2.3) than do less mobile societies, since individuals moving up the hierarchy should carry linguistic variables from lower-class dialects with them. Some of these will inevitably be received by the established members as unacceptable, but others will persist, presumably more of them when the movement of individuals is constant and numerous.[1]

2.4.4 Hungarian imperative declaratives

Kontra (1992) documented a dramatic instance of the incursion of non-standard features into the standard language as a result of upward mobility. Two of the questions in Kontra's Hungarian National Sociolinguistic Survey asked participants to judge the grammaticality of these two sentences:

> *Nem szeretem, ha elhalasszák   a   döntést*
> not   like-I   if postpone-they the decision
> I don't like their postponing the decision.

> *Ha időben   érkeznek,   ők   is   láthassák a   filmet*
> if in time arrive-they they too see-can   the film
> If they come in time, they can also see the film.

Both sentences are condemned by standard grammars, usage guides and school teachers. "In fact," Kontra (1992: 218) says, "they contain the most heavily stigmatized verb forms in Hungary today, that is the imperative forms *elhalasszák* 'they should postpone' and *láthassák* 'they should see' where standard Hungarian speakers use the indicative *elhalasztják* 'they postpone' and *láthatják* 'they can see'."

The judgements made by the random sample of 850 respondents were not as decisive as traditional sources would suggest: a majority, 55 percent, judged the first sentence grammatical, and a fairly large minority, 29 percent, judged the second one grammatical. When the educational levels of the respondents were correlated with their judgements of these sentences, they turned out to be insignificant: the first sentence, for instance, was judged grammatical by 55 percent of the lowest educational group, 59 percent of those with eight years of schooling, 52 percent of high school graduates, and 57 percent of university graduates.

The explanation, according to Kontra, lies in the communist policy of "pushing working class children into higher education" (1992: 219). From the communist takeover in 1948 until 1960, schoolchildren with one or both parents working as laborers received government aid as long as they were at school, and a similar, though less generous aid program continued until 1990, when the communist regime collapsed. While it lasted, Kontra (1992: 219) says, the "power structure . . . made it possible for members of the communist political and economic elite to retain their vernacular non-standard speech. . . . When they came to power, they may have changed some of their habits or their clothing, but there was no linguistic threshold to cross." As a result, the standard dialect underwent a broadening, with some former WC markers coming into common MC use.

The communist regime may, however, have been too short-lived for the incursions to be permanent. With respect to these grammatical features, at least, Kontra is critical of their widespread acceptability. If his attitude is representative of the academic sector, the incursions into the standard dialect will undoubtedly be eliminated, as far as possible, as was the political system that gave rise to them.

2.4.5 New York (th) and (dh)

Under ordinary circumstances, instead of carrying their WC markers into the MC, upwardly mobile individuals adjust the frequency of certain linguistic variables in order to sound more like the class they are joining and less like the one they are leaving. Labov (1966b) demonstrated the general validity of this correlation by re-analyzing his New York City data according to the social mobility of the speakers. Table 2.4 shows some of the results for two variables: (dh) is the initial consonant in words like *this*, *them*

Table 2.4 Correlation of upward social mobility (U) and stable class status (S) with two linguistic variables in two social classes (after Labov 1966b: tables 6 and 8)

Mobility	WC (dh)	LMC (dh)	WC (th)	LMC (th)	Style
U	27	17	—	26	CS
S	80	50	95	35	
U	27	09	19	18	IS
S	62	38	84	39	
U	17	06	14	06	RP
S	52	29	35	28	

and *there*, with the standard variant [ð] and non-standard [d]; (th) is the initial consonant in words like *think*, *three* and *thanks*, with the standard variant [θ] and non-standard [t]. The speakers were classified as upwardly mobile (U) if either their father's occupation or their own first occupation was a lower-status occupation than their present one, and if neither of those was higher than the present one. They were classified as stable (S), that is, neither upwardly nor downwardly mobile, if their father's or their own occupation was ranked the same as their present one. It is worth emphasizing, incidentally, that the upwardly mobile make a significant constituency: by Labov's criterion about 30 percent (43 of 148) are classified U (based on 1966b: table 3).

Table 2.4 includes the sub-set of Labov's sample with the most representatives, WC and LMC. They are also the social classes at the cusp between the basic blue collar/white collar divide. The index scores for (dh) and (th) are percentages of the non-standard variant recorded in three styles, casual (CS), interview (IS), and reading passage (RP). In order to interpret the scores in the table, it is necessary to keep in mind that the individuals classified as "U" are listed with the social class they began in, not the one they have joined. In other words, the individuals represented in the cell WC–U have moved into LMC occupations after starting out in WC occupations or growing up in WC households. If they were classified by present occupation alone, they would be placed in the LMC. Their status is ambiguous, whereas the individuals in the WC–S cells are unequivocally WC, having started out in the same social class to which their present occupations belong.

The correlations follow a familiar sociolinguistic pattern. Reading across the rows, the higher social group, LMC, consistently uses fewer non-standard variants than the WC. Reading down the columns, all groups use fewer non-standard variants as the style becomes more self-conscious, with more self-monitoring. The most important observation for our purposes is the relationship within the six cells, which shows that the upwardly mobile group (U) use fewer non-standard variants than the stable group (S) in the social class of their origin. Looking, for instance, at the upper left cell, we notice that the non-mobile working-class (WC) speakers have the non-standard variant [d] 80 percent of the time, but the mobile individuals in their class cohort (WC-U) have that variant only 27 percent of the time. This relationship holds for both variables throughout the table: the U-group always uses fewer non-standard variants than the S-group in their social class.

2.4.6   Mobility as a leveling force

A second relationship shows up consistently as well. In all the cells, the upwardly mobile members of the working class score lower than the stable members of the class above them. In table 2.4, I have shaded the relevant numbers in the first cell: the WC-U group score 27 percent but the LMC-S group score 50 percent. That is, the upwardly mobile individuals actually use fewer non-standard variants than the people in the social class they are joining. This relationship holds throughout the table: the upwardly mobile speakers not only use fewer non-standard variants than the people in the class in which they originated but also use fewer than the people in the class which they are emulating.

One plausible explanation is hypercorrection. It may be that the upwardly mobile are overzealous in their attempts at speaking a sociolect that is not native to them. So far there are too few studies with mobility as an independent variable to know whether hypercorrection might be a common characteristic of upwardly mobile speech. If it is, however, then it is interesting to conjecture the long-term effect on a highly mobile society. If a noticeable proportion of the population uses variants at a frequency beyond the norms of their social cohort – that is, hypercorrectly – in successive generations, then it seems likely that the norms themselves will come to be altered in that direction. If the upwardly mobile WC speakers use fewer non-standard variants than the LMC speakers they are joining, then the force of their example – providing, of course, their numbers are significant and their influence is persistent – might alter the LMC norms in the direction of those used by the MMC. Indeed, table 2.4 shows that the WC-U speakers are more similar to the MC-U speakers than to the MC-S speakers.

2.5 Homogenization

The most extreme case of mobility is the formation of villages, towns or
cities where formerly there was nothing. This happened on a the grandest
scale, of course, in the period of imperial conquest in the sixteenth and
seventeenth centuries. Hundreds of communities came into being, and the
founding generation was almost always a diverse lot, different from one
another in the places they came from, the social classes they belonged to,
the experiences that formed them, and, of course, the dialects they spoke.

In all of these communities an astounding linguistic homogenization took
place in the first generation. Unfortunately there were no sociolinguistic
studies made at the time: the founders were too busy clearing the land and
scratching out a living. The best evidence comes from astute observers.
Thus an English visitor to Maryland, William Eddis (quoted by Read 1933:
21), reported in a letter home in 1770:

> The colonists are composed of adventurers, not only from every district of
> Great Britain and Ireland, but from almost every other European
> government. . . . Is it not, therefore, reasonable to suppose that the English
> language must be greatly corrupted by such a strange admixture of various
> nations? The reverse is, however, true. The language of the immediate
> descendants of such promiscuous ancestry is perfectly uniform, and unadul-
> terated; nor has it borrowed any provincial, or national accent, from its
> British or foreign parentage.

Similarly, almost a century later a similar observation was made in Canada
by William Canniff (1869: 363–4), himself the offspring of founders. "Listening to the children at any school, composed of the children of English-
men, Scotchmen, Americans, and even of Germans," Canniff said, "it is
impossible to detect any marked difference in their accent, or way of ex-
pressing themselves."

If we did not have comments like these from people who observed the
homogenization, we would nevertheless infer that it happened from the
simple fact that the Englishes spoken in Canada, the United States, Australia, New Zealand and the other former colonies have much less dialect
diversity than does England.

We would like to understand precisely how this homogenization takes
place. Which features of the constituent accents are retained, and which
ones are lost? How are social traits evaluated, and what effect does this
evaluation have on the emergent linguistic system? In other words, what are
the dynamics of homogenization?

Since no sociolinguists were present – or even existed – during the

European imperialist era, we will probably have to wait for the planting of colonies in outer space for large-scale studies of the dynamics of homogenization. There are, however, small-scale colonizations taking place and these may provide insights into it.

2.5.1 /a/-deletion in Sheshatshiu

One such site is Sheshatshiu in Labrador, at the northeastern tip of Canada. There, about 600 nomadic Montagnais Indians were brought together in the 1950s to provide them with a central place for educational facilities, medical services and other amenities. Clarke (1987, 1988) initially hoped the community would provide a case study of a society in which there was no social stratification.

Table 2.5 Territorial group means and age group means for deletion of initial /a/ by Montagnais speakers in Sheshatshiu (Clarke 1987: table 1a, 1c, 83)

	14–19	21–44	46+
Northern	.95	.81	.41
Southern	.95	.79	.52
Southwestern	.79	.82	.71
All groups	.87	.81	.60

Her investigations revealed that there was in fact stratification in terms of prestige rather than material goods. Instead of a large range of linguistic variation among the founding population, as in colonial situations, Clarke found three basic regional patterns. In their speech and in some social relations, the older individuals retained allegiances to one of three territorial groups based on their traditional hunting grounds. Although everyone in the village lived in the same conditions, largely sub-standard, Clarke discovered that the southwestern territorial group was looked up to by the other two, the northern and the southern, probably as a result of their more thorough acculturation. As expected, their dialect took on prestige as well and to some extent made the directions of change predictable.

The chief interest in the study from our viewpoint is the homogenization that took place in the first generation born and raised in Sheshatshiu. Table 2.5 shows the means for variable deletion of initial unstressed /a/. Looking at the oldest groups in the rightmost column, it is clear that /a/-deletion was preponderantly a southwestern feature in the original dialects. After the groups came together in Sheshatshiu, however, /a/-deletion has become a general feature in the speech of younger people: the 21–44-year-olds, unlike their elders, show uniform frequencies regardless of their territorial origins. The mean for all of them has accelerated past the southwestern elders who provided the model. The youngest group, 14–19, show a further acceleration as the feature obviously has become a general one in Sheshatshiu Montagnais.

Interestingly, while the southwestern teenagers maintain the mean of the next older groups, the northern and southern teenagers have gone further, well beyond the means of the next older group. This appears to be another example of the hypercorrection previously noted in §2.4.6. In this case, it is not exactly a result of upward social mobility but rather of geographical mobility. In their zeal to adopt the linguistic norms of the more prestigious group, the adopters have outdone their models.

The linguistic differentiation evident in the older generation has thus been leveled in the younger generation. This is evident not only from /a/ -deletion but much more generally. Clarke (1987: table 4, 84) shows that four other southwestern phonological variants have increased significantly among younger speakers and two northern and southern variants have similarly increased in their speech. The overall effect is that the younger speakers have an accent noticeably different from their parents in several respects but similar to their peers. The homogenization is a direct result of their geographical convergence.

2.5.2   /ou/ in Milton Keynes

In the past forty years or so, British economic policy has included planned communities, called "New Towns," in regions targeted for industrial development. One of these, Milton Keynes, was incorporated in 1969 in a rural area 70 kilometres northwest of London. The site chosen encompassed two small towns with a population of 43,000, and today supports an urban population of more than 150,000.

In this new-world-style colonization in an old world setting, Kerswill and Williams (1992) have undertaken a developmental study of WC schoolchildren, 4- to 12-years-old, and their parents. The parents come predominantly from southeastern England, especially London but also elsewhere in Buckinghamshire, the county in which Milton Keynes is situated, and nearby Hertfordshire and Essex, but several others are from more distant Scotland, northern England and overseas.

Kerswill and Williams's early impressions suggest some of the mechanisms of homogenization. Comparing the vowels of the schoolchildren with those of the various parental accents, they note an absence of variants that are regional markers. From this, they draw the following conclusion (1992: 79):

> The absence of these variants is evidence of levelling towards a variety (or set of varieties) with no strongly regional features. This levelling seems to be achieved with two kinds of "strategies." First, phonetically intermediate features are adopted, and these are often a compromise between a London feature and a more standard, RP form. These features make the working-class children in our sample sound less "broad" than their peers elsewhere, such as Reading or London. Second, features which are found in the South East generally are adopted in full measure. . . . The co-occurrence of all these features gives rise to an accent that, for many people (including probably Milton Keynesians – though this has not been tested), is difficult to locate geographically, except as coming from "somewhere in the South East."

The best evidence so far of the way in which the founders' diversity gets reversed by their offspring is the quantitative comparison of parents' and children's realization of the /ou/ phoneme, the vowel in words like *rope*, *both*, *coat*, *brooch*, and *oak*. Kerswill and Williams assign a weighted score to the variants (1992: 81):

(ou)-Ø	[oː], [oʊ]	Scottish and Northern England variant
(ou)-1	[ɐʊ]	London and older Buckinghamshire
(ou)-2	[æY]	fronting
(ou)-3	[æI]	fronting and unrounding

At least ten tokens were transcribed for each of the children and their mothers, and then the vowels were assigned the score, Ø–3, and the total was averaged to determine a score for each individual. The results are plotted in figure 2.2. Note that the individuals in both lines are arranged in rank order, from highest to lowest; mothers and their children are not in the same column.[2] It is perhaps odd that the children score consistently higher than their mothers. Kerwill and Williams (1992: 81) explain this by noting that the fronting of the onset vowel, as in variants (ou)-2 and (ou)-3, is a change taking place generally in southeastern England. The children but not their parents are apparently participating in the change. Most important, the children's range of variation is much less than their mothers'. The highest- and lowest-scoring children differ by less than one point; the highest- and lowest-scoring mothers differ by two points. The children are focused on the (ou)-2 variant, [æY], but their mothers more frequently have the (ou)-1 variant [ɐʊ].

These differences between the contiguous generations in Milton Keynes undoubtedly typify the homogenization of accents and dialects that went on on a much wider scale in the era of exploration and conquest. In this

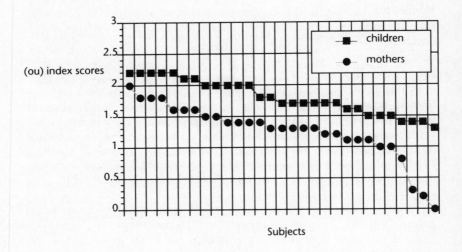

Figure 2.2 Index score for (ou) variants in the speech of schoolchildren and their mothers in Milton Keynes (Kerswill and Williams 1992: figure 1, 81)

instance, there was of course a regional dialect already established on all sides of the new town, and the influence of southeastern standards is palpable in the changes described above and in all the other changes discussed by Kerswill and Williams. Without that external influence guiding the direction of change, as in the planting of English-speaking colonies in places where there are no established dialects, the resolution of rampant variability into a few variants is much less predictable. In fact, it appears that the resolution might lead to even less variability than is found among the schoolchildren of Milton Keynes, and that the impetus toward homogenization may exert a continuing influence in the history of the dialect.

2.5.3   The persistence of homogenization

We are just beginning to understand that the leveling of dialects by the offspring of the founders of a new community is not merely a transitory phenomenon at the beginning of settlement. It appears that, as long as mobility is a vital force, homogenization may diffuse beyond the originating speech comunity and exert a persistent influence on language change.

The diffusion of homogenization was also observed by William Eddis in 1770, on his visit to Maryland and other early settlements of the United States. Eddis wrote (Read 1933: 21), "This uniformity of language prevails not only on the coast, where Europeans form a considerable mass of the people, but likewise in the interior parts, where population has made but slow advances; and where opportunities seldom occur to derive any great advantages from an intercourse with intelligent strangers." In other words, new settlements do not necessarily level the founders' dialects in unrelated and independent ways.

This should not really be surprising, since independent and unrelated leveling in adjacent new world communities would lead to diversity that would rival old world diversity. Instead, the early linguistic history of new world settlements results in homogeneity across great expanses. In Australia, Bernard (1981: 19) characterized the traditional view of Australian English as follows: "The picture is of a widespread homogeneity stretching from Cairns to Hobart, from Sydney to Perth, a uniformity of pronunciation extending over a wider expanse than anywhere else in the world." That claim of a world record cannot stand when we take into account the homogeneity of the English language in Canada. Priestley (1951: 75–6) said:

> the most surprising thing about the English currently spoken in Canada is its homogeneity. . . . It is certain that no Ontario Canadian, meeting another Canadian, can tell whether he comes from Manitoba, Saskatchewan, Alberta, or British Columbia – or even Ontario, unless he asks. . . . This emergence within fifty years of a predominantly homogeneous speech over a three-thousand-mile-long geographical area seems to me most unusual.

It should be pointed out that the homogeneity of both Australian and Canadian English is only observable when one restricts the view to urban MC speech. That is not to say that the homogeneity is trivial in any sense. In both countries, the urban MC people constitute the majority. But more comprehensive views (on Australia, Horvath 1985: chapter 2, and on Canada, Chambers 1991a) indicate rural diversity and at least incipient urban variability.

2.5.4 *(aw)-fronting in Canada*

The apprehension of homogenization as a persistent sociolinguistic force arose as a by-product of studies of a change in progress in urban, inland Canadian English that affects the /aw/ diphthong.

Canadian English includes allophonic variants (Joos 1942) widely known by the term Canadian raising (Chambers 1973). For older speakers, the allophones of /aw/ remain essentially as predicted by the Canadian raising rule: [ʌu] before voiceless segments, and [ɑu] elsewhere. The phonetic distinction occurs in pairs such as *house: houses, lout: loud, couch: gouge,* [mʌuθ]: [mɑuðz] *mouth: mouths* and all similar contexts.

The change occurs as variable (aw)-fronting. It was noticed informally in the early 1970s, and studied sociolinguistically in Toronto in 1979 (Chambers 1980, 1981). Where the older people typically have back onsets, speakers under 40 often have more fronted onsets. For the younger speakers the phonetic variation is much broader: [ɑu], [au] or [æu] elsewhere, and these plus [ʌu], [ɐu] or [ɛu] before voiceless segments. The phonetic profusion results, of course, from the interaction of (aw)-fronting with Canadian raising, so that the fronted variants are sometimes mid ([hɐus] or [hɛus] for [hʌus] 'house') and sometimes low ([hauzəz] or hæuzəz] for [hɑuzəz] 'houses'), and, significantly, occasionally [haus] or [hæus] for 'house', where the onset vowel is not raised to mid before a voiceless consonant.

Sociolinguistic analysis in Toronto revealed correlations with social dimensions of age and sex, and with the linguistic dimensions of the voicedness of the following segment. When the study was replicated in Vancouver (Chambers and Hardwick 1986) and Victoria (Hung, Davison and Chambers 1993), it was discovered that the change was underway there as well, and that it had very similar sociolinguistic dimensions.

Figure 2.3 shows the social correlates in Toronto, Vancouver, and Victoria. The fronting index on the ordinate indicates the proportion of non-back vowel onsets in all speech styles. From left to right, there are three age groups – 12-year-olds, 22-year-olds, and over 46. Each age group is further divided by sex, with the females to the left of the males. The slope of the bars shows graphically that younger speakers have more fronted onsets than older, and that females have more fronted onsets than males in the same age group. The similarity of the slope from left to right indicates that the change is progressing not only along the same social dimensions but also at a very similar pace in the three cities.

Of course, we also found some sociolinguistic differences in the cities. Most notably, the 12-year-olds in Vancouver, especially the boys, occasionally use mid, rounded vowels ([oʊt] for 'out') in fast speech, a tendency that bleeds (aw)-fronting (Chambers and Hardwick 1986: 37–41). But the similarities are more striking than the differences.

The fact that there are any similarities at all should be a source of wonder. Toronto is more than 3500 kilometers from Vancouver and Victoria as the crow flies, considerably further by ground transporation routes. Vancouver and Victoria are separated by the Juan de Fuca Strait. Toronto and Vancouver are large, industrialized, multicultural cities that dominate their regions, but Victoria is small and bourgeois.

What the three cities share is their nationality. Canada's nationhood has required extraordinary measures in transport and communications to survive the natural barriers of distance and climate and the political barriers of French separatism and British–American colonialism. The province in which Vancouver and Victoria are located, British Columbia, joined the Canadian confederation in 1871 after securing the promise of a coast-to-coast rail link,

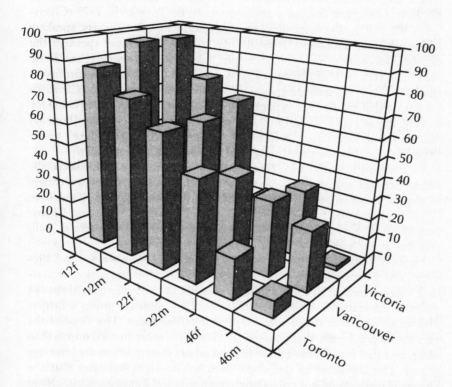

Figure 2.3 Fronting indices for three age groups (12, 22, 46+) and both sexes (m, f) in three Canadian cities, Toronto, Vancouver and Victoria (based on Hung, Davison and Chambers 1993: figure 3, 253)

and Vancouver was founded in 1886 when it was the chosen western terminus of the railroad. Since then, movement between the regions has been constant. Canadian geographical mobility stimulates and is promoted by social and occupational mobility.

The shared nationality implies common values, aspirations and attitudes. The mobility allows interaction and mixing, both horizontally from region to region and vertically from class to class. The sociocultural network appears to perpetuate homogenization as a persistent linguistic force.

2.5.5 *Dialect laws of mobility and isolation*

Although mobility has seldom been studied directly as an independent variable in sociolinguistics, dialectologists have long been aware of its power as a dialect leveler. It has the force of a natural linguistic law: **mobility causes people to speak and sound more like people from other places**.

In dialectology it was the corollary of this law that was enshrined: **isolation causes people to speak and sound less like people from other places**. Dialect geographers, in their quest for the most distinctive regional speech varieties, systematically sought the most isolated speakers as their subjects. As Orton said (1962: 15–16), describing the choice of informants for the Survey of English Dialects, "dialect-speakers whose residence in the locality had been interrupted by significant absences were constantly regarded with suspicion." His principal fieldworker, Ellis (1953) stated that the ideal informant would be "a broad speaker, with an agricultural background, born in the village of native parents, married to a wife who is herself a native of the locality." What they were seeking were people whose speech is as consistently regional as possible, that is, people who use nonregional variants as little as possible.

Weinreich (1953: viii) states these laws of mobility and isolation in terms of "contact" and "estrangement," respectively, as follows: "Contact breeds imitation and imitation breeds linguistic convergence. Linguistic divergence results from secession, estrangement, loosening of contact."

Weinreich also noted that mobility had been ignored in dialect research in favour of isolation, a bias that is only now beginning to be redressed. Mobility has been sociolinguistically underestimated as a reformative force just as it has been socially and politically underestimated.[3] Its influence is, however, implicit in numerous studies. In §3.3, I review two classic studies, one by Wolfram in inner city Detroit and the other by the Milroys in Ballymacarrett, in which the greater mobility of the women is the main factor in standardizing their accents compared to the more regionalized speech of the men in the same social groups. In the discussion of networks in the next section, I discuss several case studies in which the number and kind of ties individuals have to their peer group varies directly with their use of localized regional speech forms. In most cases, this too is ultimately a fact about social mobility, since there is a general relationship such that the tighter people are tied to their local network the narrower the range of their contacts. Mobility is a factor at numerous other points in this book as well. It deserves to be recognized and studied explicitly as a social variable with linguistic correlates.

2.6   Networks

Although social class has been the primary social variable in sociolinguistics, linguists are well aware that some social groups are not class-differentiated and nevertheless show linguistic differentiation. Clearly, within tightly structured, relatively homogeneous social clusters – neighborhoods, parishes, institutions – individuals further demarcate themselves by patterns of linguistic variation.

These micro-level social clusters are called networks. Their sociolinguistic application was most influentially introduced to the field by Lesley Milroy (1980), who reviewed the sociological background of network studies in order to establish the theoretical context for results from the Belfast survey. Basically, the network was invoked "to explain individual behaviour of various kinds which cannot be accounted for in terms of corporate group membership" (1980: 135), that is, class structure.

2.6.1 Norm enforcement

The social function of networks is epitomized succinctly as "a norm-enforcement mechanism" (1980: 136, 175, originally Bott 1957). The loyalty of an individual to the network is directly related to that person's conformity to its collective values. Non-linguistic observations are familiar to everyone: some networks such as local chapters of the Mafia, the Freemasons, the Ku Klux Klan and college fraternities require secrecy as a norm and enforce it with expulsion or, for some groups, execution; others such as neo-Nazi cells, military platoons and private schools require uniform dress as a norm and enforce it with punishment or ultimately expulsion for flagrant nonconformity; still others such as nuclear families, tribal phratries and some Highland clans require exogamy as a norm while European royalty, apartheid ethnic groups and some other Highland clans require endogamy, and in both cases the norm is enforced by marginalizing the offenders or banishing them.

Between the extremes of perfect conformity and culpable nonconformity, of course, there occur boundless degrees of individual expression, though all but the mildest deviations are usually regarded with disapproval and subject to overt comment.

The sociolinguistic correlate of network membership is analogous to the non-linguistic correlates, though the linguistic norms are largely subconscious and only in extreme cases subject to overt comment. As Milroy (1980: 175) puts it, "the closer an individual's network ties are with his local community, the closer his language approximates to localized vernacular norms." There is a gradation of linguistic conformity to local dialect correlated fairly closely with the individual's integration into the network.

2.6.2 Network and class

It will be obvious from the description of networks that they are in some ways parallel to social class divisions. Social classes are also, to some degree, norm-enforcement mechanisms. It is for that reason, in every culture, that people in the same social class share not only similar incomes and educations but also similar attitudes, tastes, recreations, fashions, and, as we have seen, certain linguistic norms.

The difference, equally obviously, is that the class system impinges less stringently on individuals. A person's circle of intimates – his or her network – can impose standards of behaviour more directly and enforce them more rigorously. Whereas the guardians of social class norms are more or less ineffable, the guardians of network norms might very well buy you a pint of ale or pass you the salt across the dinner table.

So the difference between social networks and social classes as norm-enforcement mechanisms has to do with their proximity to the individual, or the immediacy of their influence. The class structure of a town, city or nation is a confederation of an unbounded number of networks. "Network studies," as Guy (1988: 54) says, "are microsociological in focus, while class studies are macroscopic."

The similarity between the two has not always been clear. Milroy (1980: especially 79–84) reviews the work of various sociologists and social anthropologists who suggest that the solidarity ethos that reinforces network structures may have to be destroyed in order for an individual to embrace the status ethos that motivates the class system. Terms like these leave the impression that network and class are antithetical, whereas it is implicit at all other points in Milroy's work that they coexist. Network affiliations clearly do not preclude broader experiences and looser contacts beyond the network. The Belfast subjects whose networks are Milroy's focal point belong to the working class. Middle-class Belfasters, like middle-class people in all the industrial nations, are likely to participate in social networks that are less tightly knit and much less salient to them than their working-class counterparts.

This relationship is clearer in Milroy and Milroy (1992), where they observe that the "close study of networks . . . can give us some idea of the mechanisms that give rise to correlations between language and class" (p. 4). In other words, the immediacy of network influence and its directness can be extrapolated to provide clues about the more ineffable and indirect forces at play in society at large.

2.6.3   *Some network studies*

It is difficult to specify the circumstances under which a network study would be more appropriate or more profitable than a macro-level study. The social groups under study must obviously be localized and close-knit.

Usually, but not always, they are homogeneous with respect to social class, age, ethnicity, and other independent variables. Here is a summary of some of the social settings in which the sociolinguistics of networks have been applied very successfully: .

- Gauchat (1905) studied the vernacular (*le patois*) of Charmey, Switzerland, a village of 1247 in eastern Gruyères. Though the population is, he says, *relativement pure* or immobile, he chose as his main subjects five men and four women of disparate backgrounds and ages, and supplemented the data from them by interviewing other villagers as he saw fit. He deliberately maximized the social differences in order to increase the possibility of linguistic differences, and in this respect he was not disappointed. "Although all the conditions favour [dialect] unity," he says, "the diversity is much greater than I would have imagined after a short visit" (1905: 222).[4] In order to explain the differences he correlates the fine phonetic detail with the social variable age (pp. 202–21) and with network variables including incursions from neighboring vernaculars on the one hand and standard French on the other (186–93).
- Labov (1972a) studied Harlem teenagers in New York City. The subjects were all young (10–20), poorly educated, ghettoized blacks but most of them segregated themselves from one another as members of street gangs known as the Thunderbirds and Aces. Although membership in a street gang effectively isolates an individual from members of other gangs – the penalty for crossing boundaries can be extremely painful – the gang members share a set of activities, creeds and values that cut across gang lines. As a result, the gang members are more like one another socially and linguistically than are the unintegrated individuals of their age group, the loners and misfits known as "Lames" (discussed further in §2.9.3.1).
- Milroy and Milroy (1978) studied Belfast WC enclaves in three neighborhoods: Ballymaccarett, the Hammer and Clonard. The neighborhoods are highly insular – the first two are Protestant, the third Catholic – and the subjects are mainly under-educated WC whites. The men are especially ghettoized. Those who are employed usually work in the local factory and seldom venture outside the neighborhood where sectarian factions come into conflict. The women are much less restricted in their movements, both for working and for recreation (with sociolinguistic consequences discussed in detail in §3.3.2).
- Cheshire (1982) studied WC adolescents who frequented adventure playgrounds in Reading, England. The playgrounds are parks with some recreational structures and makeshift shelters where children playing truant from school could spend several hours during the day. They provided a general gathering place for boys and girls in the neighborhood.

Parents often tried to keep their children away, with varying degrees of success. (See §§2.6.5, 2.7.2)

- Eckert (1988) studied adolescents as a participant observer in several high schools in the Detroit suburbs. She identified two networks, called Jocks and Burnouts, that differed essentially in the role of the high school culture in their mundane activities: the Jocks participated in sports and school politics as well as other social and academic activities, whereas the Burnouts were outsiders, hanging out in restaurants and malls, taking drugs and generally carrying on their social lives apart from the school (as discussed in §4.4.3.1 below). These networks are so well defined that the whole high school population not only recognizes them but a significant proportion identify themselves as "in-betweens," less than full members, that is, of either group. Eckert found significant linguistic correlations depending upon network affiliations. Especially interesting was the loose correlation between the parents' social class and the adolescents' affiliations. Though Jocks tended to come from MC backgrounds and Burnouts from WC backgrounds, there were numerous cross-overs. Eckert's study probably provides the best evidence of social networks and social classes as independent (but overlapping) social entities.

- Lippi-Green (1989) studied social and linguistic behavior in an isolated mountain village with 800 residents in western Austria. The small population and its isolation made macro-level notions such as socieconomic differences irrelevant. The best social correlate for linguistic behavior turned out to be the individual's integration into one of three networks (as in §§2.6.4., 2.9.3.2 below).

- Edwards (1992) studied 66 black residents in a Detroit inner city neighborhood with high unemployment and over 60 percent of the households on welfare. The principal social correlate of the subjects' choice of either black English variants or standard English variants was age, suggesting the primacy of a macro-level factor. Beyond that, however, the most telling factor in correlating linguistic choices by people of the same economic and educational background was the extent of their participation in the neighborhood culture, that is, their integration into the local network (as discussed in §2.8.3 below).

In all these instances, the social dynamism in the community being studied revolves around a set of local values. These are social forces that impinge upon individuals with considerable immediacy – what Guy (1988: 54) calls "the uniqueness of each individual's life experiences and contacts." In a sense, they are the most intimate social pressures.

In another sense, however, they are chosen rather than imposed, at least to some extent. A student entering high school can decide whether to associate with Jocks or Burnouts, a Harlem teenager can choose between joining a gang or being an outsider, and an alpine villager can pick his closest associates by frequenting their pubs and joining their clubs. This aspect of network membership differs from macro-level ties, which are largely determined at birth. As Lippi-Green (1989: 223) says, "While age and gender are indicators of group alliance about which the individual has no choice, and within which he or she must function, the . . . network sub-sectors . . . represent a different aspect of the individual as a community member: that of a free agent."

Here again, the difference between class and network seems to be one of degree rather than kind. Socially, the path of least resistance will cause individuals to live and die as members of the social class they were born into – the social class to which their parents belonged. Even so, some individuals become central members and others peripheral. Some break out of the pattern, grasping whatever opportunities the society provides for mobility, upward or downward. By the same token, membership in networks has a deterministic element. The path of least resistance would cause individuals to follow in the footsteps of older siblings, best friends and classmates in participating in the same chain of associations. The possibility of individuals linking themselves more or less closely than their most influential peers is undoubtedly greater than with macro-level associations – at least impressionistically, for it is hard to imagine any objective measure – and this is perhaps the basis for the notion of "free agency" that Lippi-Green mentions.

Sociolinguistically, the closeness of one's bonds and the degree of integration in the network prove to have interesting consequences.

2.6.4 *Measures of network bonds*

In seeking an explication of the network ties of individuals, we are really looking at their daily associations. How many people in a certain group know them? How well do they know them?

The number of connections is the network density. Geographers first observed the significance of network density, the number of actual connections between members (or places) as a proportion of the maximum number that could exist (see Haggett and Chorley 1969). The content of those connections is the network multiplexity. Sociologists observed that the number of interconnections was no more important than their quality, what they called (using characteristic jargon) their multiplexity, as in the distinction between nodding acquaintances and brothers, work-mates, team-mates, and other kinds of intimate relations (see Boissevain and Mitchell 1973).

Beginning with Milroy (1980), sociolinguists have discussed the network

Figure 2.4   On the left, a diagram representing a low–density network, in which the individuals know the central member but not one another. On the right, a high-density network in which everyone knows all the others.

measures of density and multiplexity (for example, Coates 1986: chapter 5, Wardhaugh 1992: chapter 5) although they have not yet been applied directly in any sociolinguistic study. In their place, sociolinguists have used less abstract measures of network integration (as in §2.6.6 below). Density and multiplexity are the fundamental factors on which our intuitions about network are based.

Density, the number of links among individuals, is measured by dividing the total actual links (× 100 to reduce it to a percentage) by the total possible links. Figure 2.4 illustrates two simple networks involving six people. In the one on the left, the central member knows the other five but they do not know one another. This situation, rare in real life, might arise if a coach brought together the best players on five successive teams, or if a teacher assembled students taking private lessons for group instruction. The density is obviously low. By the formula, with five actual links out of 15 possible links, the density is 33.3 percent. In the diagram on the right, where everyone knows everyone else as is the usual situation in, say, a neighborhood, bowling team or small office, all 15 of the possible links exist, making the density 100 percent.

Multiplexity, the content of the links among individuals, is measured by dividing the number of multiplex links in a network (× 100, as before, to reduce it to a percentage) by the total number of links in the network. Obviously, the kinds of links that constitute multiplexity must be specified for each study, but some of the significant relationships that draw people closer include kinship, workplace associations, proximity of residence, and the like. (In the next section, we review several bonds that sociolinguists have used as indicators of multiplexity.) In figure 2.5, the six-member network is represented with one multiplex link, in which all six individuals

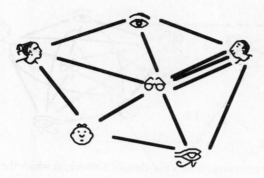

Figure 2.5 A diagram representing a network in which two members have multiplex connections as, say, brothers and workmates as well as neighbors.

are, say, neighbors but two of them are brothers and technicians in the same laboratory.

Only one of the ten links is multiplex. By the formula, the multiplexity is 10 percent. It is perhaps worth noting that the network represented in figure 2.5 is moderately dense, in between those represented above. Here, there are ten actual links out of 15 possible ones. The density is 66.6 percent. In measuring the density, the multiplex link counts the same as any other.

2.6.5 Sociometrics

Although sociolinguists have not applied formulas for density and multiplexity in their work, a couple of notable studies have applied another measure of multiplexity known as sociometrics. This method apparently originates in educational research, where the interpersonal dynamics among classmates can affect the learning environment for children.

The basic approach of sociometrics is to question each member of the network about their relationships. Each child in a class might be asked, "Who is your best friend in the class?" or "Who do you like best in your class?" The optimal answers, in terms of social relations, would be reciprocal: Jan would name Robin, and Robin would name Jan. That happens less often than one might imagine. Typically, in any group, some individuals will be named more frequently than others, so that Jan, for instance, might be named the "best friend" by four or five classmates. Other individuals might be named infrequently or not at all. The naming patterns can then be

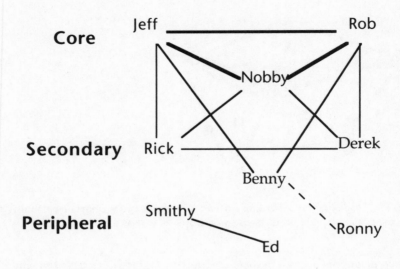

Figure 2.6   Membership status in the Orts Road group based on reciprocal naming only (after Cheshire 1982: table 38, 91)

diagrammed in a manner similar to figure 2.5, with links from each individual to the person(s) named in answer to the question. The most frequently named are the central members of the network and the others are members to varying degrees from the core to the periphery. Socially, the extremes of membership relations are widely recognized in ordinary language by terms such as the insiders and the outsiders. The naming relations can reveal many degrees of network status intermediate between these extremes as well. They can also reveal distinct network clusters within one group, each with its own central and peripheral members, often recognized in general parlance as cliques.

In sociolinguistics, sociometrics was first applied by Labov in his study of Harlem teenagers. He asked his subjects, "Who are all the cats you hang out with?" (1972a: 261–2). The sociometric diagram graphically identified the actual leaders and their main allies as well as the marginal members.

Cheshire (1982: 87–94) used the same method with the WC adolescents in the Reading adventure playgrounds. She asked the boys at a playground on Orts Road and the girls at a playground in Shinfield to name the friends they spent most of their time with. The results, like Labov's in Harlem, put the social structure into perspective, distinguishing core members from secondary members and (what Cheshire called) non-members.

Figure 2.6 diagrams part of the sociometric structure of the Orts Road group. Only reciprocal namings are considered here. Each line in the figure links the boys who named one other among the friends they spend most of their time with. Three boys, Nobby, Jeff and Rob, at the top of the diagram linked by the heaviest lines, were reciprocally named by four boys, including one another. They are the core members of the group. Three others, Derek, Benny and Rick, were reciprocally named by three boys, in each case by two of the three core members and one other. They are the secondary members. The others, Ed, Ronny and Smithy, were reciprocally named by only one other person, though not by one of the core members. In this example, it appears that not only the number of namings is relevant but also their source.

It is worth noting that the information about the hierarchical structure could not have been obtained as reliably by direct questioning, with questions like "Who are the leaders of your gang?" and "Who are the hangers-on?" Just as people are inclined to mis-report their use of language by standardizing their responses, so they are also inclined to over-emphasize their social status. The social system studied by Cheshire differed from that of Labov in that the gang structure in the playgrounds was less well established. Where the Harlem teenagers were heirs to a system in which their older brothers and sometimes their fathers had participated, the Reading teenagers were less well informed about their predecessors, similar though their behavioral patterns undoubtedly were. Few of the conventions of their playground subculture were handed down by older participants and the current group were not consciously involved in protecting their turf from traditional or long-standing rivals. Because of the looseness of the social organization, direct questioning would probably not have yielded any useful information.

In every network study, it is necessary for the investigator to define the social features that constitute a multiplex link. Sociometric patterns based on self-reported associations can provide useful divisions into a kind of pecking order based on status.

2.6.6   *Measures of network integration*

In practice, sociolinguists have usually devised a set of criteria based on local conditions in order to determine the degree of network integration of each subject. The conditions that enrich network ties are basically the same everywhere: kinship, proximity (neighborhood), occupation (workplace), and friendship (voluntary association).

Milroy (1980: 141–2), in her Belfast study, ranked her subjects according to five criteria:

Table 2.6 Network integration rankings of nine boys in the Orts Road group based on (1) carrying of weapons, (2) style in clothing, (3) job aspirations, (4) participation in minor criminal activities, (5) skill at fighting, and (6) swearing, with their sociometric status (after Cheshire 1982: table 42, p. 102, and table 38, p. 91)

	(1)	(2)	(3)	(4)	(5)	(6)	Status
Nobby	+	+	+	+	+	+	Core
Rob	−	+	+	+	+	+	Core
Jeff	−	+	+	+	+	+	Core
Rick	(+)	−	+	+	+	+	Secondary
Ronny	−	−	−	+	+	+	Peripheral
Derek	−	−	(+)	−	+	+	Secondary
Ed	−	−	−	−	+	+	Peripheral
Benny	−	−	−	−	−	+	Secondary
Smithy	−	−	−	−	−	−	Peripheral

- kinship ties with more than one household in the neighborhood;
- the same workplace as at least two others in the neighborhood;
- the same workplace as at least two others of the same gender;
- regular participation in a territorially-based activity (street gangs, bingo games, football teams, etc.);
- voluntary association with work-mates after working hours.

The subjects were assigned one point for each criterion they fulfilled. The result was a "network strength scale," an index score from zero to 5 ranking the subjects as unintegrated (∅) to highly integrated (5) with four intermediate grades.

Similarly, for her adolescent boys, Cheshire (1982: 97–102) devised a "vernacular culture index" based on six criteria: (1) carrying of weapons, (2) style in clothing, (3) job aspirations, (4) participation in minor criminal activities, (5) skill at fighting, and (6) swearing. It is instructive to compare the network integration indices with their rankings in the sociometric diagram. Table 2.6 shows the ranking of the nine boys in figure 2.6 according to the six criteria and then lists their sociometric ranking in the rightmost column. The six criteria, identified by the numbers in the sentence above, form an implicational scale such that a positive score for one criterion implies a positive score on all the criteria to its right (but not vice versa). The two discrepancies are indicated by parenthesizing the offending coefficient in Rick's and Derek's scores.

Comparing the sociometric status with their integration indices shows a perfect correspondence for the core members; they top the scale for integration just as they do for status. This result is expected because the prototypical members of any category will be, by definition, the best defined by any reasonable membership function. Below that, what appears to be fairly random is partly an artifact. Ronny, although a peripheral member by the criterion used in figure 2.6 above, reciprocal naming, actually has higher status when non-reciprocal naming and other sociometric factors are taken into account. Cheshire (1982: 91) classifies him as secondary; if he were so classified in the right column above, the two measures of network integration would have, as expected, a high degree of correspondence.

Lippi-Green (1989: 218–19) ranked her Austrian villagers on a scale with sixteen criteria, differentially weighted so that some were allotted two points and others one or a half point, to a maximum of 17 for married subjects and 16 for single ones. The criteria mainly arose from a finer breakdown of the four essential network characteristics, as in this sample:

- kinship: Is the subject's father/mother a member of a core clan? (1 point each);
- proximity: Is the subject's spouse a member of an established family in the village? (1 point);
- occupation: Does the subject work in the village (0.5 point), and has the subject always worked there? (1 point);
- associations: Indicate each organized club or group to which the subject belongs? (0.5 points each to a maximum of 1.5).

Several of the criteria recognized conditions peculiar to the alpine setting in which the study took place:

- For each grandparent who was a core member of the village and whom the subject (a) knew and (b) interacted with, give 0.5 point (up to 2.0 points);
- Is the subject's employment free of contact with tourism? (1 point).

The fine detail of Lippi-Green's network index allowed her to attempt linguistic correlations with the whole scale and with sub-parts of it. She found, for instance, that for the women in the village their integration into the local network made a significant predictor of whether their speech would be conservative or innovative, as long as integration was taken together with age and education, the macro-level factors. Men's speech correlated with the sub-part of voluntary associations (as discussed in §2.9.3.2). (For another method of constructing a network index [Edwards 1992], see §2.8.3.)

Table 2.7 Percentages of centralization for four age groups on Martha's Vineyard (Labov 1963: 22)

Age	(ay)	(aw)
76+	25	22
61–75	35	37
46–60	62	44
31–45	81	88

2.7   Linguistic Correlates of Network Integration

The consistent finding of network studies is that the best integrated individuals use the regional variants most frequently. This result is, of course, not surprising in any way. It is nevertheless the best evidence that factors below the level of social class, age, sex and region can be determinants of dialect.

Two individuals can be socially similar in all macro-level respects – say, two men of the same age, offspring of lifelong residents of the same city, former classmates and now teachers in the same board of education – and yet sound noticeably different. Most likely the linguistic difference will be the result of one speaking a more standard dialect than the other, and most likely it will be correlated with distinctly different patterns of participation in neighborhood affairs.

Following are two exemplary instances, the first phonological (§2.7.1) and the other grammatical (§2.7.2), illustrating the essential sociolinguistic fact about networks: the people at the core demonstrate their loyalty by, among other things, using regional variants.

2.7.1   Phonological markers in Martha's Vineyard

One of the earliest examples of the linguistic correlates of network integration came about almost accidentally in a study of vowel centralization on Martha's Vineyard, a small island on the northeastern coast of the United States. Labov (1963) documented the variables (ay) and (aw) in which the onset of the diphthongs in words like *white, wide, why* and *house, hound, how* occurred sometimes as the low front open vowel [a] and sometimes as a slightly centralized vowel [ɐ] or central [ə]. The centralization was a recent development, so that younger Vineyarders had more central onsets than older ones. That aspect is obvious in table 2.7, where the percentage increases from the oldest group to the youngest.

Table 2.8 Percentages of centralization correlated with subjects' attitudes toward their home environment (Labov 1963: 39)

Attitudes	(ay)	(aw)
positive	63	62
neutral	32	42
negative	09	08

Labov then tried several correlations with independent variables in hopes of discovering the social dimensions of the sound change. He found, for instance, that in the traditional occupational groups fisherman centralized most, farmers least, and others in between; that the strictly rural up-islanders centralized slightly more than the down-island villagers; and that those of Yankee and aboriginal ancestry centralized slightly more than those of Portuguese ancestry. But the conflation of these correlations did not result in a coherent view of the social significance of this feature.

What did result in a coherent view was the correlation with people's attitudes toward Martha's Vineyard. The island is a popular holiday area, and every summer its population sextuples with the influx of "summer people." The permanent residents are divided in their feelings about these summer residents even though they depend on them for their living. Many resent them as interlopers insensitive to the island traditions; some others envy them and feel the island society is enriched by their presence. Labov elicited opinions about the island and the summer people from his sample population and classified them as either positive (the majority), neutral or negative.

He then re-sorted the centralization scores according to these three groups and discovered the striking correlation shown in table 2.8. The people with the most positive attitudes toward the island and its traditions centralize the onsets of the diphthongs frequently, regardless of their age, and those with negative attitudes about their home environment centralize them very infrequently, almost not at all. In other words, the greater the allegiance to the island, the more centralization of the diphthongs. Labov (1963: 36) says, "When a man says [rəɪt] or həʊs], he is unconsciously establishing the fact that he belongs to the island, that he is one of the natives to whom the island belongs."

2.7.2 *Grammatical markers in the Reading playgrounds*

Just as grammatical variables divide social class members sharply (as discussed in §2.3.4), so they also appear to divide network participants sharply.

Table 2.9 Three grammatical variants and their occurrence in the speech of adolescents who participate in the playground subculture to different degrees in Reading (after Cheshire 1982: tables 44, 45, pp. 104–5)

	Core	Secondary	Peripheral
nonstandard *what*	92.31	18.00	0.00
nonstandard-*s*	77.36	45 (approx)	21.21
nonstandard *never*	64.71	43.00	37.50

Cheshire studied several grammatical variants and correlated their use with the speakers' involvement in the playground culture. Table 2.9 shows three of the eleven grammatical variables with the frequency of the non-standard variant in the speech of core, secondary and peripheral participants.[5] Non-standard *what* refers to its use as a restrictive relative pronoun in sentences like (1982: 73):

Are you the little bastards what hit my son over the head?

Non-standard -*s* refers to the use of suffix -*s* on present indicative verbs other than third person singular, which is the only form where it occurs in standard English. In Reading vernacular, it occurs in sentences like these (1982: 40, 43):

I just lets her beat me
You boots them, don't you?
We buses it down the town

Non-standard *never* refers to its use with the narrow meaning "not on this occasion" in contrast to the standard dialect use where it means "not on any occasion;" the non-standard use occurs in sentences like these (1982: 67):

I never went to school today
And he hit my brother over the head, and he never even went down, and his head was pouring with blood

The gradation in table 2.9 from high frequency by the core subjects to moderate frequency by the secondary subjects and lower frequency by the peripheral subjects shows that these three variables function in very similar ways to mark the degrees of allegiance to the vernacular culture. A closer look suggests that non-standard *what* is a particularly cogent marker of the playground vernacular, occurring almost exclusively in the speech of the core members. For the other two variables, the non-standard variants are used generally by all the subjects.

2.8 Interaction of Network and other Independent Variables

An individual's involvement in a network is not necessarily an isolated social fact. Some interactions between network and other independent variables are common, indeed predictable.

2.8.1 Social class

People in the middle of the class hierarchy maintain looser network ties than WC people or, for that matter, upper-class people. Both WC and UC people tend to cluster in neighborhoods, and – perhaps stereotypically – the former congregate at local bars, bowling alleys and poker games and the latter at business luncheons, racquets clubs, and horse shows. The MC, always the most mobile group and since mid-century the most amorphous, might live in far-flung suburbs, commuting to work, where they often work beside people who have commuted equally far from different directions. Their work-mates are seldom the people they meet along the sidelines as their children play soccer in the Saturday league or in the aisles at the supermarket on Friday evening.

Similarly, MC people are much less likely to reside in the vicinity of their childhood homes. At the opposite extreme, the UC often consider the home estate part of their legacy, to be handed down from generation to generation. For the MC, inquiries about the proximity of kin and the duration of residency that are among the measures of network integration would be almost meaningless in many MC neighborhoods.

2.8.2 Sex

Equally commonplace are observations of sex-based networks: sporting events, poker games and recreational contact sports tend to be male preserves while showers, bridge clubs and exercise classes tend to be female preserves. MC dinners often observe the social convention of seating men and women alternately, presumably in order to avoid fragmenting the conversation into two exclusive modes. The sociolinguistic significance of gender differences in mobility and social contacts is discussed §3.4.1.

2.8.3   Age

Regardless of sex and social class, human beings go through at least one period of their lives in which they maintain close network relations with their peers. This is adolescence. In industrial societies, teenagers notoriously maintain almost constant peer contact, hanging out together after school in malls, restaurants or clubs, spending long hours in telephone conversations, and adhering to strict norms of dress, grooming, style and speech. (For details, see §4.4.)

Sometimes network relations evolve over time, with the result that one generation may differ from the next. Edwards (1992) provides a clear example in his study of a Detroit inner city black neighborhood.

Edwards constructed his survey as a network study. For each of his subjects, he calculated a vernacular culture index based on their responses to ten statements (1992: 101). The first five statements provided an estimate of the individual's physical integration in the neighborhood:

1   Most of the members of my family live in this neighborhood or with me.
2   Most of my relatives live in this neighborhood or with me.
3   Most of the jobs I have held have been in this neighborhood.
4   Most of my friends live in this neighborhood.
5   I have frequent daily interactions with people in this neighborhood.

The other five statements provided an estimate of the individual's attitude toward the neighborhood and his racial isolation:

6   I would like to remain living in this neighborhood.
7   I do not have white friends with whom I interact frequently.
8   If I move, I would like to move to a neighborhood like this one.
9   The street culture doesn't bother me; people have to survive.
10 This is a good neighborhood to raise kids.

For each of these statements, the subjects assigned themselves a mark from 1 (strongly disagree) to 4 (strongly agree), making a range from 10 to 40.

Edwards then reported a significant difference between the oldest and youngest groups in his survey with respect to two linguistic variables. Variable (ay) has (in Edwards's terms) a "Standard English (SE)" variant, [aɪ] or [ai], in words like [bɪhaɪnd] 'behind', [faɪv] 'five' and [faɪt] 'fight', and a "Black English (BE)" variant, [aː], as in [bɪhaːn], [faːv] and [faːt]. Variable (r) has SE [ɹ] preconsonantally and finally where the BE variant is Ø.

The correlation Edwards finds is not in terms of the vernacular culture

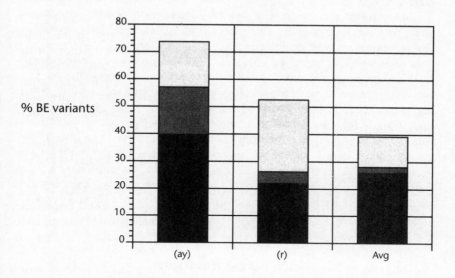

Figure 2.7 Use of BE variants in inner city Detroit by three age groups: 26–39 in darkest part of bars, 18–25 above them, and 60+ at top (based on Edwards 1992: table 5, 103)

index but in terms of age. Figure 2.7 illustrates the gap between the oldest group, over 60, and the two youngest groups, 18–25 and 26–39.[6] Each bar shows the percentage of the BE variants used by each age group, with the (ay) variable on the left, (r) in the middle, and the average scores for the BE variants of all variables on the right. For instance, the average scores show the 26- to 39-year-olds at about 27 percent, the 18- to 25-year-olds slightly higher at 29 percent, and the oldest group, those over 60, at almost 40 percent.

The relationship of these results to the network analysis is revealed when the responses to statements 1 to 10 above are linked to them. The use of BE variants correlates significantly with the scores on statements 3 and 7, so that people who have held jobs mainly in the neighborhood and do not have white friends they frequently interact with are also the people who use the BE variants of (ay) and (r) (1992: 109). So far this is just another example of the primary linguistic correlate of network integration: the least mobile people speak the most regional dialects.

What makes it more interesting for our purposes is a second correlation: the responses to statements 3 and 7 also correlate significantly with the age of the respondents, so that older people were the ones who held jobs mainly in the neighborhood and did not interact with whites (1992: 109). These facts converge, and suggest that the results shown in figure 2.7, with age as the independent variable, might have been stated with network integration as the independent variable. The graph would presumably have been similar at least in its basic findings.

If so, it provides an example in which age and network are interrelated. In this Detroit neighborhood, social patterns are undergoing a change. The racial segregation in place forty or fifty years before Edwards's study, when his oldest subjects were being educated and joining the work force, no longer holds for the current generation. With the breakdown of at least some of the race barriers – freedom to seek jobs and friendships outside the ghetto – the networks of the younger generation are less dense than their grandparents. With those freedoms has come a linguistic difference. The most distinctive linguistic markers of the local vernacular still exist but the younger people use them less frequently than the older people, and presumably have a larger linguistic repertoire.

2.9　Individuations

Sociolinguistic research has uncovered very few idiosyncratic cases. Occasionally we come upon individuals whose speech seems completely anomalous. Some of these people are suffering from pathologies, like the woman with Broca's aphasia whose speech, though otherwise fluent, was monotonal, arythmic and devoid of intonation (Ross 1982). Others defy explanation – like the native Torontonian whose English sounds foreign-accented though he has spoken it from the age of two, or the American morphologist whose syntax, especially in rather formal circumstances as when lecturing in public, becomes convoluted and disjointed.

In one sense, linguistic idiosyncrasies abound. Everyone's speaking voice is sui generis, and for that reason we can identify the voices of all our friends and many nodding acquaintances when they speak. This kind of individuation belongs to the personal characteristics discussed in §1.1.1.

Exactly how these personal characteristics are actualized has been given very little attention, probably because they appear to be almost unbounded in form. Chao (1968: 125) once supplied a charming example. "Some people . . . habitually use a wider range of pitch than others," he noted, and then offered this illustration:

Take the Chinese sentence:

```
        ng            ng        lai
    e              e        ch
    N      bu     n              ii        ?
```
Can I get up?

When my granddaughter said it when she was five, it was like this:

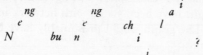

Her speech had, and still has to some extent, a wider range of pitch, so much so that Bernard Bloch . . . asked me, quite seriously, "Does Canta [that is her name] speak the same dialect as you do?" Of course she does. But in her version of Mandarin, every tone and intonation is multiplied by a personality factor.

Discovering how various "personality factors" interact to make idiolects would probably not repay the effort because they carry almost no social significance.

In a few instances, certain individuations may turn out to be socially significant. Many sociolinguists have discovered, upon analyzing their data, that there appears to be an oddball in the sample, someone running against the trends in the data. As it turns out, these people seldom remain anomalous for long. They are usually found to belong socially and linguistically to sub-groups of the sample population.

Instead of pure anomalies, then, they may fall into social sub-categories that have their own defining characteristics, linguistic and otherwise. Not surprisingly, the evidence for these relatively rare sub-groups is far from secure. In the following sections, I postulate four distinctive minorities – interlopers, insiders, outsiders and aspirers – based in each case on at least two fringe characters found in different studies in the sociolinguistic literature.

2.9.1   Interlopers

When individuals move from one dialect area to another, their ability to master the new dialect depends partly upon their age (Chambers 1992: 687–90). The best evidence we have been able to assemble so far indicates rather broad age thresholds: someone coming to a dialect region under the age of seven will master the dialect like a native, and someone coming to it over the age of 14 will always betray non-native origins. In between seven and 14, there is no telling how an individual will fare.

As always, there are intermediate degrees as well. Some people who arrive in that in-between period come to sound like natives of the new region and are almost never taken for anything but natives. It is only through fine-grained sociolinguistic studies that we discover they never master highly complex rules of the new accent.

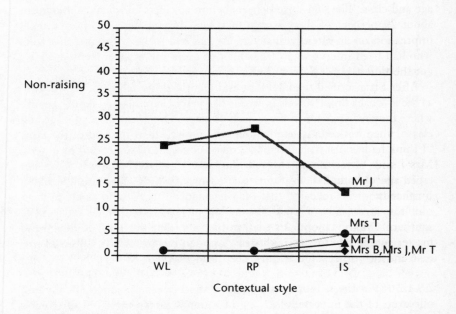

Figure 2.8 Mr J's non-raising scores in three styles compared to other MC adults in north Toronto (from Chambers 1984: figure 3, 124)

2.9.1.1 *Mr J in Toronto* An example is Mr J, who was part of the sample of MC adults in the Toronto survey I conducted to investigate the change in progress in the phonetics of Canadian raising (as in §2.5.4 above). As is well known, in standard Canadian English /au/ has a mid onset [ʌu] before tautosyllabic voiceless obstruents, as in *lout, mouse, south*, and *couch*, and a low onset [ɑu] elsewhere, as in *loud, arouse, gouge, power, bough*, and *how*. Among younger speakers, this is changing so that a range of more fronted onsets can now be heard.

Mr J, as a 56-year-old engineer–writer from North Toronto, was expected to conform to the older pattern of Canadian raising, along with the rest of his age-mates (46+) in the survey. When his interview was transcribed, however, Mr J proved to be out of line with his age-mates – and everyone else – because of a number of unraised onsets before voiceless consonants (Chambers 1984). Figure 2.8 shows the gap between him and his age-mates. The others never fail to raise apart from an instance or two in the informal interview style, when an emphatic word might get lengthened and its vowel lowered. Mr J fails to raise fairly often, especially in the more self-conscious word list and reading passage styles.

In all other respects, he sounded like a Canadian English speaker of his age and class. The non-raised onsets before voiceless consonants amount to about 20 percent of the possible instances, just enough to make a small impression on an attentive listener. At the end of his interview, his wife, who had been interviewed earlier for this same survey, commented, "He's got the tiniest bit of a drawl to his voice."

After I transcribed the interview and identified the source of the "drawl" as the low back onset vowels in words like [sɑuθ] 'south' and [skɑut] 'scout', where they never occur in the speech of native Canadians of Mr J's age and class, I then noticed a second comment by his wife at the end of the tape. "I think he has just a shade of an American accent of some kind or other," Mrs J said. "I feel he doesn't talk the same way I do." She was right: her taped speech sample had no unraised onsets at all (as shown in figure 2.8). Further inquiries revealed that Mr J had moved to Toronto as an 11-year-old from upstate New York, the region of the United States adjacent to southern Ontario. It appears that, in his case, that was too late for him to master completely the intricacies of Canadian raising. (For a review of this case and two other, similar ones, see Trudgill 1986, 32–7.)

2.9.1.2 *Newcomers in King of Prussia*

Another example, perhaps the first one ever, of the imperfect learning of a complex rule came out of Payne's work with adolescents in the highly mobile Philadelphia suburb of King of Prussia. First Payne documented the "notable success" of the out-of-state children acquiring the straightforward phonetic variables of the dialect (1980: 149–56). For example, in the Philadelphia vernacular, (uw) and (ow) require the fronting of the onsets of /uw/ and /ow/, and (oy) requires the raising of the onset of /oy/ – in all cases straightforward, context-free phonetic adjustments. For more than 50 children in twelve families that moved into the suburb, Payne showed that 52–68 percent had fully acquired the Philadelphia system, and 30–48 percent had partially acquired it.

When she looked at a more complex rule, the children's success rate indicated a different pattern. The rule called "short-a" provides a notorious instance of complexity. Essentially, it involves the tensing and raising of /æ/ toward [eːə], but the set of conditioning factors complicates it enormously. It never occurs in "weak" words such as *am*, *and*, or modal *can*; or before voiced obstruents except for the three words *mad*, *bad*, and *glad*; but it occurs invariably before final anterior voiceless fricatives as in *laugh*, *path*, and *class*, though never before non-anteriors as in, say, *smash*; and also invariably before final anterior nasals as in *ham* and *man*, though never in, say, *hang*. Elsewhere it occurs variably, before liquids as in *pal*; and before non-final anterior voiceless fricatives and nasals as in *traffic* and *hammer*.

Payne showed, perhaps not surprisingly, that none of the out-of-state children mastered this Philadelphia system. What was surprising was her discovery that children of out-of-state parents failed to master it even if they were born in King of Prussia. The subjects who did master it were those who were born there of Philadelphian parents. Of the contrasting success rates, Payne says, "The incomplete acquisition [of short-a] indicates that children do not freely restructure and/or reorganize their grammars up to the age of 14 but that they do have the ability to add lower level rules" (1980: 175).

The inabilty of individuals to master highly complex dialect features when they are exposed to them after the age of seven is one of the potential sources of anomalies in the survey sample. It is also, obviously, yet another effect of mobility on speech.

2.9.2   Insiders

There appears to be a tendency for individuals who are at the center of their social group to run ahead of the group in their use of salient markers. The notion of being at the center is not easily defined. It appears not to be a recognized social category that people comment on in casual conversations. It probably should not be equated with being a core member of a network, as in §2.6.5 above. The core members are the leaders, but the central members do not appear to be leaders, or not necessarily. What they have in common with the core members is a high degree of involvement in the affairs of the group.

2.9.2.1   *A "typical" boy in a New England village*   A simple example is provided by Fischer (1958: 49) in his pre-Labovian study of New England schoolchildren's pronunciation of present participle markers. Fischer, a sociologist engaged in research on child-rearing, noticed the variability of the present participle ending as [ɪŋ] or [ɪn] in *walking: walkin'*, *running: runnin'* and *searching: searchin'*. His instincts as a social scientist led him to explore the social correlates of the variants and resulted in a careful study that, since it was unprecedented, takes nothing for granted.

After eliciting speech samples by recording stories invented by the 24 children from lead sentences given by the investigator, Fisher counted the (ng) variants and set about correlating them with whatever social variables he could think of. Many of his independent variables have become familiar in sociolinguistic studies, such as sex (discussed in §3.2.1 below), family income level, and style. Another variable has gone largely unnoticed. Fischer compared the performances of what he called a "model" boy and a "typical" boy. The model boy "did his school work well, was popular among his peers, reputed to be thoughtful and considerate." The typical boy was "physically strong, dominating, full of mischief, but disarmingly frank about his transgressions." The difference in their use of the linguistic variants was enormous: the model boy used the non-standard variant [ɪn] less than 3 percent of the time, but the typical boy used it almost 55 percent of the time.

This linguistic difference in two individuals who are socially similar in almost every respect cries out for an explanation. Fischer (1958: 49) attributes it to a "personality" difference marked by the traits "aggressive" as opposed to "cooperative". The model boy is regarded as a model by his teacher, but it is worth wondering if he would be so regarded by the other boys, especially outside of school. He occupies the other end of the social pole from the typical boy. His use of the non-standard variant is as far below the mean as the typical boy's is above it. (The model boy would probably fit in with the aspirers in §2.9.4.) If the school provides the model boy with his favored milieu, then the schoolyard presumably provides the typical boy with his. Fischer's judgement of his "typicality" recognizes that the boy's main interest is outside the school and perhaps outside all other adult-dominated settings. He thrives in the company of other boys and is a conspicuous player among them.

2.9.2.2 *Elizabeth in Toronto*

In the Toronto sample that included the linguistic oddball Mr J, there was another individual who also used certain linguistic variants disproportionately. This was Elizabeth, a 22-year-old teacher's aide. Like Mr J, Elizabeth frequently failed to raise the onsets of /au/ diphthongs before voiceless consonants. There, however, the similarity between them ends.

Unlike Mr J, Elizabeth never had low back onsets on her unraised diphthongs. The onsets were always front, either open as in [saʊθ] or close as in [sæʊθ] 'south'. These are examples (aw)-fronting, the change under investigation. Most of Elizabeth's age group had fronted mid vowels before voiceless consonants, as in [sɐuθ] or [sɛuθ], but all but one of them also occasionally had fronted low vowels there too, as she did. Figure 2.9 shows the extent to which Elizabeth stood out from the others. She had unraised onsets 33 percent of the time, and the next highest score, Stanley's, was 14 percent. At the opposite end, Ann had no low onsets at all in this context; her speech in this respect (and others not relevant here) was similar in some ways to the adults. The group average, excluding Elizabeth, was less than 7 percent.

The essential difference between Mr J and Elizabeth is that his speech included some vowels unlike any others in the sample whereas hers included more vowels of certain kind than any others in the sample. He was qualitatively different from the others whereas she was quantitatively different.

The non-raising of fronted vowels in this diphthong was discernible as a trend in the data among the younger groups. Elizabeth was in the vanguard

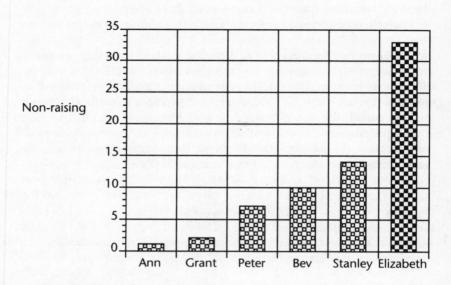

Figure 2.9 Elizabeth's non-raising score, in all styles, compared to the other MC 22-years-olds in north Toronto (Chambers 1984: figure 4, 126)

of this trend. Why she should be quantitatively different from the rest of the age group was certainly not detectable from her background. Like the other 22-year-olds in the survey, she was born and raised in the MC district called North Toronto where she attended the local public schools. Her father was an economist and her mother a housewife. At school, she participated in folk dancing, cross-country running, swimming, and a host of other activities. Her best friend was Ann, one of the other subjects, and she had known all the other 22-year-olds when they were in high school together. In her sociological profile, she was a prototypical member of her group.

Presumably, it is her very exemplariness that explains why she differs from the others in her use of non-raising. Like the "typical" boy in the New England classroom, she is a central participant in her social circle, and like him she is racing ahead of the rest in her use of a linguistic marker.

In some respects, Elizabeth and the typical boy appear to be examples of what Milroy and Milroy (1985: 367) call "early adopters." The term is apparently borrowed from sociology, and although it is certainly a misnomer the description that goes with it fits our insiders fairly well. They are "central members of the group, having strong ties within it, and . . . highly conforming to group norms; they frequently provide a model for other non-innovative members of the group." The Milroys provide no socio-linguistic correlates that would characterize these people.

There is no evidence that either Elizabeth or the typical boy adopted their favoured variants before their peers, as "early adopters" presumably do. Elizabeth may be thought of as providing a model for others in so far as her prolific (aw)-fronting is in the vanguard of a linguistic change in progress. But it is hard to see the typical boy as providing a linguistic model, in as much as (ng) is a stable variable and unlikely to increase in the direction of his own prolific use.

Sociolinguistically, these insiders appear to be identifiable as individuals who embody the social characteristics of their group prototypically and actualize the linguistic trends in the data prolifically.

2.9.3 Outsiders

If insiders represent a largely unrecognized social category, outsiders are a more familiar one. Much of this century's cultural iconography, from Kafka to Bix Beiderbecke, Leopold Bloom, Edna St Vincent Millay, Camus, Billie Holiday, Edith Piaf, Holden Caulfield, Charlie Parker, James Dean, Yukio Mishima and Yossarian, focuses on individuals apart from the crowd, un-able to join the mainstream and often alienated by it. Less dramatic exam-ples abound as well. The contribution of sociolinguistics to this iconography is the empirical evidence that being an outsider has linguistic consequences.

2.9.3.1 Lames in Harlem Adolescents notoriously form dense networks and place great value on being "part of the gang." Labov and his associates Clarence Robins and John Lewis, in their work with Harlem street gangs, viewed adolescent social behavior *in extremis*. There, peer pressure was sometimes enforced with firearms and members who were less than totally loyal might be punished mortally.

Even in these circumstances, the researchers became aware of outsiders – isolated individuals who occasionally associated with the others as fringe members but usually kept apart from them. Being apart, they cut them-selves off from the fads and fancies that characterized the insiders. Labov (1972a: 258) says, "They are not *hip*, since they do not hang out. It is only by virtue of being available and on the street every day that anyone can acquire the deep familiarity with local doings and the sure command of local slang that are needed to participate in vernacular culture." In the street argot of the gang members, the outsiders were known as "lames."

Viewed closely, the lames did not form a well-defined category. Some did not share the gang members' interests in crime, drugs and territoriality but others did. Some were forbidden to join the gangs by their parents but

Table 2.10 Four phonological variables and two syntactic variables in the speech of members of two street gangs, the Aces and the Thunderbirds, and outsiders (Lames) in Harlem (based on Labov 1972a: table 7, p. 264, with indices adjusted to show proportion of local variants; and p. 270)

Variable	Style	Aces	Thunderbirds	Lames
(ng)	IS	100	96	78
(dh)	IS	144	114	84
(r##r)	IS	94	96	79
(r)	IS	100	100	94
	RP	97	90	69
	WL	74	77	49
Dummy "it"	IS		79	9
Inverted comp	IS		80	20

others were former members who got distracted by jobs and girlfriends in their late teens.

Although they were a disparate lot – obviously more different from one another than the gang members were from one another – they nevertheless shared certain linguistic traits. One of these, as Labov mentions above, was their inability to keep up with the current slang. This is predictable, of course, since one of the sociolinguistic functions of slang is to distinguish insiders from outsiders. Because of this, its essential characteristic is that terms come into fashion and go out of fashion fairly rapidly. In order to remain fully fluent, you have to be in the right place at the right time.

Other linguistic markers went much deeper than slang. Labov compared the usage of members of the Aces and Thunderbirds with that of the lames for several linguistic variables and discovered that the gang members used much higher frequencies of the vernacular variants. This was the first empirical evidence for a result that, as we have seen, has now become familiar in several network studies.

Table 2.10 summarizes the results for four phonological variables and two syntactic ones. One obvious observation is that, for the phonological variables, where the scores of both the Aces and the Thunderbirds are available, the gangs are more similar to one another than either is to the lames. Looked at objectively, this alone should be surprising. After all, the two street gangs had very little contact with one another. Yet they are linguistically similar to one another. That similarity is emblematic of other similarities that go much deeper than their rivalry. It marks the individuals as having the same attitudes, holding the same values and participating in the same vernacular culture. It marks them, in other words, as insiders.

The linguistic differences of the lames, it follows, mark them as outsiders. Three of the four phonological variables in table 2.10 are well-studied in black English vernacular. Variable (ng) shows high use of the [ɪn] variant across the board but significantly higher use, almost categorical, in the speech of the gang members. Variable (dh), based on three variants, standard [ð], dental stop [d], and labiodental fricative [v], is calibrated so that consistent use of [d] would score 100 and consistent use of [v] would score 200. The gang members' scores show that the Aces use [v] more than the Thunderbirds but both gangs use the non-standard variants all the time, where the lames occasionally use the standard [ð]. The rarely studied (r##r) indicates the percentage of /r/ deleted when the next word begins with a vowel: 'four o'clock' as [fóəklɔk] rather than [fóɹəklɔk]. The deletion in this position is a specific feature of American black English accents, since other r-less accents of English retain the /r/intervocalically. Finally, preconsonantal and final (r) shows only slightly higher occurrences of the Ø variant in IS but the gap between the gang members and the lames widens in more self-conscious styles. The lames, unlike the gang members, adjust their speech more sharply in the direction of the standard when reading a passage of connected prose or a word list.

As expected, the syntactic variables are even more decisive distinguishers (as discussed in §2.3.4). If it is possible to dismiss the effect of (ng) as a marker, there is no chance of dismissing the evidence about dummy "it" in the same way. Dummy "it" counts the proportion of sentences with the expletive subject "it", as in *It's a policeman in that unmarked car*, where standard English has *there*. Use of "it" is a highly marked black English variant, and the lames use it very infrequently whereas the Thunderbirds use it most of the time. Similarly, though less decisively, the Thunderbirds use significantly more inverted comp, where the auxiliary of an embedded question is inverted, as in *He asked me could I go there*. The standard form, as in *He asked me if I could go there*, requires the complementizer *if* when the auxiliary is not inverted. The gap between the Thunderbirds and the lames is again enormous.

In all of these results, the outsiders subtly declare their distance from the vernacular culture of their peers. Being a lame has, as Labov says, linguistic consequences. Because the lames are themselves very different from one another socially, the most telling market of the alienation they share lies in their linguistic similarities. That may also hold for the insiders discussed in the previous section. The social characteristics of "typicality" vary from one society to the next, but the linguistic behavior of the insiders – accelerating the trends in the data of their peer group – may hold in all societies.

2.9.3.2   Ignaz in Grossdorf   Lippi-Green's finely calibrated network index, discussed above in §2.6.6, generally does not provide insights into the linguistic variation of the Austrian alpine village Grossdorf, at least not robust ones. One plausible explanation is that it is too fine to be revealing. She herself hints at that when she says (1989: 226), "the number of [linguistic] observations may have been too few to provide the contrasts needed to examine a wide range of social factors." Her social network schema may have over-differentiated the population either beyond the expressive power of linguistic variation or, more likely, beyond the sociolinguist's ability to discern it.

For one linguistic variable, however, she seems to have uncovered a subtle marker for outsiders in the small, close-knit community. She analyzes a change in progress in which the local variant [ɔ] – "a marker not just for membership in the mountain valley but also for allegiance to Grossdorf" (1989: 221) – is giving way to a low, unrounded [ɑ] variant. Her attempts at discovering the social correlates of this change are unsuccessful until she isolates the network factor of voluntary association, the extent of involvement in the social life of the village. This formed the third area of her index (1989: 219, items 14–16), determined by the individual's social activity in the village and the surrounding region, and by the number of clubs they belong to.

In looking at the use of the variants, she finds three men with relatively low scores for the local variant [ɔ]: Leo 78.8 percent, Klemens 79.2 percent, and Ignaz 79.6 percent. Two others have high scores for the local variant [ɔ]: Jodok 95 percent, and Hansaseff 88 percent. However, a comparison of their primary social characteristics indicates that these two clusters make very unlikely groupings. In the group with low scores, Leo and Klemens are highly educated and work outside of the village, but Ignaz is a local farmer with venerable local ties. In the group with high scores, Hansaseff is a student at a distant institution and Jodok is a farmer with strong local ties.

On the face of it, one would expect Hansaseff to form a cluster with Leo and Klemens, the two educated commuters, and Ignaz to form a cluster with Jodok, the other clansman and farmer. Moreover, if network density alone were the linguistic determinant, one would predict that the first putative cluster would have low scores for the local variant [ɔ], as indeed two of the three do, and second putative cluster would have high scores, as one but not the other does.

Given these predictions, Hansaseff and Ignaz are the oddballs. It turns out that what they have in common with the other individuals in their groups, besides their use of the [ɔ] variant, is their voluntary associations. Hansaseff, like Jodok, is integrally involved the village affairs. Although he "is outside local workplace network structures . . . [he] spends every possible minute of his free time involved in some village activity" (1989: 230). He receives the maximum score (3) for voluntary associations, whereas the other two educated individuals who work away from Grossdorf have low scores.

Ignaz is the opposite of Hansaseff in that he spends none of his free time in village activities. Though he is, like Jodok, the descendant of several generations of conservative homebodies, he behaves more like the educated commuters not only in his relatively frequent use of the non-local variant but also in his "disinterest or even apathy about the social life of the village." In them it seems consistent with their circumstances. In Ignaz it seems odd.

"He is not a recluse," Lippi-Green (1989: 230) says, "but he also does not join organizations which require a time commitment." Not a recluse, then, but perhaps a spectator, and in any event an outsider when it comes to participating in the social life of the village. If he were young and black in Harlem, he would be known as a lame, and like the lames he carries a linguistic marker of his peripherality.

2.9.4   Aspirers

Another set of people who frequently stand apart linguistically from their peers are those with social ambitions that stretch beyond their immediate social domain.

2.9.4.1   Samson in Anniston   Feagin (1979) found an interesting isolate among the WC teenagers in her home town when she returned there as a graduate student to conduct a sociolinguistic survey of the white community. Anniston, Alabama, is a small city in the American South with about 30,000 inhabitants at the heart of a metropolitan area that doubles the population. The people are, in Feagin's words, "mainly white native born of native-born parents" (1979: 47).

When she went to Wellborn High School to interview the WC teenagers, one of the boys, Samson, remarked to the others, "What she's doin' is she's come down here [from the North] and she's gon make – she's makin' fun of our language" (1979: 295). The statement attracted Feagin's attention first of all because the speaker corrected his use of the common local form of the future marker, *gon* pronounced [go^{w}ŋ] 'going to' (1979: 91–2). It also attracted her attention because it revealed the speaker's awareness of the gap between the local vernacular and standard speech. One of the other boys, Billy, replied, "I don't see nothin' so funny about the way we talk. I mean, I don't know it's nothin' different."

It turned out, not surprisingly, that Samson also attracted the sociolinguist's attention when she analyzed the linguistic variables. Figure 2.10 shows the

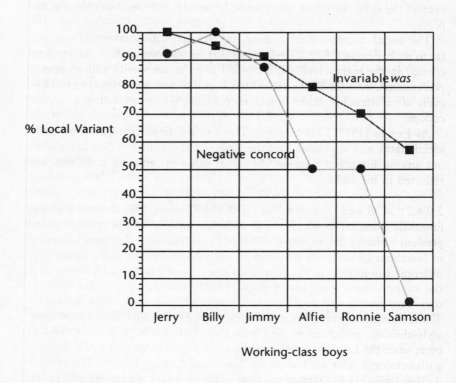

Figure 2.10 Use of local variants by six teenaged WC boys in Anniston, Alabama (based on Feagin 1979: tables 10.2 and 10.3, 272–3)

individual scores for six of the boys with respect to two variables. Invariable *was* refers to its use with plural subjects in such sentences as "I seen three, but they was all too far off to shoot" (1979: 202, spoken by the boy identified in figure 2.10 as Jimmy). This use of *was* with both plural and singular subjects is an instance of the leveling of English strong verbs also represented in the sentence above with *seen* for standard *saw* (discussed more fully in §5.6.3.1). Negative concord refers, of course, to the negation of indefinite consitituents in negative sentences, as in "I don't reckon there's no haunted house" (1979: 229, also spoken by Jimmy). In figure 2.10, the boys are arranged along the abscissa so that the most frequent non-standard users, Jerry and Billy, are on the left and the percentages decrease rightward. Samson is conspicuous as the most standard speaker: his negative concord score may be affected by the fact that his interview included only four instances of negative sentences, fewer than any of the others, but even if the drop were less cataclysmic he would still stand out among his peers.

The social correlate that accounts for Samson's distinctiveness was not far to seek. Feagin (1979: 271–2) notes that he was president of the student council in the high school. He intended to go to university and become a professional, whereas all the other boys hoped to become welders or electricians after attending trade school or policemen after attending a nearby college.

As Feagin (1979: 271) puts it, "There is a definite correlation between social status and aspiration and the scores of individuals." Samson stands out among his peers academically as an achiever, and his ambitions are reflected in his dialect.

2.9.4.2 A, B and C in Articlave Douglas-Cowie (1978) devised a sociolinguistic situation in which social ambition was one of the primary independent variables. In her native village of Articlave, four miles from Coleraine in Northern Ireland, she interviewed ten villagers in her home under two different conditions: in the first, Douglas-Cowie was the interviewer and the subjects were interviewed in pairs with refreshments; in the second, they were interviewed singly and the interviewer was "an English outsider." These contexts ingeniously set up conditions for the study of accommodation, style-shifting, group norms and individual differences, and so on. Moreover, since the English outsider in the second interviews was P. M. Tilling, a dialectologist who worked on the Survey of English Dialects (Orton and Tilling 1969–71) and was, at the time of the Articlave study, engaged in the planning of the Hiberno–English Dialect Survey, the study also has implications for the standardizing effect of non-local interviewers in dialect surveys. For our purposes here, we will concentrate on the results with respect to ambition.

The subjects' speech was quantified for seven variables in the two situations. The results for three variables are shown in table 2.11. Variable (ng) quantifies the percentage of the [ən] variant, as usual. Variable (aɪ) is a weighted index score based on the three variants [aɪ], closer [ɐɪ], and centralized [əɪ] in words like *sight*, *side* and *sigh*: invariant use of [aɪ] would score Ø, of [ɐɪ] 100, and of [əɪ] 200. Variable (yes/aye) quantifies the proportion of the lexical element *aye* for *yes* in answer to a question or as a supporting interjection when someone else is speaking.

For all three variables (and the other four included in the study), the higher the score the greater the proportion of vernacular variants. Reading the table horizontally, the scores tend to increase from left to right because the subjects have been rank-ordered, as far as possible, with respect to their use of the vernacular. Each subject has a pair of index scores for each variable, one for the interview with Douglas-Cowie and the other for the

Table 2.11 Variable index scores for ten subjects (A–J) in Articlave in two interview situations: (1) in pairs with a local interviewer, and (2) alone with an English interviewer (Douglas-Cowie 1978: tables 1, 3, 6, pp. 41, 42, 43)

		A	B	C	D	E	F	G	H	I	J
Variable (ng)	1	15	49	25	75	91	94	98	84	100	100
	2	04	05	05	35	42	75	84	75	97	100
Variable (ai)	1	48	106	84	152	184	200	196	190	200	194
	2	26	60	68	61	158	195	190	186	200	192
Variable (yes/aye)	1	0	0	0	0	71	98	82	91	100	87
	2	0	0	0	0	36	69	31	90	100	03

interview with Tilling. There is a consistent result for all variables: the scores are always higher in the first interview unless they are invariant. That is, if we disregard the speakers who never vary – who always say *walkin'*, *runnin'* and *rollin'* (as does J), or who have only the centralized diphthong [əɪ] (as does I), or who never say *aye* (as A, B, C, and D) or always say it (I) – the other speakers, the ones who do vary, always use more vernacular variants in the first interview. This is hardly surprising, of course, and would only be remarkable if it were reversed.

The controlled interview situation allowed Douglas-Cowie to draw several conclusions about the influence of context on style:

- vernacular forms increase in the second half of the interview with the Englishman (1978: 43), that is, as the subjects and the interviewer become more familiar with one another;
- vernacular forms decrease when the topic of the conversation is occupation and education (1978: 43–6); and
- vernacular forms increase when two villagers talk to one another in the presence of the English interviewer, and decrease when they are talking directly to him (1978: 47).

If none of these results is particularly surprising, they are nonetheless valuable as empirical evidence for our ethnographic impressions.

More surprising is the evidence that social ambition is a better correlate of the linguistic variation in these interviews than is social class. Douglas-Cowie obtained an index of social ambition by asking each subject to rate the others with respect to "how keen they are to get on in the world" using this scale:

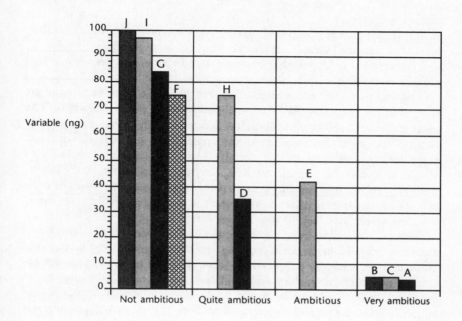

Figure 2.11 Scores for variable (ng) in the second interview for Articlave subjects grouped according to social ambition (after Douglas-Cowie 1978: figure 4, 50)

1 not keen
2 keen
3 quite keen
4 very keen

Since all the subjects knew each other well, there was "a striking amount of agreement" (1978: 48) in their answers to the question.

All the linguistic variables showed a positive correlation between standardization and social ambition. Figure 2.11 shows the correlation with (ng). The linguistic scores are those shown in the second row of table 2.11 above. The four clusters indicate the assessments of social ambition by the other subjects. At the extremes, the correlation between language use and ambition is robust. The amount of vernacular use is sharply graded from the unambitious villagers on the left to the very ambitious ones one the right.

Complementing this result is the fact that class indicators like education and occupation correlate less precisely than ambition with regard to the amount of standardization. The most ambitious group consists of subject C who is well educated and has a prestigious occupation – a prototypical member of this group – and of A and B, who are both shop assistants (salespeople) with secondary school educations. Subject I in the first group and H in the second group both have grammar school educations, so they are better educated than A, B and E, who use more standard forms. The one discrepancy is D, who has a university education and uses fewer vernacular forms than E, who is more ambitious.

Aspiring to higher social status thus has linguistic consequences of its own. It is not necessary that the individual be more than an aspirant. The most ambitious individuals in Articlave are not actively pursuing fortune or fame. They are settled members of the community, and indeed have been there for most of their lives if not all. The shop assistants are likely to remain in their jobs, and the teachers, clerks and housewives are likely to remain in theirs. It is something more subtle than their possessions or their status that makes them different from their peers. It is more like an attitude, a feeling about how they fit into the group.

Samson, the aspirer from Anniston, is just like them. He is younger and therefore actively involved in working toward his goals. But if he never made it to university or practiced medicine or law, if he were to change his mind or miss his opportunity, he would surely find a respectable position in his home town. And then he would settle down in familiar territory, surrounded by ex–classmates and aging neighbors in the town where he grew up. And for the most part he would be just like everyone else of his age and social class – except, of course, for certain subtle markers in his dialect which, like A, B and C in Articlave, are the product of his feeling about where he fits into the group.

2.9.5   The linguistic limits of individuation

So it is with all of the individuations. The interlopers, the insiders and the outsiders are all related in subtly different ways to their social groups. It may be easier to comprehend the mass only because they make a greater impression statistically and in every other way. But the edges are no less real, and our sociolinguistic instruments are already proving useful in picking them out and uncovering the correlates of their behavior.

It may turn out that the mass itself is an illusion. What our social sciences would have us perceive as an undifferentiated mass – the bell of society's curve – is presumably made up of numerous small groups with subtle, special relationships to the whole, no less real, but so far harder to discern, than that of the aspirers, the interlopers, the outsiders and the insiders.

But truly idiosyncratic speakers have never emerged from our researches. If they exist, they are so rare that no sample population to date seems to have included one. People who are reputed to speak very differently from everyone else become legendary figures. Dean William A. Spooner, Warden of New College, Oxford, became celebrated for saying things like "You have hissed all my mystery lessons; in fact, you have tasted the whole worm." Word-initial slips of the tongue are known as spoonerisms in his honor. In jazz circles, Lester Young was celebrated not only for the warm lyricism of his tenor saxophone but also for speaking a coded language. According to one of his piano players, Jimmy Rowles, "You had to break that code to understand him. It was like memorizing a dictionary, and I think it took me about three months" (Balliett 1986: 234).

They were neither among the linguistic masses nor on its edges, with Mr J, Elizabeth, Ignaz, Samson or any of the other people identified in the previous section. Perhaps they belong to a category of way-out outsiders, but we will probably never find enough of them to know for sure. What we do know for sure is that, for the most part, people sound the way you would expect them to sound given the facts about their class, sex, age, and region. The sociolinguistic evidence strongly supports George Eliot's observation, in *Middlemarch*, that "there is no creature whose inward being is so strong it is not greatly determined by what lies outside it."

3

Expressing Sex and Gender

[My aunts] told about the wild-looking town in Northern Ontario where Aunt Iris wouldn't stop the car even to let them buy a Coke. She took one look at the lumberjacks and cried, "We'd all be raped!"
"What is raped?" said my little sister.
"Oh-oh," said Iris. "It means you get your pocketbook stolen."
Pocketbook: an American word. My sister and I didn't know what it meant either but we were not equal to two questions in a row. And I knew that wasn't what rape meant anyway; it meant something dirty.
"Purse. Purse stolen," said my mother in a festive but cautioning tone. Talk in our house was genteel.

Alice Munro (1983)

In virtually all sociolinguistic studies that include a sample of males and females, there is evidence for this conclusion about their linguistic behaviour: women use fewer stigmatized and non-standard variants than do men of the same social group in the same circumstances.[1]

Over the years, this conclusion has been stated in numerous ways. Wolfram (1969: 76) says that "females show a greater sensitivity to socially evaluative linguistic features than do males." Labov (1972: 243) says, "In careful speech, women use fewer stigmatized forms than men, and are more sensitive than men to the prestige pattern." Wolfram and Fasold (1974: 93) say, "Females show more awareness of prestige norms in both their actual speech and their attitudes toward speech." Romaine (1978: 156), explaining the preference by women for a different variant from the men in her study, concludes: "The females . . . are clearly more concerned with the pressure exerted by local norms and asserting their status within the . . . social structure." Elsewhere, she summarizes the sociolinguistic results as follows (1984: 113): "women consistently produce forms which are nearer to the prestige norm more frequently than men," and she reports, furthermore, evidence for gender differentiation in choosing linguistic variants as early as six years old. Trudgill (1983: 161) says that "women, allowing for other variables such as age, education and social class, produce on average linguistic forms which more closely approach those of the standard language or have higher prestige than those produced by men." Labov (1990: 205) states it this way: "In stable sociolinguistic stratification, men use a higher frequency of non-standard forms than women."[2] Cameron and Coates (1988: 13) say that "women on average deviate less from the prestige standard than men," and add that "in modern urban societies it is typically true for every social class."

My consideration of the linguistic correlates for sex and gender will centrally involve this conclusion. I provide some of the evidence for it in §3.2, with a review of the results of variable (ng) in two widely separated speech communities. In §3.3, I look more closely at male/female variation in two communities. In §3.4, I attempt to explain the social significance for these differences. In §3.5, I look at linguistic correlates for gender in societies outside the Western world with the expectation that the comparisons will shed some light on the explanation. First, I make a distinction between sex and gender roles that will be maintained throughout the chapter.

3.1 The Interplay of Biology and Sociology

3.1.1 Sex and gender

The distinction between "sex" and "gender" essentially recognizes biological and sociocultural differences. The biology of masculinity and femininity – that is, sex differences – begins to differentiate prenatally, soon after conception. The differentiating genitalia, along with other individual identifiers such as blood type and fingerprints, develop in the fetus and remain unchanged through life (Ounsted and Taylor 1972: 250). The sociology of masculinity and femininity – gender – differentiates postnatally.

As Miller and Swift (1976: 51) put it, "At the risk of oversimplification, sex . . . is a biological given; gender is a social acquisition." The risk of oversimplification arises because the two are tightly interwoven. Gender differences are partly based on sex differences. The social role of mothering is traditionally assumed by women as a consequence of their biological functions in carrying and nursing their children. Intensely physical labor is traditionally done by men because on average they are bigger than women. Of course, sex differences do not circumscribe gender roles very rigidly. There are very few social functions that need be prescribed or determined by sex. Many of those that are, like kick-boxing and beauty pageantry, seem to be cultural excrescences.

In the fight for sexual equality, perhaps the greatest battles are fought over entrenched stereotypes. Any contention that women *must* do X whereas men *must* do Y implies a sexual basis, as if biological imperatives were drawing the lines. They seldom are. The mothering role is not incompatible with running a law practice or driving a school bus, and the laboring role is not incompatible with preparing children's lunches or ironing their clothes. In fact, sex-determined roles are fewer now than ever before. Where ditch-digging formerly required the extra girth with which men are more likely to be endowed, nowadays it is usually done by pushing buttons and pulling levers in an earth-mover, and physical strength is not required.

Sociolinguists and many other social scientists sometimes fail to distinguish sex and gender. As Eckert (1989a: 246–7) says:

> Although differences in patterns of variation between men and women are a function of gender and only indirectly a function of sex (and, indeed, such gender-based variation occurs within, as well as between, sex groups), we have been examining the interaction between gender and variation by correlating variables with sex rather than gender differences. This has been done because although an individual's gender-related place in society is a multidimensional complex that can only be characterized through careful analysis, his or her sex is generally a readily observable binary variable. . . . [B]ecause information about the individual's sex is easily accessible, data can be gathered without any inquiry into the construction of gender in that community.

I agree with Eckert's basic contention that sex and gender have not been distinguished consistently. Sex differences, being visible, are apparently taken as the independent variable to be correlated with linguistic variables regardless of gender roles in the community.

I will show below that the failure to make the distinction between gender and sex has disguised significant correlations of linguistic variation with gender on the one hand and with sex on the other. Specifically, when gender roles differ in terms of the mobility of women and men in a community, a sociolinguistic principle which I call **gender-based variability** emerges (§3.4.1). Perhaps more significantly, I will also show that male-female differences evidently persist even in the absence of well-defined gender roles. These I will ascribe to sex differences in a sociolinguistic principle that I call **sex-based variability** (§3.4.2).

3.1.2   *Gender and grammatical gender*

It is probably worth mentioning at this point that "gender" has a linguistic meaning that is quite separate from the social meaning we have been discussing. Grammatically, gender is expressed in many languages, mainly European ones, by inflectional affixes on nouns and sometimes by concord or agreement inflections on parts of speech in construction with nouns.

The traditional terms for the gender categories are masculine, feminine and neuter, but those terms are only loosely related to real-world (or semantic) gender. The arbitrariness causes some consternation for language learners, naturally, and once provoked this satire from Mark Twain (in "The Awful German Language," quoted by Miller and Swift 1976: 41):

> In German, a young lady has no sex, while a turnip has. Think what overwrought reverence that shows for the turnip, and what callous disrespect for the girl.
> . . . a tree is male, its buds are female, its leaves are neuter; horses are sexless, dogs are male, cats are female – tomcats included, of course; a person's mouth, neck, bosom, elbows, fingers, feet, and body are of the male sex, and his head is male or neuter according to the word selected to signify it, and *not* according to the sex of the individual who wears it – for in Germany all the women wear either male heads or sexless ones; a person's nose, lips, shoulders, breast, hands, and toes are of the female sex; and his hair, ears, eyes, chin, legs, knees, heart, and conscience haven't any sex at all.

Here Twain deliberately mixes up sex and grammatical gender for purposes of humor, equating masculine gender with being "male," feminine with "the female sex," and neuter with being "sexless."

Among linguists, where gender is well established as a technical grammatical term, perhaps it is the possibility of this kind of confusion that has slowed the acceptance of the use of gender as the term for a social role. Both gender roles and sex roles are often discussed together as sex roles. In this chapter, we will maintain the distinction between gender and sex as independent variables, trusting that grammatical gender is understood well enough to avoid confusion.

3.1.3 Some sex differences

Very few biological differences between males and females have an effect on language. Among the documented linguistic differences are that women are less likely to have reading disabilities, or to stutter, or to be aphasic (also see §3.4.2).

The non-linguistic biological differences are numerous. On average, women have less muscle mass than men, are shorter, weigh less, and have smaller feet. They are much less likely to be color-blind, a condition in which the perception of particular colors is defective, but they appear to be more likely to be synesthetic, a condition in which one sense activates another, most commonly occurring as a kind of technicolor hearing whereby colors are associated with speech sounds. Women are also less likely to be left-handed, and much less likely to go bald.

They usually mature earlier and more rapidly, and they typically live longer. Their advantage in hardiness is evident almost from the moment of conception, because female fetuses are less susceptible to miscarriage and stillbirth (Taylor and Ounsted 1972: 216). They are less likely to be retarded (Vandenberg 1987). They are less susceptible to almost all diseases. A notable exception is osteoporosis, loss of protein from the bones, which causes round shoulders and brittle bone in older women much more commonly than in men. Otherwise, women enjoy greater resistance to diseases, from crib death to kidney stones and gout and heart diseases of all kinds.

As a result, even though there are probably more than 110 males conceived for every 100 females, by the time each generation moves into their forties the women outnumber the men, and by the time they are in their seventies the ratio is about two to one (Taylor and Ounsted 1972: 216–17).

3.1.4   *Probabilistic, not absolute, differences*

It is worth pausing briefly at this point to consider the meaning of these comparisons. They represent physiological predispositions. Sex differences (as opposed to gender differences) may also reveal themselves in neurological predispositions, and we will have more to say about those in §3.4.

It is absolutely crucial to understand that these sex differences, whether physiological or neurological, are merely probabilistic. Females and males come in all shapes and sizes. Indeed the breadth of variation is such that there are no *absolute* sex differences. Obviously there are left-handed women with kidney stones and there are short men with osteoporosis. Biologically-based differences seem to be mild, not robust, and they should be thought of *not* as innate advantages or hindrances to one group or the other but merely as innate biases. Knowing that they exist is only useful because it allows steps to be taken to forestall any deleterious effect that the bias might have. The female predisposition to osteoporosis makes a simple example. Knowing that it exists means that dietary and other preventive measures can be put in place to compensate for whatever it is that causes it. Exactly the same goes for any other biological predisposition, whether it be neurological or physiological.

3.1.5   *Vocal pitch as a sex difference*

Linguistically, probably the most obvious physiological difference is the relative size of the male and female larynx. Men's larynxes tend to be much larger, and conspicuously so, because they cause the thyroid cartilege in the throat, called the Adam's apple, to protrude. (Because of this difference, there is no 'Eve's apple'.)

The larger larynx means that men have longer vocal cords. Longer cords vibrate more slowly, and thus produce a lower-pitched voice. The range for men is from about 80 Hz (Herz = cycles-per-second) to 200 Hz, and for women about 120 Hz to 400 Hz. The fact that these ranges overlap means, of course, that the correlation of pitch differences with sex is, like all sex differences, a statistical bias and not an absolute difference. The lower limit for a basso profundo is around 60 Hz and the upper limit for a coloratura soprano is around 1,300 Hz. Most men's voices fall between 100–150 Hz, and most women's between 200–300 Hz (Malmberg 1963: 26).

The lengthening of the male vocal cords is a secondary sexual change that takes place at puberty. Pubescent boys must adjust to the change and many of them go through a short but – for them – excruciating period when involuntary croaking sounds disturb their stream of speech (Rogers 1991: 240–1). Feminists sometimes claim that the fact that the pitch of women's speech is similar to children's contributes to their stereotyping in male-dominated societies. Typical average pitches are 120 Hz for men, 225 Hz for women, and 265 Hz for children (Rogers 1991: 127). The difference between women and children is great enough that listeners are seldom confused about which one they are actually hearing, but the relative difference between them is much less than that between men and women.

To the best of my knowledge, no one has yet devised a means of testing for stereotyped attitudes based on vocal pitch. It is evident, however, that individuals with atypical pitches can thrive even in highly sex-dependent roles – fans can readily name macho athletes with high-pitched voices and torch singers with low-pitched ones. These are not sociolinguistic variables but individual ones (as discussed in §1.1.1), of the same order as, say, lisps and soft-spokenness. They differ from person to person.

The next section considers variables of more general social significance. They are less readily observed than vocal pitch or other personal characteristics but, paradoxically, much more important as markers of sex and gender.

3.2   Gender Patterns with Stable Variables

Stable variables are those that are well established as indicators in a community and are not undergoing change. In the prototypical pattern for a stable variable, each age cohort of the same class, gender, ethnic background, and other social characteristics, will be similar to older and younger groups in the use of variants and the amount of style-shifting.

3.2.1   Variable (ng)

One of the best-studied stable variables is (ng), the pronunciation of the English participial suffix on forms such as *walking, running* and *jogging*. In careful styles in perhaps all standard accents of English, this suffix is pronounced [ɪŋ], that is, with a velar nasal consonant. The standard pronunciation also invariably has the high front lax vowel [ɪ], as shown, but that is an accidental factor, because English includes a phonotactic constraint such that syllables with the velar nasal in the coda always have lax vowels.[3] In casual MC speech and in all styles of WC speech, (ng) has a variant form that sounds like either [ɪn], [ən] or [in]. The essential feature of the variant is the alveolar nasal; the range of possible vowels is greater partly because /n/ exerts no phonotactic constraints on its preceding vowel as /ŋ/ does. Generally, speech communities have either [ɪn] or [ən] as their characteristic variant. For instance, Norwich, England, has [ən] (Trudgill 1974), and Sydney, Australia, has [ɪn] (Horvath 1985).

3.2.1.1   The variant [in] *as a hypercorrection*   The third variant, [in], with a tense vowel before the alveolar nasal, has been reported as the characteristic variant only in Ottawa, Canada, but it occurs sporadically in Toronto, where the characteristic variant is [ɪn], in Milwaukee, and no doubt in many other parts of North America. Woods (1991: 140) notes that in Ottawa speakers frequently make homophones of pairs such as *being* and *bean*, *paying* and *pain*, *playing* and *plain*, and *saying* and *sane*. If it were found only in words like these the tense vowel in the suffix could be analyzed as an assimilation to the preceding high front tense vowel or /j/-glide, but it is not so restricted.

The provenance of this variant appears to be not assimilation but hypercorrection. In Toronto, the [in] variant, though infrequent, occurs in very careful MC speech, and is not at all confined to more casual contexts. In other words, it patterns stylistically as an alternative to [ɪŋ] rather than an alternative to [ɪn] or [ən]. As Woods (1979: 109) says of his Ottawa sample, "It is the opinion of the author that /in/ is an attempt towards the pronunciation /ɪŋ/ and away from /ən/."

As a hypercorrection of [ɪn] or [ən], that is, a more careful alternative to those casual variants, the acoustic properties of [in] make it a plausible substitute for [ɪŋ]. Houston (1991: 253), in an attempt to explain how *ing* could have replaced historical *ind* as the participle marker in Middle English, notes that the first two formant loci for high vowels like [ij] are similar to those for velar stops, whereas those for central vowels like [ə] are similar to those for alveolar stops. Applying these acoustic facts to dialects with the variant [in] as a hypercorrection of [ɪn] for [ɪŋ], it is palpably a fudge

(Chambers and Trudgill 1980: 132–7), that is, it retains the essential articulatory feature of the casual variant but alters the acoustic properties so that they are similar to the careful variant. So far there have been no other systematic studies involving the [in] variant, although it is quite widely distributed.

3.2.1.2 The variant [ɪn] *or* [ən] *as a gender marker* Several studies of (ng) provide sufficient information about their sociolinguistic parameters to make an instructive survey of male–female behaviour when other social variables are shared.

The first study to bear resemblances to modern sociolinguistics, Fischer's (1958) sociological study of child-rearing in a village near Boston, investigated variations of *-ing* and *-in* in participles. When Fischer became curious about "certain inconsistencies" in the speech of the children in his sample, he inquired about it among linguists and was told that it was merely "free variation," the standard answer at the time. Fortunately, Fischer was not satisfied. As he (1958: 47–8) later observed:

> "Free variation" is of course a label, not an explanation. It does not tell us where the variants came from nor why the speakers use them in different proportions, but is rather a way of excluding such questions from the scope of immediate inquiry. Historically, I presume that one could investigate the spread of one of these variants into the territory of another through contact and migration, and this would constitute one useful sort of explanation. However, another sort of explanation is possible in terms of current factors which lead a given child in given circumstances to produce one of the variants rather than another.

Fischer's simple statement expresses the most fundamental motivation for sociolinguistics, and the basis of sociolinguistic analysis.

Fischer proceeded to analyze the differences in *-in* and *-ing* usage by his subjects by correlating them with a number of independent variables including socioeconomic status, individual traits (the "model" boy contrasted to a "typical" boy discussed in §2.9.2.1. above), style (formal vs. informal), mood (relaxed vs. tense), lexical root ("formal" verbs like *criticizing* contrasted to "informal" ones like *chewin'*), and, of course, gender. For his positive results he postulated "socio-symbolic" significance. The gender correlation, for instance, "suggests that in this community (and probably others where the choice exists) *-ing* is regarded as symbolizing female speakers and *-in* as symbolizing males" (1958: 48).

The growth of sociolinguistic research has amply supported Fischer, as in so many other aspects of his prescient study, by demonstrating that (ng) carries exactly the same socio-symbolic significance in numerous communities. We will now take a closer look at (ng) in the urban dialects of Norwich

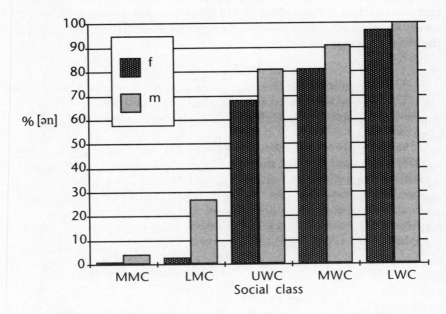

Figure 3.1 (ng) indices for men and women in five social classes in Norwich, in formal speech (based on Trudgill 1974: table 7.2, 94)

and Sydney, communities thousands of kilometres from Fischer's New England village and, of course, thousands of kilometres from one another.

3.2.2 Norwich (ng)

Trudgill (1974: 91–5) provides a classic instance of sex-graded variation in his study of (ng) in Norwich. Figure 3.1 plots the male and female (ng) indices for all five social classes in interview style – what Trudgill calls formal speech. The (ng) index is calculated as the percentage of [ən] variants among all instances of participles in the interview. In other words, a speaker who had only [ən] endings throughout the interview would score 100 percent, whereas someone who had only the standard [ɪŋ] would score 0. Strikingly, the Norwich results cover the entire range, from 0 for MMC women to 100 percent for LWC men.

As we move down the social hierarchy from MMC on the left, the bars of the graph increase progressively from class to class. Most important for our purposes, in each of the classes the men score higher than the women.

The gap between men and women is greatest in the LMC (m 27, f 3), and narrowest in the LWC (m 100, f 97). It is worth noting in passing that the social groups on the cusp between the major divisions, MC and WC, show the greatest divergences in usage.

3.2.3 Sydney (ng)

Turning to Sydney, we will look at the two main (ng) variants, standard [ɪŋ] and non-standard [ɪn]. Horvath lists a third variant, [ɪŋk], with the other two but she notes (1985: 97) that it "may only be associated with lexical items containing the morpheme *thing*," that is, the compounds *anything*, *everything*, *nothing* and *something*. This variant occurs in England as well, and is associated there only with the *-thing* morpheme. It is not a participial variant at all (and is appropriately omitted from a study of Sydney verbs by Eisikovits 1991).[4]

Leaving aside the the [ɪŋk] variant, Sydney presents a pattern for (ng) that is similar in many respects to Norwich and different from it in one respect. The Sydney results in figure 3.2 show the three social classes divided not only into men and women but further into teens and adults. As in the Norwich pattern, there is a relatively steady increase in the (ng) indices from the MC on the left to the LWC on the right, although the pattern is slightly disturbed by the MC teen boys, whose score appears to be some ten points higher than it would be if the pattern were perfectly regular. That aside, the [ɪn] variant appears to be partly a class indicator, as it is in Norwich.

Looking more closely, some differences impose themselves. First, the absolute scores in Sydney are considerably below those in Norwich, ranging between zero and 43, where Norwich, as we mentioned, covers the entire range. Second, the adults in all classes except for the LWC men (with index 32) are hardly involved in this variable at all: MC men and the adult women in all social classes score zero, and the UWC men score only 3. Third, as a complement to that, the teens are highly involved. Without the scores of the teenagers, figure 3.2 would be very flat and uninteresting.

Although Horvath suggests (1985: 103) that this "feature looks like a possible candidate for a language change in progress study," presumably basing her suggestion on the evidence for age-grading in the contrast of adults and teens, it looks at least as much like an incipient marker of ethnic background. A further correlate of Sydney (ng), though a minor one compared to class, gender and age but probably important for understanding the results, is the fact that people of Italian and Greek ancestry in Horvath's sample show higher frequencies of the non-standard variant. As second- and third-generation Italian and Greek Australians diffuse throughout the

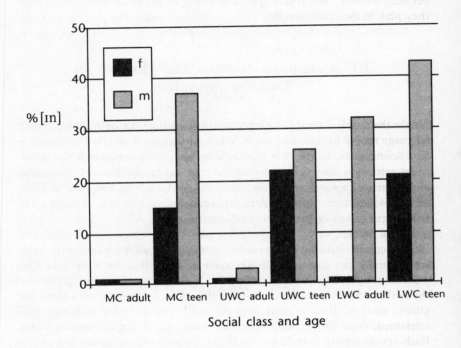

Figure 3.2 (ng) indices for men and women in three social classes in Sydney, with teen groups separated from adults (based on Horvath 1985: table 7.3, 101)

social matrix, their accents might perpetuate higher frequencies of the [ɪn] variant while in other respects falling into line with the features characteristic of their class and age. In any event, the instability discernible in Horvath's results for (ng) may take a generation or two to resolve into a fully coherent pattern.

For our purposes, the most important observation about figure 3.2 is that in those social groups that are involved in (ng) variation the males invariably outscore the females. Standard [ɪŋ] occurs invariably in the speech of three female groups but only one male group. In other words, in the six pairwise comparisons of class–age–gender groups, one (MC adult) is even and the other five all show the men outscoring the women.

That pattern is one of the most familiar in the sociolinguistic literature. In stable variables, women use fewer non-standard variants than men of the same social class and age under the same circumstances. So far, it appears to be an isolated fact. In the next section, we will look at the relationship between women's and men's speech in the light of the different social roles they play in two communities.

3.3 Language, Gender, and Mobility in Two Communities

Unlike the purely formal sub-disciplines of linguistics, sociolinguistics studies language rooted in time and place. When the linguists involved are humanistic scientists or, failing that, scientific humanists their research can sometimes convey to the reader not only the rigorous results but also something of the sense of place in which they were pursued – a "real glimpse," as Shuy (1983: 345) puts it, "of the living, dynamic, social, variable, exciting thing that language can be" in a fieldwork situation.

In this section, we take a look at two communities, inner city Detroit and Ballymacarrett Belfast, that have become part of the sociolinguistic landscape, familiar to many people who have never visited them, because they were investigated by linguists, Wolfram and his associates in Detroit and the Milroys in Belfast, who conveyed the social framework with their linguistic analysis. Both regions have the advantage of being relatively self-contained, especially considering their locations in large, complex cities. Both reveal strong correlations between gender and language use in the results.

3.3.1 Inner city Detroit

Wolfram (1969) selected 48 field records of Detroit blacks from the random sample of over 700 interviews in the large, bi-racial project in which he had served as a fieldworker (Shuy, Wolfram and Riley 1968). His sample is symmetrical: 12 people in each of four social classes, upper middle (UM), lower middle (LM), upper working (UW) and lower working (LW), equally divided by gender.

He isolated four phonological variables and four grammatical variables. Among the most striking features of his results was the discovery of gender grading for all eight variables. We will look briefly at four of them, two phonological and two grammatical, as representative of the gender correlations.

3.3.1.1 Variable (th) First, morpheme-medial and final /θ/, symbolized (th), is realized in Detroit Black English Vernacular (BEV) with four possible variants: standard [θ], labio-dental [f], stop [t], or nothing Ø (Wolfram 1969: 82–4, 91–2). In initial position it apparently occurs regularly as the

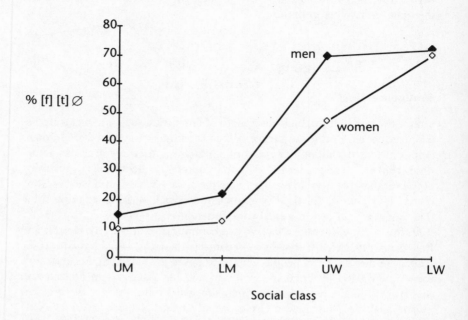

Figure 3.3 (th) indices for men and women in Detroit, as a percentage of [f], [t] and Ø variants as opposed to standard [θ] (from Wolfram 1969: 92)

standard variant [θ], and so that position is excluded from the analysis. Medially as in *nothing* and finally as in *tooth* the possible realizations are as follows (using Wolfram's notation):

CATEGORY	nothing	tooth
θ	[nəθɨŋ]	[tʰuθ] or [tʰutθ]
f	[nəfɨn]	[tʰuf]
t	[nət²ŋ] or [nə²ŋ]	(infrequent) [tʰut˺]
Ø	[nəɨn]	([wɪ#mi] 'with me')

The variants [t] and Ø occur almost exclusively in the words *nothing* and *with*, which are very frequent in the interviews. The primary variation is between the other two variants, [θ] and [f].

In figure 3.3, the gender differentiation is shown by calculating the percentage of non-standard variants as opposed to the standard one. Speakers with only [θ] would score zero on the graph and speakers with only [f], [t] or Ø would score 100. Obviously none of the social groups reaches either of

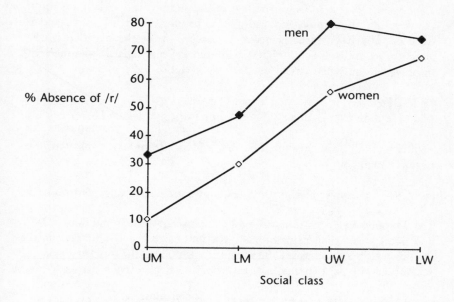

Figure 3.4 (r) indices for men and women in Detroit (from Wolfram 1969: 117)

those extremes, but there is a notable stratification between the MC groups and the WC groups, with the former under 20 percent and the latter over 47 percent. This variable is clearly a social class indicator.

It is also clearly a gender indicator, as the gender groups in each social class are consistently stratified, with the women scoring lower than the men, that is, with fewer non-standard variants.

3.3.1.2 Variable (r) Gender differences are also evident in figure 3.4, representing variable (r), the presence or absence of postvocalic/r/. Phonetically, the /r/ may be pronounced or not in preconsonantal position, as in *barking* or *bird*, and in final position, as in *car* or *mother*. Wolfram (1969: 109–10, 116–17) counted any constriction as a realization and opposed it to the complete absence of constriction.

. Compared to the (th) indices, the (r) indices do not as sharply mark the two major social classes. In the figure, the lines slope quite steadily upward from the UM instead of making the abrupt rise that we noticed for (th). The gender differentiation is, if anything, sharper, with the gap between the women and the men wider. Again, the women are consistently closer to the abscissa, that is, they are more r-ful than the men.

3.3.1.3　Multiple negation　The first of the grammatical variables is multiple negation, a common and widespread feature of English non-standard dialects. The basic form is negative concord, with the negative marker attached to every indefinite in the sentence. In standard grammar, the negative can only be marked once, as in the following sentences:

BEV　　　　　　　　　　Standard
He didn't do nothing　　= He didn't do anything OR He did nothing

Wolfram (1969: 153) cites the following sentence from his datafile, with five negative markers:

We ain't never had no trouble about none of us pullin' out no knife.

He also notes two constituent negations that seem to be found only in BEV and not in other dialects of English: the first has a negative marker on the auxiliary verb as well as on the indefinite preceding the auxiliary, and the second has the negated auxiliary inverted in a declarative sentence:

Nobody can't step on her foot　　= Nobody can step on her foot
Didn't nobody knew it　　　　　= Nobody knew it

In the tabulation for figure 3.5, Wolfram counted the number of realized multiple negations among the total negated sentences in the interview, and calculated the percentage. The graph shows a now-familiar pattern, with a steady and in this case sharp rise from UMC to LWC, and clear stratification of the genders, with the women always having fewer non-standard forms.

　　Grammatical variables stratify groups more sharply than phonological variables, as we have seen (§2.3). This observation was first made by Wolfram (1969: 203–4) in his analysis of these Detroit variables. It holds here for multiple negation but the effect is partly masked in the group averages, which give the appearance of a fairly regular increase. Actually, the groups include some individuals with maximum scores – 100 percent multiple negation – and some others with minimum scores – no multiple negation at all. Of the 48 subjects, seven have categorical multiple negation and 15 have complete absence of multiple negation. These two sub-groups fall into the social categories exactly as expected: the seven with categorical multiple negation are all WC, and five of them are men; the 15 with no multiple negation are all MC, and nine are women.

3.3.1.4　Copula deletion　The final variable is zero copula, one of the markers of BEV wherever it is spoken (Wolfram 1969: 165–79). In BEV it is possible

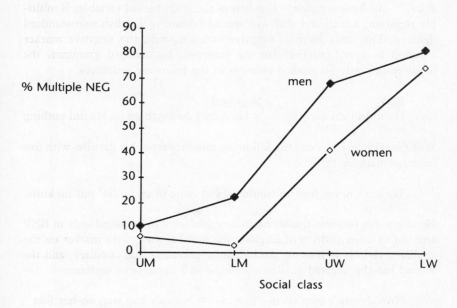

Figure 3.5 Percentage of multiple negation by women and by men in Detroit (from Wolfram 1969: 162)

to delete the present tense form of the copula, *is* or *are,* in several syntactic environments, including these:

He busy right now.
She a nurse.
If we getting beat, I rather one of my friends to jump in.
Some say you gonna die.

The constraints on copula deletion are complex, but Labov (1969) discovered that they follow the constraints on copula contraction in standard dialects.

In the tabulation for figure 3.6, Wolfram counted instances of the complete absence of the copula as a proportion of the total number of present-tense existential sentences including those with full copulas and those with contracted copulas. The results make a familiar figure, with a notably rapid rise between the MC groups and the WC groups, and of course with the stratification of men and women following the expected pattern.

3.3.1.5   Gender roles in inner city Detroit   These results along with those from Wolfram's four other variables present a striking picture of a gender

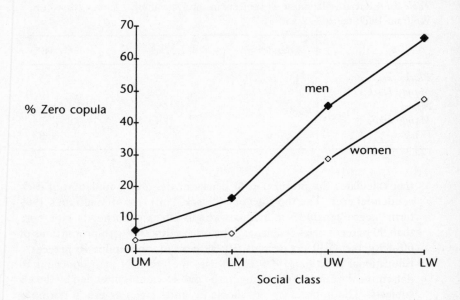

Figure 3.6 Percentage of zero copula realized by men and women in Detroit (from Wolfram 1969: 178)

difference that runs consistently through this speech community. While subsequent studies in other communities have confirmed the general tendency, few others have found the correlation so pervasive. It is worthwhile locating some of the social parameters in which this linguistic pattern is embedded.

Unique among sociolinguistic studies, Wolfram's Detroit survey includes among the independent variables a measure called racial isolation (1969: 25–31). As Wolfram says, "Patterns of Northern segregation are a main source for transforming many southern [Black] speech characteristics into ethnic and class patterns of speech in Northern cities." In other words, the extent of an individual's segregation from other racial and social groups is likely to increase the use of ethnic markers, or, put positively, the number of regular interactions beyond one's immediate neighborhood is likely to expand the repertoire of linguistic variants.

In order to measure racial isolation, Wolfram estimated the amount of contact each of his subjects had with members of other races in the three social contexts shown in the top row of table 3.1.

• Residential isolation (1969: 26–8) has the five categories in the leftmost row, representing degrees of racial contact based on census information

Table 3.1 Racial isolation of 48 subjects in the Detroit BEV survey (based on Wolfram 1969: tables 1, 2 and 3)

	Residence	School	Peer Group
Black	15	25	25
Mainly black	27	10	16
Mixed	5	9	5
Mainly white	1	4	2
White	0	0	0

that calculates the proportion of blacks in the total population of each residential area. The top category ("black," in place of Wolfram's 1969 term "negro") includes individuals who live in neighborhoods with more than 90 percent black residents. The others descend with proportions of 60–89 percent, 40–59 percent, 10–39 percent, and under 10 percent.

- Educational isolation (1969: 28–9) uses the same set of proportions to determine the amount of mixing in the public schools attended by the 48 subjects. The importance of schools in enforcing peer group norms is nicely underlined by one of Wolfram's UMC women subjects who said she was ridiculed when she arrived at an exclusively black junior high school for "talking like a white person."
- Peer group isolation (1969: 29–31) was estimated from a part of the interview that dealt with the individual's friends and acquaintances. It includes direct questions such as "Is there a group of people you used to associate with?"; "Do you still see them a lot?" (1969: 224).

Table 3.1 shows that the subjects preponderantly occupy the top categories, black or mainly black, with some significant seepage into the middle categories notable in the school category. Although Wolfram's inclusion of racial isolation is innovative, I think it is fair to say that it is not exploited in the study. No metric is devised that would integrate the three components into a weighted index score, and the individual subjects are not in any other way identified as participants in one or other of the categories. It would make some difference, as unlikely as it is, if the 25 subjects who attended the black schools were not among the 15 who live in black residential areas, and so on. A reasonable inference is that the females will more likely be found in the lower categories, that is, the less isolated sub-groups, because of a time-honoured tendency to remove girls more often than boys from social situations where they are more vulnerable. The amount of mixing of categories would be a strong dilutant of racial isolation and the amount of consistency of individuals-per-category a strong reinforcement, but those aspects are not recoverable from the analysis.

Moreover, there is another category that is clearly relevant. Interactions in the workplace may be monochromatic or not. Unlike interactions with neighbors and peers, these are socially asymmetrical either with bosses or underlings, but they are nonetheless significant because of their direct relationship to subsistence and success. These too tend to be differentiated by gender. Men in factory jobs, whether LWC labourers, UWC fork-lift operators or LMC supervisors, may go some months without exchanging more than a few words with someone of another race, but women in the same social categories, whether LWC cleaners, UWC check-out clerks or LMC receptionists, can hardly avoid conversing with other races in a workday.

The unequal distributions of men and women both in the lower categories of Wolfram's racial isolation variable and in workplace interactions will come up again in §3.4. First, though, we will review some results from another community where men and women also differ strikingly in their use of standard variants.

3.3.2 Ballymacarrett, Belfast

In the 1970s, the Milroys began studying the speech of Belfast, Northern Ireland, in three working-class enclaves. One of the enclaves, Clonard, is Catholic and the other two, the Hammer and Ballymacarrett, are Protestant. Because of Belfast's rigid ethnic divisions – "to call this division *religious* is misleading," L. Milroy (1980: 71) says – it was necessary that the fieldwork be carried out by a woman, Lesley Milroy, rather than a man, and important that she find her way into each district not as a complete outsider but as "a friend of a friend." These conditions proved seminal in working out the methods for undertaking sociolinguistic studies within a social network (as discussed in detail in §§2.6-2.8).

Among the phonological variables the Milroys analyzed, several showed a striking pattern of gender-grading (L. Milroy 1976, Milroy and Milroy 1978, J. Milroy 1980). I will be using data from Ballymacarrett to illustrate this pattern, but it is noteworthy that this pattern also shows up in the other two neighborhoods as only slightly less clear cut. Moreover, I might have illustrated the same point using other variables from the Belfast survey because several others show similar patterns.

Entirely fortuitously, the index scores for the four cited here – (a), (ε), (th) and (Λ) – do not overlap. As a result, figure 3.7 plots all four of them on the same figure. It is important to realize that their lack of overlap is merely a methodological accident and has no linguistic significance whatsoever. The four lines on figure 3.7 represent independent observations, and if the variants had been weighted differently in their analysis their lines might have overlapped. Nevertheless, the fact that they happen not to

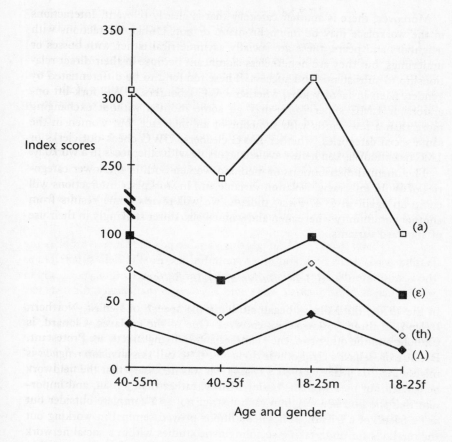

Figure 3.7 Index scores on four phonological variables for women and men in two age groups in Ballymacarrett, Belfast (based on Milroy and Milroy 1978: figures 1, 2, 4, 7, 26, 28, and 30)

overlap and can be represented simultaneously, so to speak, serves a useful rhetorical purpose here because it dramatically represents the similarities that exist in the gender grading.

Figure 3.7 shows a recurring zig-zag shape for all four variables, like the first three strokes of a W. The highest scores for each variable belong to the middle-aged (40–55) and young (18–25) men, and the two lowest to the middle-aged and young women. In all instances, the young men's scores are higher than the older men's scores, and thus represent an increase in the use of non-standard variants.

3.3.2.1 Variable [ʌ] The variable represented closest to the abscissa in figure 3.7 encodes the vowel of a lexically defined set of 22 items including *pull, took, look,* and *would* which occur with either the standard Belfast [ʉ] or with non-standard and stigmatized [ʌ]. The non-standard variant causes embarrassment for speakers when their use of it is drawn to their attention. Maclaran (1976: 47) says that all Belfast natives are conscious of the pronunciation because "their teachers or grandmothers used to correct them for using it." In spite of that, it persists quite hardily among Belfast men. Even in linguistic interviews they use it more than 30 percent of the time, whereas the women in their social groups use it less than 20 percent of the time. Beyond a doubt, the men's use is considerably greater in more private settings. Milroy and Milroy (1978: 25–6) note: "There can be no doubt that the [ʌ] variant has conscious vernacular prestige; it is almost prescribed amongst adolescent and other close-knit male peer groups."

3.3.2.2 Variable (th) Although this variable has the same symbol as the familiar variable in BEV and other communities, in WC Belfast it refers to the voiced interdental fricative /ð/, which can be deleted intervocalically in words such as *bother, mother, other,* and *together,* so that *mother,* for instance, is pronounced [mɔːər]. The gender difference is even more striking for this variable, with both male groups deleting the fricative over 70 percent of the time. The older women are at 37 percent but the younger women are down at 25 percent, making a considerable difference between them and their male age-mates. This variable has almost exactly the same pattern in the Hammer and Clonard as in Ballymacarrett, and in all three neighborhoods the men who have the lowest scores for this variable still have higher scores than the women with the highest scores.

3.3.2.3 Variable (ɛ) This variable encodes the vowel in monosyllables with a final voiceless stop such as *step, bet* and *peck,* which occurs in Belfast with a regional variant [æ] as well as standard [ɛ].[5] As figure 3.7 shows, all the men in Ballymacarrett use the regional variant all the time. For them, it is not a variable at all. The women, however, use both, and the younger women use the standard variant almost half the time, making, again, a striking discrepancy between them and their age-mates.

3.3.2.4 Variable (a) For this complex vowel variable, the variants involve fronting in one environment and backing in another. The MC standard vowel is [a], the low front open vowel, in words such as *pat, pap, pan* and *pack.* Although figure 3.7 documents only the back variants, it is worth noting in passing that the front variants occur in Belfast before velars, such as *back* and *bag,* where the vowel is fronted and raised to [bɛk] and [bɛg]. In this respect, the change resembles part of the northern cities sound shift in the United States (Labov 1991: 14–16), where the MC standard vowel /æ/ is also raising and fronting to [ɛ]. The back variants in Belfast have no counterpart in the northern cities shift. They occur in non-velar environments, where the standard vowel [a] is sometimes heard as back [ɑ], or back centralized [ɑə], or rounded [ɔ], or rounded centralized [ɔə]. Hence, in figure 3.7, invariable use of the standard vowel [a] would score 0, and invariant use of rounded, centralized [ɔə] would score 400. The men's scores for both age groups are just above 300, meaning a preponderance of [ɔ] vowels with some instances of [ɔə]. The men are again greatly at odds with the women. The middle-aged women, with scores around 240, and the younger women, around 200, both have fewer centralized vowels and occasional occurrences of standard [a] where the men have almost none.

3.3.2.5   Gender roles in Ballymacarrett   When we look at the social structure in Ballymacarrett (L. Milroy 1980: 70–84), the possible sources of these linguistic differences at first appear to be puzzling. All the subjects are members of a tightly-knit, working-class neighborhood. Many live close to relatives, sometimes in houses where they were not only born and raised but their parents were too. Outsiders are looked upon with some suspicion when they first come into the area. Considerable value is attached to local loyalties and the maintenance of local ties.

However, as is typical of high-density social networks, gender roles are clearly defined. L. Milroy (1980: 79) says, "the sexes tend to polarize in these communities, with a sharp distinction being recognized between men's and women's activities." Ballymacarrett is near the most highly industrialized sector of the city, so that the men do not have far to travel to work. In fact, all of the Milroys' male subjects in Ballymacarrett were currently or formerly associated with the local shipyard (1980: 76). The men almost never leave the neighborhood: they use local pubs and clubs exclusively. The boys hang around together on street corners, and a sense of territoriality is attached to their corner. "If the boys strayed outside territorial boundaries," Milroy (1980: 80) says, "they tended to become involved in fights with other corner groups; sometimes indeed they went beyond their area of three or four streets exactly for that reason."

The women's movements are much less constrained. In Ballymacarrett nearly all of them travel outside the neighborhood to work, and consequently they have no qualms about shopping downtown or, especially the younger ones, meeting friends there for lunch or the cinema. The Milroys had some difficulty finding women as subjects for their 18–25 year age group because they tended to marry men from other parts of the city and move into the suburbs (1980: 81).

Clearly, the women of Ballymacarrett have much looser neighborhood ties than the men. In the course of their work and their recreation they mix with a more diverse population. Their fellow workers are varied in origin, and, as clerks or cleaners, they necessarily speak to people with accents different from the ones they grew up with.

In Ballymacarrett as in inner city Detroit, then, women and men play very different roles in terms of their geographical and occupational mobility. The women move much more freely and intermingle with a much broader social cross section. It should not be at all surprising under these circumstances to find that they have a wider repertoire of linguistic variables at their command, including a mastery of those variants that have currency beyond their home communities. The importance of these different roles will obviously prove to be one important factor in explaining the linguistic variation that expresses sex and gender roles, to which we now turn.

3.4   Causes of Sex and Gender Differences

3.4.1   Gender-based variability

The observation that women master standard speech better than men is by no means new. It was made as early as 55 BC by Cicero in *De Oratore* (III, 12) in a dialogue in which his mouthpiece, Crassus, sardonically contrasts his mother-in-law's elegant accent (translated here as "tone of voice") with that of Sulpicius, his interlocutor. This passage is Cicero's argument in favor of the standard accent. Parenthetically, he also proposes an explanation as to why women and men differ linguistically:

> As there is a certain tone of voice . . . peculiar to the Roman people and city, in which nothing can offend, or displease, nothing can be liable to animadversion, nothing sound or savour of what is foreign, let us cultivate that tone, and learn to avoid not only the asperity of rustic but the strangeness of outlandish pronunciation. Indeed when I listen to my wife's mother Lælia, (for women more easily preserve the ancient language unaltered, because, not having experience of the conversation of a multitude of people, they always retain what they originally learned,) I hear her with such attention that I imagine myself listening to Plautus or Nævius; she has a tone of voice so unaffected and simple, that it seems to carry in it nothing of ostentation or imitation; from whence I judge that her father and forefathers spoke in like manner; not with a rough tone . . . nor with one broad, or rustic, or too open, but with one that was close and equable and smooth. Our friend Cotta, therefore, whose broad manner of speaking you, Sulpicius, sometimes imitate, so as to drop the letter I and pronounce E as full as possible, does not seem to me to resemble the ancient orators, but the modern farmers.

This passage is interesting in its own right because Cicero cites a couple of variables – I-deletion and E-diphthongization – that occurred in classical Latin, but it is especially interesting for our purposes because he makes the sociolinguistic observation that men were more likely than women to use the "broad" variants – a situation very familiar to us from the preceding sections of this chapter. Although we used contemporary situations to establish these points, there is every reason to believe that the same situations obtain virtually everywhere, and it is reassuring to have Cicero's testimony on classical Rome.

In another matter, however, there are grounds for objection. In suggesting that Crassus's mother-in-law's accent preserves the equability of her father's and forefathers' accent, Cicero apparently assumes that the Latin of the immediately preceding generations had no variants. This assumption seems bizarre, in as much as we have yet to find a society without linguistic variation. Furthermore, we have just noticed that Cicero's contemporaries used linguistic variants in very similar ways to our contemporaries some two thousand years later, and it seems highly improbable that one generation or two before him might have been any different.

3.4.1.1 *Isolation and gender roles*   His putative explanation for the gender difference is based on the relative isolation of women of Lælia's class. Because they do not commingle with "a multitude of people," he says, their accents remain pure. As we have seen in the discussion of mobility (especially §2.5.5 above) the most isolated speakers tend to be the most consistent dialect speakers. If it were true that women of Lælia's class were isolated to the same degree as, say, fourth-generation villagers in the heart of an agricultural district – that is to say, the archetypal informants in a dialect geography survey – they would undoubtedly, as Cicero contends, be highly consistent speakers of their class accent.

Whether or not Cicero has correctly appraised the social situation of Crassus's mother-in-law is a moot point. I find it hard to resist questioning, if only in passing, his assumption that the best educated, most liberated women of the day in the cosmopolitan cultural capital of the Western world led such overprotected lives. Cicero did not really know Lælia or the social circles in which she moved. She was very old by the time he became prominent, and was dead by the time he extolled her accent in *De Oratore*. In her prime, she was known far and wide as a gifted conversationalist, and was "surnamed the wise" (Smith 1850). Surely she did not gain such a reputation in the rarefied setting Cicero imagined for her.

For the moment, let us accept Cicero's claim at face value. It is then possible to integrate it with the evidence we turned up for inner city Detroit and Ballymacarett into the following generalization about gender-based variability. **In societies where gender roles are sharply differentiated** such that one gender has wider social contacts and greater geographical range, the speech of the less circumscribed gender will include more variants of the contiguous social groups. In Detroit and Ballymaccarett, the less circumscribed gender, the women, use more variants of the social groups above them. In Rome, the less circumscribed gender, the men, used variants described as "broad, or rustic, or too open," presumably from the social group below them.

One clear advantage that this explanation has over previous attempts to explain linguistic differences between men and women is that it attributes nothing at all to gender itself. It does not claim that women are likely to be "more conservative" than men, or "prestige-oriented," or anything else. As Eckert (1989a: 248) says, "Not only is it a mistake to claim that women are more or less innovative than men, but at this point in our research it is a mistake to claim any kind of constant constraint associated with gender." Instead, the dynamic variable is mobility. Sociolinguistic patterns, according to the principle of gender-based variability, are to some extent determined by the breadth of social and geographical contacts.

3.4.1.2 Shifting roles in coastal South Carolina   This point emerges very clearly from a study by Nichols (1983) that takes careful account of occupational and geographical mobility among residents of an all-black island community along the South Carolina coast. This region of the United States was settled by blacks in the seventeenth century and the basilect, Gullah, is well known to linguists because of a classic study by Lorenzo Turner (1949).

Nichols discovered a shifting pattern of dialect use, with the middle-aged and younger adults sharply gender graded but the older adults consistent. Her results are summarized in table 3.2. The older women and men are more similar to one another than the other age and gender groups. The other age groups are differentiated by gaps of almost 20 to 30 percent. It is worth noting in passing, before discussing Nichols's explanation, that in all cases the men in each age group exceed the women in the percentage of creole usage, that is, in the frequency of regional dialect variants in their speech. This, of course, is consistent with results we have seen in the other studies cited, further confirming one of the most robust results of sociolinguistic research.

Nichols notes that these speech patterns reflect individual and community differences in mobility. The oldest group, both women and men, were largely immobile, working on the island as well as living there. They speak a common dialect. The middle-aged group, after they became adults, began taking advantage of the improved transportation to the mainland in order to work there, and the younger group, as a matter of course, travel back and

Table 3.2 Use of creole forms by women and men in three age groups in coastal South Carolina (from Nichols 1983: 60)

Age/Gender	Individual creole %	Gender group creole %
older f	38	
older f	23	31
older m	35	
older m	39	37
middle f	0	
middle f	8	4
middle m	15	
middle m	31	23
younger f	33	
younger f	0	17
younger m	52	
younger m	42	47

forth for work and recreation. In both groups, the speech is correlated with gender.

"In general," Nichols says (1983: 61), "the amount of travel and exposure to a wide range of language varieties affects the percentage of creolized speech *within the gender groups*, but not across them." For example, the two young women in the sample differ considerably both linguistically and otherwise: the first speaks creole dialect proportionately similar to the older people and she is herself a high school student with no further mainland ties as yet, whereas the one with no creole forms works after school in a mainland store as a sales clerk where she "interacts with tourists from all over the east coast." Together they make a textbook illustration of mobility as a standardizing factor on the speech of individuals regardless of gender.

The gender differences have a further explanation. While both the middle and the younger groups, women and men, have in common the geographical mobility of working on the mainland, their occupations characteristically differ. Nichols (1983: 62) says, "Men from the island often work with each other on their mainland jobs, while the jobs of island women tend to be isolated from other island women and from other members of the larger black speech community." The men usually work in construction as carpenters and bricklayers, while the women work as motel maids, sales clerks and mail carriers. Younger women are pursuing white collar positions in sales, nursing and teaching much more actively than men.

One young man told Nichols (1983: 63) that he could make more money laying bricks than a woman could make teaching school. In this sense, the men's occupations are much more circumscribed in terms of their social contacts, and their speech reflects that exactly as the principle of gender-based variability predicts it should.

3.4.1.3 Mobility and gender roles Implicit in the claim of gender-based variability, and crucial to it, is the ancillary claim that norms of mobility are likely to be defined differently for women and men. As we saw in the comparison of the two younger women in Nichols's study, differences in mobility need not be correlated with gender. However, they usually are. The reason this kind of variability is called "gender-based" is because it is a common determinant of female–male differences in speech.

In modern industrialized societies, in the lower social echelons gender roles typically differ in terms of geographical range and social breadth. As in inner city Detroit, working-class Belfast and coastal South Carolina, the difference is that women have the greater range and breadth. So far, to the best of my knowledge, there has been no documentation of a community in which the men rather than the women have the greater range and breadth. If and when such a community can be found and studied, its predicted sociolinguistic patterns will reverse the pattern that has become a common-place in our studies.

These differences in characteristic mobility patterns between the sexes may themselves follow from the inherently greater linguistic adaptability of women. The evidence for this inherent adaptibility arises from situations where gender differences occur in the absence of mobility correlations. It is to those we now turn.

3.4.2 Sex-based variability

It is probably safe to say that Cicero's claim is too poorly documented to make an entirely convincing illustration, except in theory. In fact, the socio-linguistic record as well as the historical record strongly suggests that we should not accept his claim about differentially circumscribed gender roles for upper-class Romans. The linguistic difference he indicates seems more similar to the one we find among MC men and women in modern societies, where the roles of men and women do not differ noticeably in terms of restrictions on social contacts.

3.4.2.1 MC blurring of gender roles As Milroy (1980: 79–80) notes, the converse of dense networks having well-defined gender roles also holds: loose-knit network structures as found in the MC go together with the blurring of gender roles. MC women and men, under ordinary circumstances, have the same range of acquaintances and contacts. Either one might plausibly take the car to the garage for repairs, or arrange the delivery of a pizza, or attend a benefit ball for the opera society. Women, that is to say, do not lead more or less protected lives than men. Yet we consistently find the same linguistic difference between men and women as Cicero found.

Evidence of this absolute linguistic difference, not correlated with any obvious social fact such as sharply circumscribed gender-role differences, has caused considerable speculation and some controversy. Labov (1966: 312) suggested that the women's wider range of variants in New York was the result of "hypercorrection," without further explanation. Later, when other sociolinguists had added similar evidence for male–female differences from other surveys, Labov (1972: 301–4) returned to the point, stating that "our answers at the moment are not better than speculations," and suggesting that the crucial influence of women on children in the first stages of language acquisition equipped them with a "special sensitivity." "Women," he says (1972: 243), "are more sensitive than men to overt sociolinguistic values."

3.4.2.2 "Status consciousness" These speculations still beg the question why – why would women hypercorrect, why would they be more sensitive? – and it fell to Trudgill (1972) to attempt the first detailed explanation. Trudgill's main point was that MC men, but not MC women, ascribe "covert prestige" to WC speech features. Now established as a functional principle in linguistic variability, covert prestige is discussed in detail in §5.4.1.

Although covert prestige takes up about two-thirds of Trudgill's original article (1972: 183–93), subsequent linguistic comments have devoted almost as much attention to an additional, unelaborated suggestion Trudgill made – he calls it "necessarily speculative" – that occupies about half a paragraph. I quote it here in its entirety (1972: 182–3):

> Women in our society are more status-conscious than men, generally speaking, and are therefore more aware of the social significance of linguistic variables. There are two possible reasons for this:
>
> (i) The social position of women in our society is less secure than that of men, and, usually, subordinate than that of men. It may be, therefore, that it is more necessary for women to secure and signal their social status linguistically and in other ways, and they may for this reason be more aware of the importance of this type of signal. (This will be particularly true of women who are not working.)
> (ii) Men in our society can be rated socially by their occupation, their

earning power, and perhaps by their other abilities – in other words by what they *do*. For the most part, however, this is not possible for women. It may be, therefore, that they have instead to be rated on how they *appear*. Since they are not rated by their occupations or by their occupational success, other signals of status, including speech, are correspondingly more important.

This passage, along with the statements by Labov and others cited above and at the beginning of this chapter, has attracted some feminist criticism. A good summation of the debating points, which will not be reviewed in detail here, may be found in Spender (1980) and Trudgill's response (1983: chapter 9); more generally, for the feminist critique, see Cameron (1990). Suffice it to say that "the reasons for such feminist dissatisfaction," according to Cameron (1988: 5–6), have been "that methodology, measuring instruments and scoring systems, theoretical assumptions and individual interpretations have been, in sociolinguistics as elsewhere, riddled with bias and stereotype; and that this bias must not be ignored, because studies of 'difference' are not just disinterested quests for truth, but in an unequal society inevitably have a political dimension."

Specific reviews have generally criticized interpretations of the sociolinguistic results on male–female variability. I know of no reviews that have questioned the use of methods, tabulations or indexing of data in such a way as to taint the results. Cameron and Coates (1988: 21) point out, for instance, that Milroy's network strength scale gives points for a couple of criteria that men are much more likely to fulfil than women. As a result, men are likely to get higher scores because of "a scoring system that throws the differences into relief by giving women low scores unless they take on male roles." The objection here is not that Milroy's network scale shows men and women to be different but that the difference is likely to be indicated by men scoring more points than women. The raw scores are, of course, arbitrary, and the criteria could readily be restated so that the women were more likely to score more points and the men fewer. In that event, higher scores would mark looser network ties whereas in Milroy's formulation they mark denser ties. The social facts underlying the scores would, obviously, remain exactly the same. It is important to note that Coates and Cameron are not – here or elsewhere – questioning Milroy's results or the facts underlying her results. The same point holds for the other sociolinguistic studies they cite. As they put it (1988: 21), "Women and men differ in their speech patterns; that is agreed."

3.4.2.3 "Face" Deuchar (1988) puts forward an interpretation of male–female differences specifically intended as an alternative to Trudgill's "status consciousness" interpretation. In her view, the mechanism that determines women's greater use of standard speech is an interpersonal strategy known as "face," the maintenance of self-esteem in social exchanges. The notion is extrapolated from Brown and Levinson's interpretation (1978) of politeness levels in discourse. They see an interactional tension between the desire for individual autonomy or self-reliance ("negative face") and the desire for approval or cooperativeness ("positive face"). Social intercourse normally requires paying attention to the other participant's face while protecting one's own.[6]

The balance between the two is tipped when the participants have unequal power. To take an extreme example, a pauper interacting with royalty is likely to ignore his own face and be excessively polite or obsequious, and the royal person is likely to ignore the pauper's and be rude or arrogant. In more equal circumstances, as when one friend requests a loan from another, the exchange is likely to be suffused by reciprocal politeness ("Geez, I hate to ask . . . ," "No problem, really . . .") intended to protect one's face in making the imposition and the other's in delivering the favor.

To this framework, Deuchar adds the assumption that women are less powerful than men. The social challenge they face in interacting with men is to pay due attention to the men's faces while at the same time maintaining their own. Deuchar (1988: 31) says, "The use of standard speech, with its connotations of prestige, appears suitable for protecting the face of a relatively powerless speaker without attacking that of the addressee." The adoption of standard speech forms by women thus saves face by adhering to prestige norms but does so so subtly that the men they are speaking to do not recognize it as detracting from their own face.

In its present formulation, Deuchar's framework is little more than a sketch. Its implications need to be tested. One of them, clearly, is that women should use a much greater proportion of standard forms when speaking to men than under any other circumstances. Another is that women in unequivocally powerful positions should use proportionately fewer standard forms in speaking to their male underlings than to their peers, male or female. Both of these seem eminently testable.

3.4.2.4 Sociolinguistic ability

3.4.2.4 Sociolinguistic ability Although Deuchar's framework meets the approval of at least one of Trudgill's critics – Cameron (1988: 11) says, "Deuchar's assumption is that any useful account of gender differentiation in language must explicitly discuss the question of *power*: a point that can hardly be overemphasised" – it seems to me to suffer from the same essential flaw. No less than Trudgill's account in terms of linguistic insecurity or, for that matter, Labov's in terms of hypercorrection, Deuchar's explanation in terms of face-saving is essentially a negative attribute. The presupposition of all three interpretations is that women are somehow compensating for shortcomings. To Trudgill, they are affecting the trappings of social status that they otherwise do not have; to Labov, they are exceeding the norms appropriate to their stations; and to Deuchar, they are offering subtle apologies to their overlords. All of these are basically negative motives.

And yet, the linguistic behavior for which these interpretations are proffered is not by any criterion negative. Certainly any objective observer – a Martian perhaps, if no one else really qualifies – would be perplexed by the discrepancy between the empirical evidence and these interpretations of it.

The empirical evidence clearly shows women as much more able performers than men in the whole spectrum of sociolinguistic situations. For one thing, they command a wider range of linguistic variants. WC women in Ballymacarrett have a linguistic repertoire that allows them to converse on equal linguistic terms with the sluggards from the shipyards living next door and with the toffs from the law office across the corridor at work. For another, they have the linguistic flexibility to alter their speech as social circumstances warrant. WC women in inner city Detroit deal with situations where their husbands would often struggle to make themselves understood, as in meetings with the principal or negotiations with the landlord. Moreover, the sociolinguistic abilities of women often function as a legitimizing factor in upwardly mobile families. In North America, influxes from the WC into the MC are common, and they often entail linguistic asymmetries in which the male's speech, to a far greater extent than the female's, remains marked by the foundry or the farm, often to his helpless annoyance. In all these respects, the women have a clear advantage over the men in terms of their sociolinguistic competence.

3.4.2.5 Verbal ability   There is, in the psychological literature, a long record of evidence of female verbal superiority. The formerly recalcitrant facts about the sociolinguistic difference between men and women suddenly do not seem so odd when we view them as female advantages rather than shortcomings. In various tests over many years, women have demonstrated an advantage over men in fluency, speaking, sentence complexity, analogy, listening comprehension of written material and of spoken material, vocabulary, and spelling (see the summary in Maccoby and Jacklin 1974: 75–85; also Denno 1982, Halpern 1986). Their sociolinguistic superiority appears to be just another manifestation of it.

The extent of this advantage is very slight, and must not be overstated. The following statement by Maccoby and Jacklin (1974: 75), whose survey of the sex-difference literature remains the standard reference, is notable for the hedges and qualifiers in almost every phrase as well as for its appraisal of the narrowness of the difference. "It is true that whenever a sex difference is found, it is usually girls and women who obtain higher scores," they say, "but the two sexes perform very similarly on a number of tasks in a number of sample populations."

Slight though it is, the advantage is real. Perhaps the best indicators are standard tests of various kinds. The Graduate Record Examinations, for instance, are a battery of aptitude tests taken by undergraduates from several nations intending to go on to graduate studies in the United States. Although this is a relatively narrow sample, it is nevertheless large, being taken by thousands of people every year. It also has the advantage of neutrality because it is not designed in any deliberate way to reveal sex differences. The verbal portion of the test demonstrates the female advantage. In 1973-4, the last year that sex differences were reported, the mean for women was 503 and the mean for men was 493. This difference, though tiny in absolute terms, is statistically significant for this large sample (Hoyenga and Hoyenga 1979: 238). Similarly, among students taking the Scholastic Aptitude Test in hopes of being accepted into American medical schools, the mean verbal score for women was 554 and for men 531 (Notman and Nadelson 1973). On another standard test, the vocabulary portion of the Wechsler Adult Intelligence Scale, a sample of 850 females and 850 males between 16 and 64 showed the overall female advantage as statistically significant (Sherman 1978: 43).

Results like these, based on large samples and designed for independent purposes, seem relatively invulnerable to charges of bias, misinterpretation, or skewing. If it is true that the tests were conceived and designed by men, and if that fact in itself constitutes a bias, then why should the test scores persistently reveal a female advantage in verbal ability?[7]

Results from standard tests are reinforced by various statistics showing that the distribution of verbal disorders heavily disfavors males. As mentioned in §3.1 above, men are more likely to stutter and to have reading disabilities. They are also much more likely to suffer aphasic speech disorders after brain damage (Kimura 1983). To these could be added the fact that males are four times more likely to suffer infantile autism and dyslexia than are women (Taylor and Ounsted 1972: 224).

3.4.2.6 Psychological explanations These facts about the female's superior verbal skills seem to sit rather uneasily among psychologists and others, as do similar facts about the male's superior spatial skills (see, for example, Hoyenga and Hoyenga 1979: 243–49 and references therein). The discomfort apparently resides in the inability of social scientists to come up with an explanatory principle that underlies the differences.

Much of the literature reviewed in the previous paragraphs is suffused with half-hearted attempts to attribute the male–female differences to differentiated socialization when in fact the samples are so diverse geographically and culturally as to make socialization quite unconvincing.

Another tentative explanation, more convincing as far as it goes, claims that female precocity in verbal skills beginning in infancy predisposes them in that direction. As Sherman (1978: 40) says, "the early female advantage bends the twig toward female preference for verbal approaches to problem solution. This bent is then increased by the verbal emphasis of the educational system and by aspects of sex roles that do not encourage girls' development of visual–spatial skills." This explanation is also in terms of socialization but it evokes verbal precocity as the impetus for it. The obvious problem with predicating the difference on precocity is that it leaves the essential question unanswered. Where does the precocity come from? What causes it? We have really only moved the question back one level. What is the root of the female–male disparity in verbal skills? Female verbal precocity. What, then, is the root of female verbal precocity?

3.4.2.7 Sex differences The psychological literature also includes a long history of speculations about chromosomal, metabolic, hormonal or neurological factors that might be at the root of the differences (reviewed in Sherman 1978: 88–134, Hoyenga and Hoyenga 1979: 23–57, 85–114, Kimura 1987). These, then, are not gender differences but putative sex differences.

Many attempts at establishing sex differences should be viewed skeptically. Consider, for instance, the "Gout Hypothesis" (Sherman 1978: 88), which attempts to correlate the level of uric acid in the blood with professional achievement. The hypothesis gets its name from the fact that excessive uric acid is the cause of gout and kidney stones. For many years it has been known that men have higher levels than women and, it follows, more gout and kidney stones. Initial attempts at relating urate levels to achievement seem to consist of claims that certain male geniuses suffered from gout. Later attempts measured urate levels in various occupational groups and tested correlations between high achievement occupations and urate levels. The results showed higher levels in businessmen than in skilled laborers and professors – ambiguous results at best.

Endocrinal secretions have provided a rich source of hypotheses based largely on the association of androgens like testosterone as "male" hormones and estrogens like progesterone as "female." No hormone, apparently, is unique to either sex (Briscoe 1978). The scientific riddle, then, is to unravel potential effects on sex from a common but fluctuating and partly cyclic endocrine system. Recent research suggests that, even if there are no sex-specific hormones – even if, as Briscoe (1978: 45) says, "the endocrinology of sex is not separate but hermaphrodite in the human species" – quantitative differences of particular hormones at particular moments are crucial determinants of sexual differentiation. Presence of androgens in the first weeks after conception determines the development of male genitalia, and their presence later in the gestation period appears to determine sex-appropriate behaviour (Gorski 1987, McEwen 1987). The fact that these developmental stages are not simultaneous predicts that there will be individuals who are physically one sex and behaviorally the other. As Kimura (1987: 134) says, "This finding obviously has some interesting implications for the origins of variations in sexual preference in human beings."

Equally important, it provides a mechanism for sex differentiation of brain organization. Numerous effects suggest sex-based brain differentiation, including different tendencies in handedness, stuttering and aphasia. There is also experimental evidence indicating male–female differences. In dichotic listening and viewing tests, for instance, where a stimulus is presented to either the left or right ear or eye but not both, leading to its processing in one hemisphere or the other, females usually show better equivalence between the two sides than males.

For many years, neuropsychologists have hypothesized what is called "sexual dimorphism in brain asymmetry – that is, in the degree to which the left and right hemispheres are specialized for different functions" (Kimura 1987: 135). In particular, women's brains appear to be more globally organized for specific functions whereas men's brains are more highly lateralized with verbal functions in the left hemisphere and spatial functions in the right (see Sherman 1978: 108–34 for an overview). In other words, in the female brain linguistic functions are more diffusely represented than in the male.

One consequence that follows predictably from this difference is the lower incidence of aphasia in women. If the language functions are shared throughout the cortical area, then damage to one part of the female brain is less likely to disrupt their capability for using language. Kimura (1987) provides striking support for dimorphism in brain asymmetry with a very large sample of brain-damaged patients. In addition to the lower incidence of aphasia among women, she also identified enormous discrepancies between the sexes in the location of damage causing aphasia. Men were afflicted after damage to almost any part of the left hemisphere whereas women were usually spared unless the damage was extensive in the anterior region. Sex-based brain asymmetry provides the simplest explanation for the aphasia profiles. More generally, it provides a basis for the female's advantage in linguistic wellbeing and in verbal skills.

3.4.2.8 Insignificance of individual differences   Our search for a principle that might underlie the female's sociolinguistic skills has taken us fairly far into a vast ancillary area in an attempt to link it with the much more general verbal proficiency that accrues to women. Because this is generally outside the realm of sociolinguistics, it is probably worthwhile to emphasize that the postulated sex difference in terms of language (and, for that matter, anything else) is merely statistical. Individual differences are almost as extensive as sex differences. Maccoby and Jacklin (1974) estimated that the range in favor of females in verbal tasks was between 0.1 to 0.5 SD (standard deviation), the standard score of the difference between means, with the typical difference about 0.25 SD (confirmed by Hyde 1981).[8] Graphically, that means that the populations of females overlap with the males except for one quarter of one percent. In other words, for any array of verbal abilities found in an individual woman, there will almost certainly be a man with exactly the same array. Nowhere are there groups of women with totally different verbal abilities from groups of men.

It is important to recognize that these innate predispositions are small and surmountable. They do not program individuals for some inevitable social role or otherwise circumscribe their destiny. This basic fact cannot be overemphasized. The historical record is overburdened with atrocities predicated on bogus genetic theories, from Hannibal to Hitler and beyond. Claims about sex and racial differences have repeatedly been invoked as vindications of sexism and racism, and they are always fraudulent. The biochemist Briscoe (1978: 41) makes their absurdity bitingly clear by asking: "What blood level of androgen is the cut-off point above which one gets to be a junior executive and below which one is relegated to a secretarial position?"

If educators, upon learning about the sex-based aptitude differences we have just been discussing, proposed because of them to make distinctive school streams for boys and girls, their proposal would be categorically and indefensibly sexist. Its only real purpose would be to discriminate rather than to educate. The reason, of course, is that the male and female populations are not sufficiently differentiated by sex-based differences to make streaming productive. It is not only that there is only one quarter of one percent difference, but, more important, that the human being, regardless of sex (or race, or age, or any other criterion), is enormously adaptable. Education serves individuals, not statistical entities, and individuals, whether female or male, vary across the whole range of human possibilities.

As a general factor about human nature, putative lateralization differences allow for an interesting hypothesis for explaining the minor but persistent differences in verbal ability that have been accumulating since the inception of systematic testing almost a century ago. For a fraction of that time sociolinguistic research has also turned up a persistent discrepancy between women and men in the frequency of their use of standard and stigmatized variants. Sometimes, those differences – or a large part of them – are explicable in terms of differences in gender roles, as we saw in the cases of inner city Detroit and Ballymaccarett.

Sometimes, notably when they are found in MC groups in modern industrial societies where gender roles overlap almost entirely, they seem to be simply inexplicable. In these instances, it is plausible to speculate that we are seeing another effect of the sex-based difference: **the neuropsychological verbal advantage of females results in sociolinguistic** discrepancies such that women use a larger repertoire of variants and command a wider range of styles than men of the same social groups even though gender roles are similar or identical. The tendency for women to take on gender roles requiring greater mobility may be a *result* of their innate sociolinguistic advantage rather than a *cause* of it.

Since women have this innate advantage, it should follow that comparable discrepancies reveal themselves in various societies and cultures, whenever gender roles are not the obvious cause. In the final section, we turn our attention to sociolinguistic studies that have been carried out beyond the Western world.

3.5 Male and Female Speech Patterns in Other Societies

The observation that men and women use language differently in different societies goes back several years. The assumption that usually accompanies such suggestions is that the differences are gender-based. That is, even before the development of sociolinguistics, observers who noted female–male differences in speech usually assumed that the differences in their behavior followed from differences in the sociocultural roles they fulfilled. That assumption, of course, is a version of our hypothesis about gender-based differences.

3.5.1 Limits on female–male differences

Now that we have added a second hypothesis about sex-based differences, we should expect some limit on the kinds of differences that can possibly occur. Female–male differences are no longer understood to be only the result of gender roles. They are now seen as the result of innate differences as well. The interaction of these two hypotheses should limit the actual female–male differences that can occur.

In particular, what we would not expect to find is a situation, regardless of the sociocultural situation, where women's speech is markedly or consistently more limited than men's in terms of the repertoire of variants or the extent of stylistic shifting. That is, if it is true that women generally have an innate verbal facility different from men, that difference should override cultural, political or social bounds. In certain – probably unusual – social structures, we should perhaps not be surprised to find well-defined situations or contexts in which the men's speech regularly evinces more standard variants than the women's. But we should not expect to find, in any society, regardless of its social organization, gender differences for a representative sample of the population whereby men invariably use a larger repertoire of variants and command a wider range of styles. In other words, we should not expect to find a society that reverses the results of, say, Ballymacarrett or inner city Detroit.

These predictions follow from what I take to be the strongest possible interpretation of the hypothesis about sex-based variability. As always, the strongest interpretation is the most interesting because it is testable and refutable.

As it happens, the sociolinguistic literature includes a number of claims for female–male differences which do seem to overturn the sociolinguistic roles of women and men. On close examination, as we shall see, none of them makes a convincing case, though for different reasons. The first one, about Japan, cannot be substantiated. More recent ones, about Middle Eastern societies, have been re-analyzed in interesting ways. All of them, besides being interesting in their own right, offer some support for the sex-based difference hypothesis.

3.5.2　*Putative differences in Japan*

One of the strongest early claims contrasted the speech of Japanese women with European women according to E. R. Edwards in 1903 (quoted by Jespersen 1921: 243, presumably translated by him from French). Although Edwards's comments are not sufficiently documented to pose a serious challenge to the hypothesis, they are interesting both as an example of astute observation and for Edwards's awareness of linguistic variability, decades before it figured seriously in linguistic analysis. He described the Japanese female–male difference in the following terms:

> In France and in England it might be said that women avoid neologisms and are careful not to go too far away from the written forms: in Southern England the written sound *wh* [ʍ] is scarcely ever pronounced except in girls' schools. In Japan, on the contrary, women are less conservative than men, whether in pronunciation or in the selection of words and phrases. One of the chief reasons is that women have not to the same degree as men undergone the influence of the written language. As an example of the liberties which the women take may be mentioned that there is in the actual pronunciation of Tokyo a strong tendency to get rid of the sound (*w*), but the women go further in the word *atashi*, which the men pronounce *watashi* or *watakshi*, "I". Another tendency noted in the language of Japanese women is pretty widely spread among French and English women, namely, the excessive use of intensive words and the exaggeration of stress and tone-accent to

mark emphasis. Japanese women also make much more frequent use than men of the prefixes of politeness *o-*, *go-* and *mi-*.

The last few points are of course similarities rather than differences. They are interesting partly because they are reminiscent of points introduced by Lakoff (1975) in her feminist critique which have often been elaborated since.[9]

More important for our purposes are the differences Edwards cites. Japanese women, he claims, are less "conservative" than French or English women because they use new words and certain phonetic processes more frequently than men. The cause of the difference, according to Edwards, is gender-based: "women have not to the same degree as men undergone the influence of the written language." By that, he is probably referring to differences in the educational level typically attained by women and men. However, that cannot be the whole story, because at the time women in France and England were also generally less well educated than men, although the differences, especially in literacy, may not have been so great. Of course, the Japanese culture of a century ago seemed to Western observers enormously exotic, partly because it was largely closed to Westerners and uninfluenced by them.

Edwards's claim does not challenge our hypotheses but provides, at best, an indication of where one might seek such a challenge. Unfortunately, the contrary sociolinguistic behavior of Japanese gender groups is apparently not discernible today. The largest sociolinguistic study using methods comparable to other studies discussed in this book, by Hibiya (1988) in Tokyo, unluckily found no significant gender correlations for any of the variables. It is not surprising, of course, that Edwards and Hibiya, more than eight decades apart, got different sociolinguistic results. As is well known, Japanese society underwent cataclysmic changes in the second half of this century by emulating Western industrialized societies so successfully as to become a leader among them. Cultural differences remain as a result of millenia of independent development but social differences are undoubtedly much less disparate than they once were. The sociolinguistic ramifications of these differences remain to be discovered.

3.5.3 The Middle East

More recently, strong claims have been put forward for gender differences in sharply distinguished social circumstances in several Middle Eastern societies. These claims have now been revised, as we shall see, but the gender differences appear to be well established throughout the Middle Eastern region.

Many Middle Eastern nations are diglossic. The linguistic situation is well known mainly from the work of Ferguson (1959a, 1959b, 1970). Literary Arabic functions as the "high" language, used in sermons, lectures, newspaper editorials, news broadcasts, and other formal situations,[10] and modern colloquial Arabic varieties function as the "low" language, used in informal conversations with family and friends, in folk songs and poetry, and other homely situations. Literary Arabic, as the language of the Qur'an, high literature, and education, is the prestige variety, and is openly lauded for its logic, expressiveness and beauty, sometimes even by people, Ferguson (1959a: 328) says, whose command of it is not very extensive.

3.5.3.1   (q) in Cairo, Amman and elsewhere   In several communities, sociolinguistic results clearly show that women use fewer of the literary Arabic forms than men.[11] Figure 3.8, from Haeri (1987: 174), brings together the results for one variable from three different sample populations: Cairo, Egypt (Schmidt 1974), Amman, Jordan (Abd-el-Jawad 1981), and an international group from Egypt, Syria, Palestine, Jordan and Lebanon (Salam 1980). The variable is (q), probably the best studied variable in the language, which has three variants: the uvular stop [q], the standard or classical variant; the glottal stop [ʔ], the urban speech variant; and the velar stop [g], the low-level variant, considered casual in some communities and stigmatized in others.

The proportions in figure 3.8 differ quite considerably in each of the communities. The international group on the right (Inter f and m) has the highest proportion of standard [q], as might be expected from the fact that they must neutralize (as far as possible) regional norms in order to communicate with people beyond their regions. They also have the highest proportion of nonstandard [g], presumably because some of the speakers in the sample come from regions where it is is colloquially acceptable. The Cairo sample has proportionately the least standard [q], with Amman in the middle.

3.5.3.2   A gender-based explanation   The greatest consistency, and the one that has drawn attention to the data, is the relative proportion of [q] among women and men. In all three surveys, the men score higher than the women. This result, along with similar results for other variables, led investigators to conclude that in these Middle Eastern communities the women and men reversed the proportionate use of standard variants found in Western societies. Abd-el-Jawad (1981: 324) noted that women "do not use prestigious forms as often as men", thus "contradicting patterns reported in Western communities." Bakir (1986: 6), in a study of gender variation in Basrah, Iraq, concluded: "Women in the community under discussion do not lead in the use of forms that they consider to be better. They, furthermore, associate these better forms with men's language."

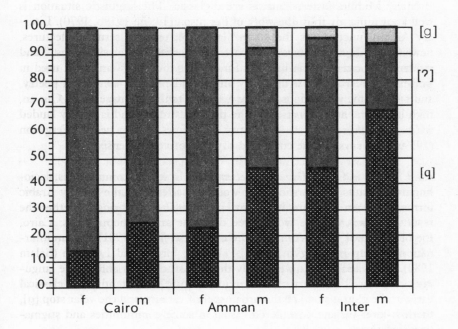

Figure 3.8 Proportions of (q) variants for women and men in three Arabic communities (from Haeri 1987: figure 1, 174)

The reason proffered for this difference was in all cases gender-based, as determined by the roles played by women and men in these communities. Bakir (1986: 6) says:

> The structure of this Arab community is such that the place and existence space of women is still the house. It is the man who deals with the outside world and handles public situations. Women are not generally required to communicate with this outside world, with its cares and concerns. This is done by the man of the family. Besides, the social structure of the Arab communities is still segregative in essence. Although there are many types of institutions where men and women meet and work together, the men's society and the women's society are still separate, and women are expected not to trespass on men's grounds by doing men's work or assuming roles and participating in functions that men are expected to perform.

More generally, Labov (1982: 79) says, "It appears that where women have not traditionally played a major role in public life, cultural expectations will lead them to react less strongly to the linguistic norms of the dominant culture." Elsewhere he suggests that this pattern may represent "a Near- and

South-Asian *Sprachbund*, a linguistic area that has developed a distinct pattern of sexual differentiation, possibly under Muslim influence" (1983: 7).

3.5.3.3   Prestige and standard varieties   Soon after this gender-based interpretation became established, other sociolinguists began questioning its premises. The re-analysis began with Ibrahim's observation that "the questions of Arabic sociolinguistics are usually stated and discussed in terms identical with those of typically non-diglossic European languages" (1986: 115).

The problem of interpretation has its roots in the equating of the "prestige" variety with the "standard." In Western societies they seem to be the same thing. Most people, asked to evaluate speakers using standard and non-standard speech forms, will judge the standard users more favorably, attribute to them higher status and material success, and generally associate with them the trappings of prestige. Whatever attraction the non-standard may have – and it is, as we shall see in §5.4, sufficient to perpetuate it – is tacit or covert.

In Arabic societies, however, the notions of standard and prestige varieties must be kept separate. There is no question that literary Arabic is the prestige variety. It may be thought of as an international standard, or perhaps super-national, in the Arabic-speaking world. But it is not the standard variety nationally.

The diglossic situation entails that literary Arabic be a superimposed variety. It is not a mother tongue. It is thoroughly codified, and as a result, highly stable and unchanging. Its prototypical contexts are formal ones, such as religious ceremonies, classrooms and lecture halls, and high literature. It is not appropriate for neighborly conversations among families on the way to mosque, or in the playground at recess, or in topical verse. Ibrahim (1986: 118) notes that literary Arabic cannot even be acquired by upwardly mobile individuals because it is "inseparable from education." People who did not attend the best schools or move in the upper circles in their youth will not master it as adults. What they will master, if they rise in stature socially and occupationally, are features of the urban vernacular as they lose features of their neighborhood vernacular.

I take that to mean that literary Arabic does not form part of the linguistic continuum in Arabic communities but is removed from it by a gap. As a result, it cannot fill the role of the standard variety in social stratification.

3.5.3.4   (q) in Nablus and Baghdad   Abd-el-Jawad (1987: 360–64) adds further reasons for keeping the prestige and standard varieties apart. He documents regional developments whereby changes are diffusing through the vernaculars in patterns that are familiar from changes in progress in other languages. From their distribution in the sample populations, it seems clear that they are functioning to develop indicators – he calls them "stereo-types," but one of his main points is that they are not (regionally) stigma-tized – of regional standards. One involves the variable (q) in two regions, the first on the West Bank in the city of Nablus and the other in Iraq dominated by the city of Baghdad.

In Nablus, the former standard variant [q], the prestige form in literary Arabic as we have seen, is being replaced by the variant [ʔ] in the speech of younger people, with the women leading the innovation (as in Amman, figure 3.8 above). In Baghdad, the variant [g] is increasing in frequency in the speech of the younger members of the dominant social group and [q] is considered old fashioned. Neither of these changes is touching the prestige variety at all, but both are socially significant changes below that level, in the stratification of the standard variety.

Obviously, if literary Arabic were truly the standard variety, these changes observed by Abd-el-Jawad would all be changes away from the standard. But the social strata involved in the changes indicates that they are stand-ardizing. The convergence of all these arguments splits literary Arabic, the prestige variety, from the vernaculars, which include the standard variety and other socially restricted varieties. As Haeri (1987: 175) says, "Classical Arabic is not a synchronically relevant variety of modern day Arabic on a par with the living vernaculars."

3.5.3.5 Lexical variants in Baghdad   Some appreciation of the complexity of the linguistic situation comes from Abu-Haidar's description (1989: 473–4) of the status of various lexical forms of the literary Arabic term *sidq* "truth", summarized in table 3.3. Five variants are in active use. The lowest level forms, *sidig* and metathesized *sigid*, are stigmatized as semi-literate usage. The most frequent form, *sidug*, is presumably the one that Abd-el-Jawad observed diffusing as the variant [g] establishes itself as a Baghdadi indicator. The next most frequent, *sidiq*, has the literary Arabic variant [q] and is apparently spreading socially among Muslims, possibly at the ex-pense of the literary form *sidq*. The social stratification of Baghdadi Arabic, in Ibrahim's terms, encompasses the gradation from the lowest levels to *sidiq*, excluding the highest level, literary Arabic form. The standard form, as opposed to the prestige form *sidq*, is *sidug*, the Muslim form and the most frequent.

3.6 Linguistic Evidence for Sex and Gender Differences

When the linguistic situation in the Middle East is re-analysed in this way, taking into account the social ramifications of diglossia, the discrepancy

Table 3.3 Variants of *sidq* "truth" in Baghdad with their social significance (based on Abu–Haidar 1989: figure 2, p. 473)

Form	Phonology	Social Stratification
ṣidq	[q], monosyllabic	literary Arabic, used by educated people
ṣidiq	[q], epenthetic [i]	originally non-Muslim, now used by some Muslims approximating literary Arabic, very frequent
ṣidug	[g], epenthetic [u]	Muslim form, most frequent
ṣidig	[g], epenthetic [i]	used by illiterate and semi-literate, all ages
ṣigid	[g], metathesis	used by illiterate, elderly people

between male and female responses in Middle Eastern and Western societies disappears. Ibrahim (1986: 123) believes that the social differences formerly considered to be its determinants may not really be so different. "It is wrong," he says, "to conclude that because women in a particular society might be in a social position that is inferior to that of men, they would necessarily use an inferior language variety. If this were the case, then women in most societies, including the Western ones, would be using inferior language varieties."

In both worlds, women use more standard forms than men of the same social group. So far, sociolinguistic studies of the Middle East have gone through two stages: they concentrated, first, on establishing social correlates, including male–female differences, and, second, on revising the original interpretation of those differences.

The revised results are consistent with the hypothesis of a sex-based difference in the linguistic behaviour of females and males. Although the sociocultural organizations differ remarkably from the Western world, the sociolinguistic behaviour is essentially the same. The female advantage in verbal abilities apparently overrides the sociocultural differences.

What is missing, or at least not yet obvious, from these studies is any evidence that impinges on the hypothesis of gender-based differences. Middle Eastern societies, as is well known, range along a continuum from traditional or "fundamentalist" at one pole to liberal at the other. The point where a nation places itself along the continuum partly shapes cultural institutions and determines numerous social conventions. The internal differences between Middle Eastern societies may or may not be greater than the differences between, say, Western European societies, but one of the sociocultural variables that appears to differ more sharply than in Europe is the definition of gender roles. If the socially defined constraints (or lack of them) on women or men are really systematically reflected in their language as the hypothesis of gender-based differences maintains, then the Middle East should prove to be a rich source of inference about the validity of the hypothesis.

4

Accents in Time

How do we measure present time, since it has no extent? We must measure it as it passes by, but once it has passed by what would be measured no longer exists. From where does it come, and by what path, and to what place does it go? From where, except from the future? By what path except by the present? To what place, except into the past? In other words, it is from that which does not yet exist, by that which lacks space, and into that which no longer exists.

St Augustine Confessions XI

We ain't what we wanna be, and we ain't what we're gonna be – but we ain't what we wuz.

South Carolina mountain proverb (Shaw 1952)

Like class and sex, age exerts an irrepressible influence on our social being. Our age is an immutable social fact, and it is proving, with advances in social organization and medical science, to be the most immutable. Social classes may be altered in political economies that allow for mobility so that individuals need not live their days in the class they are born into, and gender roles become less confining under exactly the same conditions, with a wider range of possibilities for the sexes. The impact of social and sexual categorization can thus be altered by political action – but our ages remain fixed.

Age plays an almost autocratic role in our social lives and, it follows, in our linguistic development. In this chapter, we begin by looking at the general indicators of age in our lifespans (§4.1.1) and at some of the linguistic indicators that accompany them, especially vocal pitch (§4.1.2). Then we consider the three sociolinguistically crucial ages, first generally (in §4.2) and then specifically: the first exposure to social pressures from parents and peers (§4.3), the hyper-sensitive norm enforcement of adolescent networks (§4.4), and the accommodation of speech to style of life in early adulthood (§4.5).

Cutting across these normal progressions through time is the mutability of language itself, constantly changing, partly – probably largely – in order to keep functioning as a meaningful social emblem (§4.6). One kind of change, age-grading (§4.6.1), is relatively rare – or at least infrequently reported – and appears as a regular, maturational change repeated in successive generations. The other, much better studied and perhaps the most striking single accomplishment of contemporary linguistics, is the apprehension of sound change in progress (§4.6.2), in real time and apparent time.

4.1 Aging

The adults in any society can normally guess the ages of their fellow citizens from their appearance, give or take a few years, and individuals who for one reason or another foil the guesswork hear about it endlessly. Commenting that people appear younger than their years is a common brand of flattery, usually cliched and often duplicitous but widely accepted as harmless. Commenting that people appear older than their years is an insult except to adolescents impatient for the onset of adulthood.

4.1.1 Physical and cultural indicators

By and large, the physical indicators of age are shared by all people in all cultures. Childhood is marked by superficial androgyny with boys and girls similar in height, weight, musculature, and other physical characteristics. Adolescence, when the most visible sex differences emerge, often marks its onset with momentary gawkiness caused by height gain without commensurate weight gain and growth of the extremities prior to commensurate body development. Early adulthood sees the resolution of these adolescent disparities into a kind of unified physical entity, or as nearly so as individuals ever get to it. This is the point in our physical development that has been exalted, sometimes cynically, in all the industrialized nations: the idealized 25-year-old – wrinkle-free, clear-eyed, slim-waisted – is held up as a paragon by the clothing, dietary and cosmetics industries. These are normally the reproductive years – appropriately the organism best reproduces itself when it is at its own physical peak – and consequently the period of greatest sexual vigor, a fact not lost on the advertisers for the "youth" industries.

The physical equability of young adulthood is of course transitory, and advancing age brings wrinkling skin, weight re-apportionments in chest and abdomen, greying hair and, for men, receding hairlines. All these signs are apparently discernible in finer detail than most people are ever aware because, although they emerge very gradually, indeed imperceptibly, our ability to infer ages within a few years is hardly less astute in this period than in the others. These are the years euphemistically called middle age, from about 35 to 55. Old age consummates the gradations begun in middle age – men with receding hairlines become bald, faces with crow's-feet become furrowed, and so on – and carries additional markers of its own: decreasing size partly from stooped skeletal features and partly from metabolic reversal (catabolism), receding gums making people "long in the tooth", and slowing of gait, coordination and reflexes.

This entire sequence of physical change from infancy to dotage is determined prenatally. The onsets of puberty, adulthood, middle age and old age are very similar in all normal people, and they apparently remain fixed regardless of changes in life expectancy. The increase in human lifespans is perhaps the most dramatic biological change in the past two centuries.[1] In this century alone, in the Western industrial countries, men and women born in 1894 could expect to live to the ages of about 46 and 49, respectively, but those born a century later, in 1994, to about 72 and 79 (Hustead 1989: 10, 70). The ravages of plagues and infectious diseases are much less, with the result that young adults and middle-aged people are less likely to be enfeebled or disfigured by diseases than they were a century ago, but there is no reason to believe that the greatly increased life expectancy brings with it anything but a prolonged old age. Puberty is not delayed, young adulthood is not extended, and the onset and progress of middle age seem to be the same as they always were. The robust health that prolongs old age is also what makes it worth prolonging.

Although physical clues are far and away the most important in our ability to estimate the ages of people we meet, they are not the only ones. Clothing is one of the cultural trappings that is partly age-graded, with certain attire characteristic of certain age groups in successive generations. Only old women dress in solid black to go shopping, only young men wear team sweaters, only little girls wear buckled sandals, only teenagers wear ripped jeans, only old men wear felt fedoras to sit in the sun in the park – infallible indicators of this kind are hard to find because to some extent they are creatures of fashion, but the idea is clear, and familiar.

More subtle cultural and social markers of age can also be found. Certain activities are age-graded, like skipping for girls, quilting or lace-making for middle-aged and older women in rural settings, recreational ice hockey for young adults in Canada and recreational non-contact ice hockey for middle-aged men, and lobby-sitting at the shopping mall in the mornings for older men.

Attitudes can also be markers of age. When Hemingway said that T. S. Eliot was "born middle-aged," he was not referring to his physiognomy. Stereotypically, people are said to become more conservative as they grow older. This does not suggest that everyone starts out liberal-minded, but only that someone who starts out conservative could be ultra-conservative in the end. How general this is may not be really calculable, but there are some celebrated examples – Arthur Koestler, Jack Kerouac, perhaps Fidel Castro, Malcolm Muggeridge, to name a few – of people whose leftist leanings veered sharply right as they grew older, and there are no iconic examples of shifts in the opposite direction. The shift does not entail politics exclusively or even primarily, but generally older people are thought to be less flexible and less tolerant than young people.

It is interesting to wonder if this age-graded conservatism, so familiar in industrialized societies, occurs in other societies, especially those in which old people are said to be venerated. If it does, it could exert a continuous, and perhaps insidious, effect in, say, patrilineal East African societies where the oldest men automatically become councillors (Gibbs n.d.: 96–7), if their attitudes led to policy decisions marked by conservatism and inflexibility.[2]

All of these aspects of aging play a part in our ability to estimate people's ages – what they are doing and wearing and saying as well as how they look. Any one aspect might suffice by itself, but they normally come together. Another one that enters into it, usually as part of the complex but sometimes by itself, is their speech.

4.1.2 Some linguistic indicators[3]

A person's speech is such a reliable indicator of age that we can usually guess the age of telephone callers within seconds of hearing their voice for the first time. This seems to be possible because we are so sensitive to the effects of aging on the complicated physiology that produces speech. The articulatory organs and the larynx are subject to wear and tear, and the timing of muscular activities and respiratory activity is subject to slippage. These things, like all the normal characteristics of aging, happen gradually and imperceptibly, so much so that they are apparently beyond the capacity of physiologists and phoneticians to observe and describe with pinpoint accuracy. But ordinary people, with no training of any kind, can judge the gestalt of their effects with extraordinary precision.

One of the indicators of age is progressive creakiness in voice quality. Creaky voice occurs in some African languages as a distinctive feature and in RP accent as a kind of variable terminating juncture (Rogers 1991: 247). It is the result of speaking with the vocal cords closed except in the anterior part, where they vibrate slowly (Hardcastle 1976: 84). The progressive

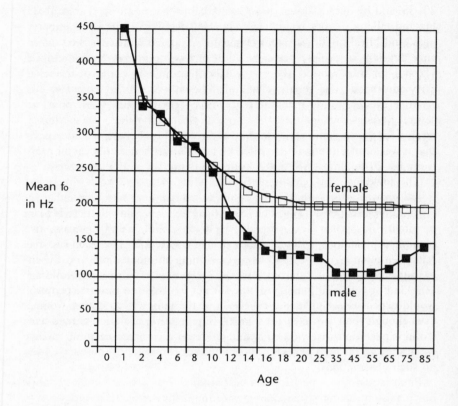

Figure 4.1 Fundamental frequency for females and males from birth to old age (based on Helfrich 1979: figures 2 and 3, 81–2)

creakiness of aging voices is the result of changes in muscle tone. In advanced old age, when the speech rate slows, the voice quality often becomes tremulous.

Another of the primary indicators of age in speech is pitch. We have already noted (in §3.1.5) the significance of pitch as a sex difference resulting from the growth of the male Adam's apple at puberty. Pitch is produced by the rate of vibration of the vocal cords, measured in cycles per second or Herz (Hz). The average pitch of a person's voice is called the fundamental frequency (f_0), and the mean f_0 is the average for a group of subjects. For both females and males, the f_0 decreases with age in the first two decades until adulthood.

Figure 4.1 plots the f_0 for various age groups. Note that the age scale on the abscissa is asymmetrically represented by twos from 2–20, by fives from

20–35, and by decades after that. Crying babies have a mean f_0 around 500 Hz and talking infants around 450 Hz (Helfrich 1979: 80). Until puberty, girls' and boys' pitches are indistinguishable, and then the marked difference develops in adolescence. The adult means for women are around 225 Hz and for men around 120 Hz, but both show continuing decreases in early adulthood. The general shape of the curves is similar from 1 to 20.

After age 20, for women there are no systematic changes in pitch for several decades, but for men the average continues to decrease slightly. If pitch were the *only* indicator of age in the voice, these results would suggest that it was nearly impossible to infer a woman's age from her speaking voice from age 20 to almost 85, but of course it is not the only difference.

The lowering of pitch for both sexes after maturity, when the larynx is full grown, is presumably the result of muscle and coordination losses beyond the peak period. For men over 60, as figure 4.1 shows, there is a rise in pitch. This is harder to explain. Helfrich (1979: 81–83) suggests two possible explanations, without a great deal of conviction. The pitch rise may reflect either the relative ratio between diminishing body size and the invariant larynx size, or, alternatively, the weakening of hormones in old age as a kind of converse puberty. If the former explanation were correct, one would expect to see at least a reflection of the same effect among women, even though their larynxes are smaller. The latter explanation carries with it the expectation that women would undergo a comparable pitch change when they go through periods of hormonal adjustment, but there have been no such observations.

Pitch is just one – perhaps the best studied – of several similarly subtle but persistent changes that characterize linguistic aging. It is important to recognize that these are indicators of aging, not markers. Because they affect the whole population with little variation they do not carry any special social significance – they cannot be stigmatized, criticized or prescribed out of existence. They happen equally to speakers of non-standard dialects and to speakers of standard dialects, and they cut across stylistic and social boundaries. They are accidental features of the language faculty, but the language faculty itself remains intact through the whole enormous range of physiological and sociological changes that accompany normal aging.

4.2   The Acquisition of Sociolects

A key to understanding the social aspects of language acquisition by children is the obvious truth – readily observed but often overlooked in technical discussions – that language is not acquired out of need or necessity. Children acquiring their mother tongue are not engaged in survival exercises.

The symbiosis of parents and infants is strong enough under normal circumstances that most children would survive perfectly well even if they never learned the words for apple juice or bowel movements.

Instead of using language to look after their physical needs, children appear to learn it so that they can join the conversation, put in their two cents' worth, and pass the time of day. Just as adults spend a very small proportion of their linguistic energy on purely functional activities – asking for directions, making a purchase, instructing a colleague in some routine – so children spend very little of theirs on functional matters. Yet the theorists in such areas as pragmatics, acquisition and even language origins, when they have considered the roots of the activities they study, have assigned functionality a primacy that is not evident in sociolinguistic observations.

Among the theories of language origin, only Langer's (1942) is rooted firmly in the kind of social nexus that underlies most sociolinguistic activities.[4] Where Hockett (1960) and many other linguists seek the origins of language by trying to derive it from animal call systems, Langer relates it instead to the distinctly human instinct for vocalization. As Langer (1942: 102) says, "Between the clearest animal call of love or warning or danger, and a man's least, trivial *word*, there lies a whole day of Creation – or in the modern phrase, a whole chapter of evolution." Infants are babblers from the beginning, whereas chimps and other higher primates grow taciturn at about four months (105–6).

Infants' strongest responses, verbal and gestural, are to vocal games – songs, rhymes, and nonsense syllables. Their first uses of real language are not demands for service but names for things, at first for things present but soon after for things absent (125–6). The need to categorize objects stimulates language development more than the need to gratify appetites, and rudimentary storytelling, jokes and fantasies soon follow.

The social groundwork of Langer's theory is derived from Sapir (1933: 15; quoted by Langer 1942: 109–10). "The primary function of language is generally said to be communication," Sapir says. "There can be no quarrel with this so long as it is distinctly understood that there may be effective communication without overt speech and that language is highly relevant to situations which are not obviously of a communicative sort." In fact, communication is a derived function of language. Sapir goes on to say, "It is best to admit that language is primarily a vocal actualization of the tendency to see realities symbolically, that it is precisely this quality which renders it a fit instrument for communication and that it is in the actual give and take of social intercourse that it has been complicated and refined into the form in which it is known today."

In the same article, Sapir (1933: 15) says: "Language is a great force of socialization, probably the greatest that exists. By this is meant not merely the obvious fact that significant social intercourse is hardly possible without language but that the mere fact of a common speech serves as a particularly potent symbol of the social solidarity of those who speak the language."

Its symbolic potency is one of the topics discussed in the next chapter (especially §5.4). In this chapter, we will take a look at three significant stages in the development of "a common speech" in the sense of a sociolect, a dialect that includes features characteristic of the people with whom one wishes to show solidarity, either densely or loosely.

4.2.1 *Labov's six stages*

In the only comprehensive acquisition schedule posited in sociolinguistics so far, Labov (1964: 91) proposed a model with six stages in what he called "the acquisition of the full range of spoken English." By the "full range," he apparently meant the use of standard variants as well as vernacular or regional variants, with systematic style-shifting mediating the variation as appropriate to various social situations.

Labov's acquisition schedule has not fostered productive research since he first proposed it, very early in the sociolinguistic enterprise. As we shall see, subsequent research has not lent it empirical support. Labov himself has never referred to it in his subsequent work either to repudiate it or for any other reason, but some of his research is incompatible with it (as we will see at the end of the next section).

Our three stages do not coincide perfectly with his six. Nevertheless, it makes an instructive starting point here, because by over-differentiating certain aspects of the acquisition process, it prompts discussion of some aspects that might otherwise go unnoticed.

Labov sees the acquisition of standard English as a "process of acculturation" (1964: 89) in which adolescent linguistic behavior becomes more similar to "the predominating pattern of the adult community," by which he apparently means MMC adult standard. He says that the increasing linguistic similarities beween the young people and the adults "measure . . . the extent to which the young person has grasped the norms of behavior which govern the adult community."

The six stages in the process of acculturation (1964: 91–2, with Labov's terms in bold) are as follows:

- Acquisition of the **basic grammar** in childhood, normally under parental influence.
- Acquisition of the **vernacular**, from about five to 12, under the influence of peers in school and in the neighborhood.
- Development of **social perception**, beginning at age 14 or 15, under the influence of adult contacts, such that the youngsters may still be

vernacular speakers but their responses on subjective reaction tests (of the kind discussed in §5.1.1 below) become more similar to their parents.

• Development of **stylistic variation**, probably also starting around age 14, under the influence of wider contacts with peers beyond the neighborhood or high school, such that they begin to make adjustments in the frequency of particular variants in appropriate social contexts.

• Ability to maintain the **consistent standard**, presumably in young adulthood and presumably under pressure from the still wider contacts at work or university, such that individuals are capable of maintaining standard speech consistently for as long as the situation warrants – a stage, Labov says, "often not acquired at all" except by MC groups.

• Acquisition of the **full range**, evidently attained by a minority in most communities, for Labov notes that in New York it is attained only by "college educated persons with a special interest in speech."

In a footnote, Labov offers a caveat about attempting to generalize his results, saying that "the data . . . as a whole apply primarily to New York City" and that "New York City informants differ from those who were raised outside the city," but, confusingly, in the same footnote (89n) he also says that "the principles of sociolinguistic organization illustrated here are . . . more general than the limitation to New York City would imply."

In fact, every stage that Labov posits presupposes a linguistic situation in which, first, the neighborhood vernaculars are disparate, plentiful and influential, and, second, the standard dialect is not the vernacular of any neighborhood. If those conditions hold for New York, they surely do not hold in many other cities: the first probably holds for London and perhaps the second, the second for Buffalo but not the first, and neither holds for Sydney, Toronto, and perhaps Chicago.

With hindsight, it is clear that Labov's proposal was premature. When he proposed it, the only large-scale sociolinguistic results available to him were his own on New York. His adolescent sample is so disparate – the 58 subjects range in age from eight to 19 – that he admits he lacks a "high level of confidence in the conclusions" based on their speech (1964: 88). His terms of reference are fairly unusual too – talking about the "full range" of a language, the "adult norms" for the norms of a single social class, and so on. Two years later, when the publication of *The Social Stratification of English in New York City* (1966) set the early standard for the sociolinguistic enterprise, these terms had been abandoned.

Looking critically at his six stages as we do in the next section will show that none of his stages survives in the terms he used. However they make a useful frame of reference for the discussion of the developmental stages that follows.

4.2.2   Development of stylistic and social variants

Labov's evidence that adolescents progressively speak more like adults appears to be partly an artifact of his methods. Romaine (1984: 85) first noted the inherent contradiction in Labov's aggregating the linguistic indices of young people of three different classes (MC, WC and "Lower Class") and then comparing their scores to those of MC adults. The fact that the young people never reach the adult norms appears to support the result on which Labov bases his developmental schema, namely, that the young peoples' speech is an approximation of adult speech. But clearly some of those young people, the WC and LC subjects, have a different set of adult norms against which their development should be measured. Attainment of the fifth step, **consistent standard**, as Labov agrees, does not figure in their linguistic development at all.

The following three examples shed light on the development of style-shifting and vernacular norms, which come into being much earlier than Labov proposed and in fact seem to develop from the earliest stages of language acquisition.

4.2.2.1   Style-shifting by Edinburgh schoolboys   It has now been demonstrated in several studies, contrary to the **stylistic variation** postulate, that children are capable of style-shifting before reaching adolescence (Andersen 1990; also Romaine 1984: 99–100).

Reid (1978) studied the speech of 11-year-old boys in three different schools in Edinburgh. His results for the variable (ng), with its familiar variants, are shown in figure 4.2. His subjects belong to three social classes, MMC, UWC and MWC. Their speech was recorded in four situations on a continuum of self-monitoring: the reading passage (RP) is the most self-conscious, followed by an individual interview with an adult (IS), and then by two casual situations, in the playground (PG) with a portable microphone and in group discussions (GP) with two classmates.

The shape of figure 4.2 dramatically refutes Labov's **stylistic variation** postulate. These pre-adolescent boys evince style-shifting in a manner consistent with their social classes. The pattern is not distinguishable in any way from numerous other examples we have seen with adult style-shifting. As Reid (1978: 169) puts it in his conclusion, "It is as true of these eleven-year-old Edinburgh boys then as of older informants . . . that there are features of their speech which relate in a systematic way to their social status and to the social context in which their speech is produced."

Moreover, although Labov distinguished between the **basic grammar** phase and the **vernacular** phase, the two seem to be indistinguishable. There is no period in the language acquisition sequence when individuals

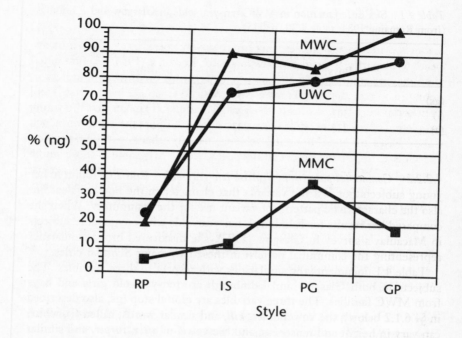

Figure 4.2 Stylistic variation by Edinburgh schoolboys (Reid 1978: figure 6, 168)

do not use socially significant linguistic variants. Labov's distinction implies that class markers and other features develop only after the grammar is developed at some maturational level, but Reid's eleven-year-olds, to no one's surprise, already reflect the vernacular of their respective classes.

Romaine (1984: 113) lowered the age for the development of socially sensitive linguistic variation when she "found some evidence for sex differentiation in the use of certain variables by children as young as six years old." As we will see in §4.2.2.3, Wolfram (1989) found evidence for regional vernacular variants in three-year-olds.

Labov himself contributed persuasive evidence for the indistinguishability of these two phases twenty-five years later (1989). In studies of the acquisition of the variables (CC) and (ng) by families in a Philadelphia suburb, he discovered that the "active period" for the acquisition of regional vernacular patterns was between four and nine, often actually preceding the acquisition of general grammatical constraints. "There is little evidence to support the notion of a language-learning faculty isolated from social and historical developments," he says (1989: 96). "On the contrary, children appear to focus sharply on the pattern of social variation, and so reproduce the historically preserved variable patterns."

Table 4.1 Sex differentiation in MWC ten-year-olds in Glasgow and Edinburgh (from Romaine 1984: table 4.30, p. 115)

	Glasgow		Edinburgh	
	Boys	Girls	Boys	Girls
(gs)	92	79	84	78
(i)	302	280	210	177
(a)	238	233	246	224

4.2.2.2   Communal patterns in Scottish ten-year-olds   Romaine found in her young subjects not just the variants that characterize the home dialect but also the characteristic patterns of variant use for the community. When she compared her results for Edinburgh ten-year-olds with comparable subjects in Macaulay's survey in Glasgow (1977), she discovered broad similarities representing the communal pattern in these two major Scottish cities.

Table 4.1 documents the similarities with respect to three variables. The subjects in both Glasgow and Edinburgh are ten-year-old girls and boys from MWC families. The three variables are glottal stop (gs, also described in §4.6.1.2 below), the vowel of *bit, kill*, and similar words, called (i), which can vary in height and tenseness, and the vowel of *after, carpet*, and similar words, called (a), which can vary from open [a] to close [æ]. The patterns in both cities reveal that the boys use the non-standard variants more than the girls, exactly as we would expect from the adult pattern (see chapter 3). More interesting is the high degree of similarity of both the increments between girls and boys, and the absolute scores in both places. Variables (i) and (a) have four variants and thus range from 0–400, but the Glasgow and Edinburgh youngsters occupy similar parts of that large range.

4.2.2.3   Emerging BEV phonology in Washington children   So far, there are very few acquisition studies of socially significant variables by infants. In one such study, Wolfram (1989) tentatively tracked the progress of twelve WC black children in Washington, DC, with respect to final nasal syllables. In black English vernacular (BEV), final syllables with an underlying vowel and nasal consonant can occur phonetically as a nasalized vowel. For instance, *run, rum* and *rung* can all be pronounced [ɹʌ̃] (Wolfram and Fasold 1974: 143). There is no counterpart for this in standard English, although nasal consonants often result in anticipatory nasalization of the vowel without, however, loss of the consonant.

At the earliest stage, 18 months, Wolfram (1989: 307–8) found that /n/ and /m/ were not yet represented in final position, although they were well established by then in initial position. At the next stage, 36 months, nasal consonants did occur in final position, and for all the children they alternated with occurrences of the same words without the nasal consonant. When the consonant was not pronounced, the vowel was nasalized. Wolfram notes (1989: 310) that this "is a pattern very different from that found for [Standard English] speakers." Put positively, it is the pattern found in adult BEV. Moreover, the nasalization/deletion process is more frequent with a following /n/ than the other nasal consonants, as it also is in adult BEV.

At the earliest age at which observations of this process are possible, then, the children show clear evidence of distinctive BEV phonology. As soon as they master the phonological features relevant to the phonology, they show evidence of the processes that apply to them.

Results like these leave no doubt that sociolinguistic competence – the individual's use of communal patterns of variation and ability to shift appropriately according to social context – develops very early. There are no studies documenting a time gap between the acquisition of linguistic competence and the development of sociolinguistic competence. In fact, there is no reason to consider them to be different from one another. When children acquire their mother tongues, they evidently acquire the local variants and the norms of their usage too. The content of language acquisition is socially determined, though its schedule is biologically determined.

4.2.3   Three formative periods

Evidence of the kind discussed in the previous section suggests that Labov's original schema was over-specified with respect to the available evidence. As we have seen, **stylistic variation** emerges much earlier than he postulated, and there appears to be no basis for distinguishing an acquisitional phase for **basic grammar** from one for **vernacular**, since they appear to be simultaneous and inseparable. The final phase, **consistent standard**, appears to be an idealization of uncertain applicability and little or no generality. Another of his postulates, not previously discussed here, **social perception**, has never been tested despite the fact that it appears to be a straightforward hypothesis for anyone carrying out subjective reaction tests with both adult and teenaged subjects.

An alternative proposal for sociolect acquisition is long overdue, and on the basis of accumulated evidence from numerous studies its general shape seems to me to be evident.

It is clear, in the first place, that vernacular variables and style-shifting develop along with phonology and syntax from the very beginning of acquisition. From that point, there appear to be three formative periods in the acquisition of sociolects by normal individuals. First, in childhood the vernacular develops under the influence of family and friends (§4.3). Second, in adolescence vernacular norms tend to accelerate beyond the norms established by the previous generation, under the influence of dense net-working (§4.4). Third, in young adulthood standardization tends to in-crease, at least for the sub-set of speakers involved in language-sensitive occupations in the broadest sense of the term (§4.5). After that, from middle age onward, speakers normally have fixed their sociolects beyond any large-scale or regular changes.

4.3 Family and Friends

Sociolinguists know that schoolchildren speak more like their peers than like their elders. This fact is not always received with equanimity by older people, especially authority figures, but the fact remains: classmates and close friends are linguistically more influential than teachers and parents. Although the family circle normally provides the first speech models for infants, within a few years it is replaced by a more significant one, the circle of friends.

In the most common social situations, the disparity between family and friends as linguistic influences is inconsequential because family and friends are natives of the same speech community. It is when we look at the situations in which the parents belong to a different speech community from the one in which the children are being raised that the primacy of age-mates over elders becomes very obvious. Then, the children have two models of dialect transmission, at least in theory, but one of those models, the parents, is never adopted under normal circumstances. To take an extreme case, when monolingual Italian adults immigrate to Sydney, Aus-tralia, they learn English and end up speaking an ESL dialect that includes some broad Australian features and some "foreign" features – an "inter-language" (Tarone 1988) – but their Australian-born offspring obviously do not perpetuate their parents' ESL dialect. Similarly, when Scots school-teachers settle and work in London, England, they retain most features of their native Scottish accents, but their London-born offspring do not retain their parents' Scottishness in their own accents. A similarly extreme but less well-known situation involving sociolectal displacement occurs in the plant-ing of new world settlements (§2.5) where none of the highly divergent founders' dialects gets transmitted to the offspring.

In all these instances, the children sound more like their playmates than like their parents. The Italo–Australian youngsters grow up speaking Aus-tralian English that is largely indistinguishable from native Australians of the same age and class. The children of the Scots schoolteachers sound like their parents' students of the same age and class rather than like their parents. And the new world children, as we have seen, sound unlike any of the adults in the community but like one another.

All of this takes place so naturally and so seamlessly that sociolinguists have largely ignored observing it systematically. An obvious empirical application arises in the kind of instances represented by the Scots schoolteachers in London. If any social situation requires Labov's distinction between **basic grammar** and **vernacular** steps (in §4.2.1), then it should be found in developmental studies of displaced sociolects like these. In the example given, the children of the Scots parents should have Scots dialect features – at least some – up to around age five, and should lose them – probably rapidly – thereafter. By carefully studying situations like these, we might expect to discover subtle patterns of dialect-shifting, comparable to style-shifting in unmixed dialect situations, as the children make the transition away from parental norms to their peers.

We might also expect to elucidate the relative influence of parents and peers, since parental models must count for something in the acquisition stages and perhaps exert discernible effects not yet understood or appreciated beyond that.

4.3.1   Dialect acquisition

Developmental studies bearing some resemblance to these have been carried out on older children moving into places where they must try to acquire a different accent. In these studies, the children's native accents have already developed, and they must learn to cope in a region where the local dialect is different from theirs. In all cases, the dominant impression is one of fitful progress, indicating the powerful effect that the native accent, once established, exerts on the acquisition process.

As we have already seen with the interlopers (§2.9.1), it is simply impossible for latecomers to a region to master accent features that are phonologically complex. So Mr J, though he arrived in Toronto at 11, still had some low back onsets in diphthongs before voiceless consonants – [saʊθ] rather than [sʌʊθ] for 'south' – because of incomplete internalization of the Canadian raising rule (Chambers 1984). Youngsters in Philadelphia suburbs fared even less well in their attempts to master the complex conditions on short-*a* that result in pronunciation differences like [beˀd] 'bad' but [sæd] 'sad', among many others. Unless those youngsters were not only born in the suburb but also had parents from there, they never got short-*a* exactly right (Payne 1980).

4.3.1.1   Six Canadians in England   Age interacts crucially in more subtle ways as well. In a developmental study of dialect acquisition by six Canadian youngsters whose families moved to southern England (Chambers 1992), the youngest children in the group were more proficient acquirers in

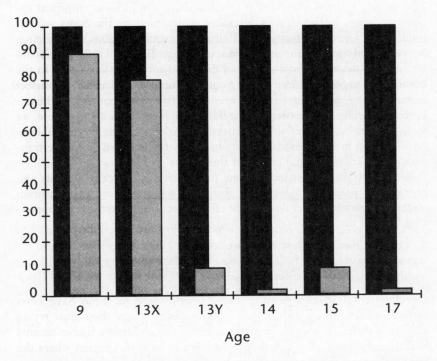

Figure 4.3 Absence of merged low back vowels in the speech of six Canadians, from youngest to oldest. In background, the scores of their English peers (Chambers 1992: figure 7, 688)

every respect, from the replacement of lexical items ("queue" for "line-up", "trousers" for "pants", etc.) and pronunciation variants ([hɑf] for [hæf] "half", [tʰəmɑ́to] for [tʰəméɪdo] "tomato", etc.) to phonological features (lack of T-voicing in "better", "city", "putting", etc.).

A dramatic example is shown in figure 4.3, which charts the progress of the six Canadians in unmerging the low back unrounded vowel of their native accents. In most dialects of English, pairs of words like *bobble/bauble*, *Don/Dawn*, *tot/taught*, *hock/hawk* and *knot/naught* have different vowels. In southern England, where these Canadians now live, the difference is very noticeable, with /ɒ/in the *bobble–Don–knot* set and /ɔ:/in the *bauble–Dawn–naught* set. For the Canadians this poses an acquisition problem, because Canadian English has merged these vowels as /ɑ/so that the words in the two sets are homophones. If the Canadian youngsters are going to sound like their southern England peers, they must learn to distinguish these

Table 4.2 Monthly progress of Debbie and Richard replacing British (B) features of three vowels with Australian (A) or variable (AB) features (based on Trudgill 1986: tables 1.4 and 1.5, pp. 29–30)

	/ou/		/ei/		/iː/	
Month	Debbie	Richard	Debbie	Richard	Debbie	Richard
1	B	AB	B	B	B	B
2	B	AB	B	AB	B	A
3	A	AB	B	AB	B	AB
4	A	A	A	A	B	AB
5	A	A	A	A	B	A
6	A	A	A	A	A	A

pairs. Figure 4.3 shows how well or poorly they are succeeding at it. The background bars represent the scores of their peers, age-mates born in the region; all score perfectly (100 percent) in distinguishing the two sets of words, as expected. The foreground bars represent the scores of the Canadians, from the youngest, nine, on the left to the oldest, 17, on the right. The bars drop off sharply after the two youngest: the four older subjects have made minimal progress or none at all. Age is clearly a determining factor.

Further evidence of the vagaries of age in figure 4.3 comes from the observation that two of the Canadian subjects are the same age, 13, but are obviously acquiring the vowel merger at very different schedules. One of them, shown as 13X, has made considerable progress, but the other one, 13Y, has barely begun the unmerging. This kind of discrepancy between age-mates is also characteristic in dialect acquisition beyond the critical age, a factor that is discussed after the next example.

4.3.1.2 British twins in Australia Trudgill (1986: 28–31) reports the case of twins, Debbie and Richard, who moved from the south of England to Australia at the age of seven. Their speech was recorded monthly for the first six months, using word lists. The results for three of the 15 segmental phonemes analyzed by Trudgill are shown in table 4.2. The rates at which they change their British (B) pronunciations to Australian (A) are strikingly different: for /ou/, the vowel in words like "low", Debbie makes the change in the third month but Richard is in a sense both earlier, using variants (AB) from the beginning, and later, retaining some British variants into the third month. For /ei/, the vowel in words like "face", the general pattern for each youngster is similar to their pattern for /ou/ but slightly delayed; and for /iː/, the vowel in "see", there is evidence of resistance not only in Debbie's slow response but in Richard's muddled one.

Although Debbie and Richard appear to be similar to the Canadians in the previous example, a closer inspection shows that they are really very different. The most important difference is that Debbie and Richard both end up at the same place in their acquisitional progress, with Australian reflexes across the row in the bottom line of the table. In a six-month span, they appear to be well on their way to acquiring their new accents. This is clearly not so for the Canadians in figure 4.3, and it becomes even clearer when you know that at the time of their interviews the Canadians had all been in their new homes almost two or three years, much longer than the twins.

The Canadian youngsters at the right end of the figure, the older ones, will never sound as if they belong in their new dialect area. The reason for that is their age. They have crossed an invisible but very real threshold that has been documented in several studies in addition to these (see Chambers 1992: 687–93, Trudgill 1986: 31–8, Payne 1980: 155–6). Children seven or under will almost certainly acquire a new dialect perfectly, as Debbie and Richard appear to be doing and also as the youngest Canadian, nine at the time of his interview but seven when he arrived in England, appears to be doing. People over the age of 14 almost certainly will not, and the oldest Canadians appear to be heading for lifetimes with non-native accents. In between the ages of seven and 14, people differ in their ability to acquire accents, apparently unpredictably. The Canadian case provides an example of that as well, in the huge discrepancy between the two 13-year-olds. Although both had been in the new region more than two years, one of them had made much greater progress than the other.

4.3.2 Generational differences in bilingual situations

One of the common observations about bilingual situations where one language has more uses and greater prestige than another is the sharp attrition of the second language (see Preston 1989: 38–52). Immigrant languages of all kinds face extinction as early as the second or third generation unless extraordinary initiatives are taken in the communities where their preservation is deemed culturally important. Even societies where bilingualism is well established as in border regions or diglossic communities (as described in §3.5.3) can suddenly be struck by an attitude shift exactly equivalent to the attitude shift in the offspring of immigrants, as in the striking example that follows.

4.3.2.1 Language shift in Oberwart, Austria Gal (1979) documented the sociolinguistic basis of second-language attrition in Oberwart, Austria. In this border region, two languages, German and Hungarian, coexisted for centuries, but in the last two decades the balance has been threatened by a

Table 4.3 Choice of German (G) or Hungarian (H) by women of various ages in Oberwart, Austria, when speaking to God, grandparents (gran), parents (dad), age-mates (peer), brothers and sisters (sibs), salespeople (clrks), husband (hus), children (kids), government officials (govt), and doctors (docs) (selected data from Gal 1979: 121).

Women's ages	Interlocutors									
	God	gran	dad	peer	sibs	clrks	hus	kids	govt	docs
14	H	GH	G	G	G	G			G	G
15	H	GH	G	G	G	G			G	G
25	H	GH	GH	G	G	G	G	G	G	G
27	H	H	GH	G	G	G			G	G
39	H	H	H	GH	GH	G	G	G	G	G
40	H	H	H	GH		GH	G	G	G	G
50	H	H	H	H	GH	GH	GH	G	G	G
52	H	H	GH	H		H	GH	G	G	G
60	H	H	H	H	H	H	GH	GH	G	H
61	H	H	H	H	H	H	H	GH	H	G
66	H	H	H	H	H	H	H	H	H	G
71	H	H	H	H	H	H	H	H	H	H

massive shift to the use of German cutting across factors such as the ethnic background of speakers, rural or urban orientation, and family traditions – the factors that formerly determined when a person would likely use one or the other language. Now certain elements of society use German most or all of the time, and those elements are overwhelmingly young people, especially young women.

Gal (1978) observes that young women with rural backgrounds who would certainly have used Hungarian as their primary language a generation or two ago now seek German-speaking mates and avoid Hungarian-speaking ones. Their behavior is one symptom of the deep-seated feeling in Oberwart that Hungarian is the language of hicks and bumpkins. It is a symptom that resounds throughout the district because it, in turn, forces Hungarian-speaking men to seek their mates in neighboring towns, which are German-speaking. So the Hungarian-speaking women take German-speaking mates and eschew their Hungarian-speaking peers, thereby forcing the Hungarian-speaking men to court women from nearby towns, who, as it happens, are usually German-speaking. The long-term linguistic repercussions are the same in both cases: the offspring will speak German as their dominant language, and perhaps their only one.

The massive shift in Oberwart language use is documented in table 4.3, which shows how women of different ages choose German (G) or Hungarian (H) in various social situations. Several domains of language use are indicated by the columns, ranging from familial on the left (grandparents, parents, friends and siblings) to official on the right (clerks, bureaucrats and professionals). The categories that seemingly interrupt the gradation are instructive. Husbands are listed to the right of center, away from the familial side, because of the propensity, described above, for Oberwarter women to marry German-speaking men. Children are also on the right, even further, although under normal circumstances one might expect adults to address them familiarly; in Oberwart, the age-sensitive language shift apparently causes people 60 and under to assume that children they are not acquainted with will speak German.

The most obvious observation about table 4.3 is that the women's responses form a scalogram with only a few discrepancies (plus a few more in the complete data set in Gal 1979: 121). The shaded cells mark the interactions in which the subjects vary their language use, and they move rightward as the subjects get older. To the left of those cells they use Hungarian, and to the right they use German, with few exceptions. For any individual, the first interlocutor group to whom she uses German marks the starting-point on the continuum for her use of German to other groups. The youngest women use it almost everywhere, and the oldest women use it almost nowhere, but in between these extremes is a highly variable, but systematic, pattern of language shift.

The pattern, assuming it is sustained as the women grow older, will clearly result in the sharp diminution of Hungarian in Oberwart within the next generation, and could result in increased marginalization and perhaps complete loss in another generation.

4.3.2.2 Loan words in Spanish Harlem The pattern of generational attrition does not occur in stable bilingual situations, by definition. In these conditions, two languages coexist not necessarily as equals but as complementary, each with its own functions, or as contextual equivalents. But stable bilingualism is a relative term, as the example of Oberwart proves. Language changes constantly, as we know, and so do the social circumstances it serves.

Sociolinguistic methods provide a more discerning tool for locating distinctions than has hitherto been available, and in at least one instance appears to have uncovered an incursion by the predominant language, or at least an incipient one, that does not threaten the stability of the bilingual situation, at least not imminently.

East Harlem in New York City became a significant Puerto Rican community in the United States in the early 1940s. The Harlem community has maintained stable bilingualism for three generations, partly because it is

Table 4.4 Indices for English loan words in Harlem Spanish (selected data from Poplack and Sankoff 1984: table 3, p. 126)

	Children	Adults
Proportion English	62.6	51.2
English only	56.4	44.4
English first	64.2	52.6
Nativization	107.2	115.6

highly segregated but also because the citizens maintain close ties with their ancestral home and because the influx of immigrants into the community is continuous (Poplack and Sankoff 1984: 105–6).

The stability of the two languages is especially noteworthy because the Spanish speakers are inundated by English in the media, the schools, government services, and indeed all but their most local contacts. Nevertheless, Poplack demonstrated the grammatical autonomy of the Harlem Spanish vernacular from English incursions in several studies (for example, 1981, 1983). Even though code-switching (Poplack 1980) and lexical borrowings are common, they apparently do not undermine the integrity of the vernacular or threaten its continued vitality.

The nativization of loan words is an important means by which the vernacular speakers acknowledge the presence of the dominant language but keep the vernacular structure intact. Poplack and Sankoff (1984: 100), in a study of loan words in Harlem Spanish, set out to discover "the mechanisms by which an item is gradually converted from a foreign element to a nativized one."

Poplack elicited lexical responses for 45 common objects by showing pictures individually to eight parents and 14 children and asking them (in Spanish) to name them: *Qué es esto?* The objects included things like a *baseball bat, jeans, hamburger, lipstick, pig, sweater, tape,* and *zipper.* In naming the objects, the subjects used either Spanish or English lexical roots, and if they used English roots they sometimes nativized them with Spanish phonological adjustments or Spanish inflectional morphology. Poplack recorded the responses and then indexed them according to the root (Spanish or English) and its integration (degree of nativization).

For our purposes, the important indices are the ones listed in the left column of table 4.4: "Proportion English" is the percentage of English roots in the set of elicited roots; "English only" is the proportion for which only English roots were offered; "English first" is the proportion of the mixed responses in which the English root was offered first, as presumably the most salient; and "Nativization" indicates the group mean for the degree to which the English root was adapted to the vernacular.

By the first three measures, the children outscore their parents. This should not be particularly surprising since the children are at one further remove from their Puerto Rican cultural roots than their parents. Perhaps as a corollary, the children are much more immersed in American culture, their native culture. In any case, the difference between the parents and children is consistent. The children volunteered about 11 percent more English roots, diluted them with about 12 percent fewer Spanish variants for the names, and offered the English root first about 12 percent more frequently when they did give variants. Although it is impossible to know how these differences on a naming task might transfer into normal language use, it seems reasonable to assume that they would amount to a perceptible difference between the generations.

The fourth row in table 4.4 quantifies the average degree of nativization of those roots. By this measure, the parents outscore the children. The difference is very slight, but it perhaps also amounts to a perceptible difference because the quantification is made on fewer items for the parents than for the children. So the first three rows show that the children use proportionately more English roots in their Spanish and the fourth row shows that they nativize them proportionately less.

These differences are not, apparently, socially significant in the generations being studied. Poplack and Sankoff (1984: 130) state that their results, including the sub-set cited here, prove that "the younger speakers are not agents of importation of foreign phonological and morphological patterns into the recipient language in the context of a stable bilingual community." If they are not, then the incremental changes from parents to children are not great enough to register as "foreign". But if the situation were perfectly stable, we should expect that the measures should not only be almost the same for both generations (and they are) but also that the slight differences that show up should not reveal uniform trends (but they do). That is, the slight differences between generations all lead to the same conclusion – that the younger people's speech is more anglicized than their parents' speech.

At the moment of the study these tendencies were apparently not socially significant. For that reason, the researchers ignored the fact that the tendencies in the data suggested a developing trend. That trend, subtle though it is, appears ominous because it shows younger people adopting aspects of the dominant language. Perhaps the insignificant differences in Spanish Harlem are comparable to differences that might have been detected in Oberwart a few generations ago, before they accelerated into breakdown.

4.3.3   Parents versus peers

All these examples make the same essential point. Sociolinguistically, people of the same age, class and sex have more influence on how people sound and how they use language than do older people. The six Canadian young-sters in England and the British twins in Australia (§4.3.1) do their best to sound like their new friends and acquaintances. Although their success will be limited by the age at which they arrive in the new situation, whatever success they have will distinguish them linguistically from their parents. In Oberwart, young people's attitudes toward German and Hungarian are so widespread that they are altering the stable bilingual situation that existed for several generations (§4.3.2.1). And in Spanish Harlem, though there is not yet any noticeable change in attitude between the generations, there are consistent differences in their bilingual behavior that might presage an attitude change (§4.3.2.2).

Thus the generations are sometimes pitted against one another linguisti-cally. So they sometimes are in non-linguistic matters as well, marked by what sociologists have sometimes called a "generation gap" (McCormack 1985). In normal situations, of course, the generations do not differ from one another in attitudes, etiquettes and language so much as to create a gap across the generations.

I have used extreme situations to document the discrepancy between friends and family. This makes a useful expository device, because extreme situations often provide dramatic results against which the normal situation, with its more subtle or perhaps just more blasé results, can be understood. But in fact I used extreme situations in this section mainly because there are as far as I know no studies of normal situations.

In the normal situation, children probably carry some markers of their elders' speech in their earliest years, especially in situations in which their most intense and only sustained social contacts are with those elders. The earliest exposure to a peer group – presumably exposure that is sustained and brings a measure of independence to the child – should then bring with it as a concomitant of other social adjustments the replacement of linguistic features wherever they differ from those of the peer community.

My impression is that this adjustment takes place naturally and very rapidly at the age of four or five, when most children in industrialized nations are first enrolled in classes or some other kind of organized educa-tional setting. One obvious kind of linguistic replacement at this stage is lexical, where children who have been encouraged at home to use nursery terms for excretory and other matters – euphemisms of one sort – soon learn to use the communal terms – usually euphemisms of another sort.

There is almost certainly much more going on at this important sociolin-guistic juncture. It may also be that our research methods are now adequate for discovering them, however subtle they may turn out to be.

In any case, at this first formative period of language development the important influences are families and friends. Where those two influences are at odds with one another, as is obvious in extreme cases and presumably present, though very subtle, in ordinary cases, then there is inevitably tension.

The learners normally resolve the tension in favor of their peers. This situation is so commonplace that any such situation resolved in favor of the parents rather than the peers would certainly be marked as socially aberrant and perhaps abnormal. In any case, the earliest stage in the acquisition of a sociolect – and, indeed, in the acquisition of language – takes place in a social milieu clearly divided between two generations, parents and peers, in a usually amicable arrangement.

The next important sociolinguistic juncture, adolescence, sees the balance of power tip decisively away from the elders into forceful, sometimes autocratic pressure from peers.

4.4 Declarations of Adolescence

Essentially, adolescence is the transition to individuation. In prototypical circumstances – now hardly typical – young people must extricate themselves from the family nucleus, where everything from the food they eat to the place they live is decided for them, and relocate themselves in circumstances in which they make those decisions not only for themselves but potentially for dependents of their own.

For most animals, the transition from childhood to adulthood passes rapidly and almost imperceptibly. So it was until recently for human beings. But in modern industrialized societies the transition is relatively long, occupying all the teenage years and, more vaguely, as many as two or three years on either side. Indeed, prolonged adolescence is one of the most significant – though probably unintentional – effects of social reform in the last century. Labor laws prohibiting children in the work force, compulsory education to the age of 16, the raising of the age of majority from 18 to 19, 20 or even 21 for purposes of voting, drinking alcoholic beverages, getting married without parental permission, driving a car, or serving in the military – these and many other laws have the effect of cocooning adolescence, extending the chrysalid state by insulating it against adult anxieties and premature responsibilities.

The transition from childhood to adulthood is cataclysmic, especially when embedded in societies with complex urbanization and high mobility, and that presumably accounts for the fact that our societies permit younger people to take longer and longer to accomplish it.

4.4.1 *An adolescent majority*

One of the seminal sociocultural events of this century took place in the 1960s, when for the first time in human history the generation of adolescents formed a plurality in nearly all the industrialized nations. In 1960, at his Inauguration as President of the United States, John F. Kennedy (1917–63) declared

> that the torch has been passed to a new generation . . . , born in this century, tempered by war, disciplined by a hard and bitter peace, proud of our ancient heritage, and unwilling to permit the slow undoing of those human rights to which this nation has always been committed, and to which we are committed today at home and around the world.

The "new generation" Kennedy meant was of course his own, the people in their forties, but in fact the one that made the most impact during his presidency (1960–3) and immediately afterwards was not the generation "tempered by war" but the one conceived during and immediately after it.

This was the generation of the "baby boomers", born in the 1940s and early 1950s. Under the force of their numbers, education became the fastest-growing service industry in the world. But other industries flourished as well. The baby boomers formed a significant leisure class, shorn of responsibilities but affluent in the relative peace and unbroken plenty of the post-war decades. They were free spenders and, notwithstanding President Kennedy's idealism, many people of *his* generation dedicated their lives to supplying them with concerts, movies, magazines, books and records.

Popular culture and teenage fashions, based originally on American models, became global. Adolescent entertainment became a multi-billion-dollar international industry and it remains so long after the baby boomers grew old, to the point where opera, symphony, jazz, ballet, drama and other forms of mature art struggle for existence almost everywhere in societies in which tastes were formed – and often arrested – in adolescence.

The adolescent years of the demographic bubble brought into high relief the character of those transitional years, full of tensions, resolutions, inanities and epiphanies. Presumably it has always been thus since the beginning of time, but never before was it so visible.

4.4.2   Outer markings including slang

The transition from childhood to adulthood is often, almost characteristically, accompanied by extremism. Extrication from the family circle is often enacted as a rebellion against suffocating authority, and independence is sometimes enacted as an embracing of radical creeds. With adolescence as a starting-point, it is perhaps not surprising that attitudes tend to become more conservative as people grow older (as discussed in §4.1.1). The extremism of adolescence may render retrenchment as the most reasonable direction of change.

Rebellion can be expressed superficially in distinctive outer markings such as green-dyed hair, nose-rings and purposely torn jeans. It is also marked in a linguistically superficial way, by the use of a distinctive vocabulary called slang, in which terms become fashionable and serve as markers of in-group membership, and then quickly become outmoded in order to mark their users as outsiders.[5]

In order to serve their social purpose, these outer markings must fulfil two requirements. First, they must be deemed frivolous and/or extravagant by elders. They must be, in teenage terms, "far-out" or "way-out", "awesome", "crazy", "fabulous", the "most", the "max" (< maximum). If the markers gain general popularity, as did shoulder-length hair and pony tails for men in the 1960s, it is then incumbent upon adolescents to change their style, by, say, shaving their heads. People in authority are automatically regarded with suspicion, and teenage slang always includes derisory terms for them, such as "pigs" (police), "peeps" (parents; Munro 1989) and "mindfuckers" (manipulators). In the adolescent world-view, all adults are likely to be "anal", "uptight" and "beige".

Second, it is essential that these outer markings be approved and shared by other adolescents. Distinctive markings that are not approved lead readily to ostracism, and teenage slang provides numerous terms for peers who do not conform, such as "dweeb", "dork", "nerd", "geek", "lame" (as in §2.9.3), "jerk", "nimrod", "square", "quad" (< quadrangle, i.e., square), and "woos" ([wʊs]).

Because many adolescents have few responsibilities, they are often preoccupied with a few narrow concerns. School is one of them, and many adolescents spend inordinate energy appearing casual about their schoolwork while working hard enough to succeed at it. Classmates who are notably cooperative in school are known as "suck-holes", "brown nosers" or "browners" and "swots", and those who are notably gifted are "brainiacs", "cram artists" and "left-brainers". Intoxicants are another preoccupation, either because they belong to the recently forbidden pleasures of adults, as in the case of alcoholic beverages, or because they belong to the legally forbidden pleasures of drugs. Teenage slang predictably includes numerous expressions for intoxication – being "baked", "blasted", "blitzed", "fried", "gapped out", "juiced", "stoned" or "zoned", whether from "quaffing suds" (beer-drinking), "toking" (smoking marijuana) or "dropping acid" and "neils". Popular music is another preoccupation, driven by fads in which "grunge" and "hip hop" replace "heavy metal" and "rap" as the favored styles, leaving behind the succession of "disco", "acid rock", "rockabilly", "Motown", and numerous others. One of the social functions of teenage music is to envelop listeners in sound and shut out the hostile adult world, as seen most obviously in "thumpers", cars with sound systems turned up so loud that the bass reverberates through the traffic noise, and in "headbangers", portable sound systems with headphones that cannot quite contain the volume being pumped into the listener's ears.

The main feature of teenage style in all these matters, including teenage slang, is evanescence. Keeping up with the fashions is more important than the fashions themselves, and people who fall behind are "fashion risks", "fly-girls" and "hippies" (the term for fashionable people in the 1960s now the generic term for fashion laggards). People who try to keep up but fall short are "posers", "wannabees" (< "want to be") and "tods".

Adolescent networks, unlike the more stable networks discussed earlier (in §2.6), require active, ongoing involvement. The measure of membership is being up-to-date. Adolescent networks belong to the rites of passage, and the constant turnover of arriving 13-year-olds and departing 21-year-olds gives the networks a turbulent, hyper-active instability in their surface characteristics even though they are, at a deeper level, entirely familiar and predictable from one generation to the next.

4.4.3 Adolescent networks and linguistic variation

Since adolescence requires a purposeful divergence from adult norms in favor of alternative norms instituted and reinforced by age-mates, we should expect that dialect and accent – as the most telling social markers – will come into play. The slang lexicon in the preceding section obviously involves language but at a superficial level – exactly as superficial, in fact, as spiked hair or purple mascara.

Linguistic markers go much deeper. In adolescence, young people are exposed to a greater inventory of linguistic variants because they are exposed to a wider circle of acquaintances. Where the locus of activity was formerly the neighborhood, centered on local primary schools and recreational grounds, it suddenly expands in secondary schools and colleges that amalgamate students from several primary schools. The closest relationships with childhood friends usually grow cooler as relationships develop with new groups. In the later teen years, mobility increases greatly with the use of cars, and without the fetters of adult supervision. Conformity to peer group norms and distinction from adult norms leads to the adoption of regional linguistic variables beyond the neighborhood and sometimes a preference for variants not favored by adults.

4.4.3.1 Jocks and Burnouts in Detroit   In a seminal study of adolescent culture in the United States, Eckert (1989) participated in the daily affairs of students in a suburban Detroit high school. The social structure, according to Eckert, is based on a bifurcation into two polar groups. The Jocks, as they are known in her school, center their lives around the school and its activities, while the Burnouts reject the centrality of the school and seek their pleasures outside it. In other schools the former are sometimes known as collegiates, soshes [sófəz] (< socialites), preppies, or sloanes. The latter are sometimes called hoods, greasers, freaks, or spacers.

Though the Jocks and Burnouts get their names from sports and drugs, respectively, membership in either group does not absolutely require athleticism or narcotics. Sports are only one of the school activities that Jocks might participate in, along with school politics, social events, journalism and yearbook. Burnouts are associated with drugs as symbols of alienation, and that association is also made by driving old cars or pick-up trucks, playing ear-shattering music, and wearing nose-rings or tattoos.

The association with sports and drugs is so tentative, Eckert (1988: 189) says, that to make it explicit one has to refer to a "jock Jock" or a "burned-out Burnout."

Most high school students regard themselves as neither Jocks nor Burnouts but as "In-betweens," belonging to neither pole. They can readily name prototypical members of both groups, and they readily characterize themselves as members of one group or the other to a certain degree.

The distinction is largely class-based with the Jocks as MC and the Burnouts as WC. The "peer-based social structure . . . will eventually emerge as an adult class system," Eckert (1988: 188) says. Students who dominate school activities tend to come from the higher social strata in the community and those from the lower strata tend to dissociate themselves from it. A few move obliquely away from the class they were raised in, as upwardly mobile Jocks or downwardly mobile Burnouts.

The Jocks progress through high school by assuming greater responsibility in its affairs from year to year. The Burnouts often work part-time after school and mix with slightly older people, taking earlier interests in adult recreations such as smoking, drinking, dating and sex. The Jocks move on to universities where they build new networks and again, as in the transition to high school, leave behind most of their old networks. The Burnouts move into the work force full time, taking their places alongside adults.

These social differences have linguistic implications. One of the variables Eckert analyses is (uh), the rounding and raising of standard /ʌ/ in words like *mother, butter, lumber,* and *supper.* In Detroit and other northern American cities such as Buffalo, Cleveland and Chicago, this vowel sometimes occurs as [ɔ] or [ʊ] as well as [ʌ]. The higher vowels are heard more frequently in the urban centres than in the suburbs, and, in turn, more frequently in the suburbs than in towns further removed from the big cities.

Figure 4.4 shows a correlation between the height of the vowel and the social categories in the suburban Detroit high school. Eckert (1988: 200) analyzed tape recordings of interviews with those students who identified themselves explicitly as Jocks, Burnouts or In-betweens. For the (uh) variants,

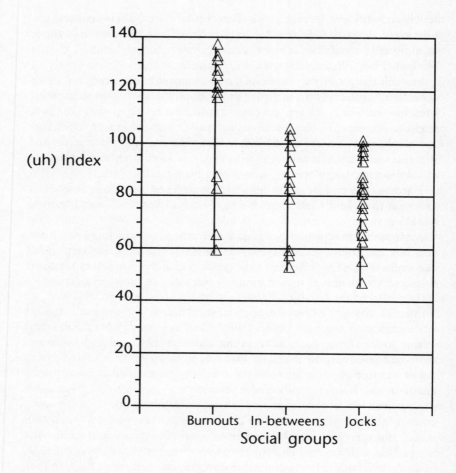

Figure 4.4 Indices for (uh) by Detroit high school students in three social catego-ries (after Eckert 1988: figure 2, 200)

the index scores on the ordinate in figure 4.4 can be interpreted roughly by thinking of zero as consistent use standard [ʌ], 100 as consistent use of [ɔ], and 200 as consistent use of [ʊ]. These are only rough indicators because, perhaps obviously, an individual can attain an intermediate score by using all three variants in some proportion. Consistent use of any one variant would be very unusual. In any case, people who score under 100 must use [ʌ] sometimes and people who score above 100 must use [ʊ] sometimes.

Although there is considerable overlap in the linguistic behavior of the social groups, their tendencies are distinct. The Burnouts cluster nearer the high end and are therefore more innovative. The Jocks cluster nearer the low end and are therefore more conservative. The In-betweens are, uh, in between: although their range is similar to the Jocks, their lowest score is not quite as low and their highest score is slightly higher.

Eckert (1988: 206) explains these differences in the social groups in terms of their allegiances to the region. The Burnouts, she says, seek a "direct connection" to the urban center of the region and adopt the variants associated with it. The Jocks are less committed to the region as many of them anticipate leaving it in the immediate future for post-secondary education. As a result, they are less motivated to adopt the regional markers. These differences are similar to those that showed up more dramatically among the adolescents on Martha's Vineyard (discussed in §2.7.1). For the Vineyarders, the differences in allegiance were extreme. Those intending to stay on the island were quite consciously choosing an insular life with limited opportunities, and those intending to leave for further education were aware that they would probably never return as permanent residents once they had been trained beyond the needs of the local economy. The situation in the Detroit suburb is a dim reflection of the distinction between adolescent social groups on Martha's Vineyard, but it is perhaps more nearly typical of the social difference.

Although the linguistic difference exists between the groups, what is more significant for our purposes is the general similarity. The adolescents, whether Jocks, Burnouts or In-betweens, all adopt the urban variants to an extent that goes beyond their parents' use of them. In that regard, they present a unified front in their social setting: their speech differs from their parents in the frequency of certain variants, and is similar to their age-mates, whatever the peer network of the individual.

4.4.3.2 Burnouts and Rednecks in Farmer City

A pattern very similar to the one Eckert discovered showed up under different social circumstances in a study by Habick (1991) in Farmer City, Illinois, a town of 2,200 in the farmlands of central Illinois. The community is largely MC, comprised of farmers and small businessmen, but Habick's sample of 20 high school students showed the same polarization as Eckert's densely populated, comparatively heterogeneous suburbanites. In Farmer City, the polar groups were known as Burnouts and Rednecks.

The Burnouts, as in Detroit, are young people with a distaste for school and a taste for alcohol, mild drugs, and loud music. The Farmer City Jocks are called Rednecks by the Burnouts, a hyperbolic use of the term that usually refers to conservative, prejudiced WC white men in the American South – originally a metonym based on their sunburnt necks. In Farmer City, the term is used more generally. As one of the Burnouts told Habick (1991: 187): "A Redneck is a person, like in this age group, who goes to all the school things, goes out for all the sports, gets good grades, or else brownnoses good enough that they get good grades, and they talk to the teachers all the time, and just general brownnose, and they don't, they won't associate with people like me."

Besides these two groups, there are a few WC or lower-class students known as "scruffies," but they are outsiders (in the sense of §2.9.3 above), belonging to neither social group.

The key linguistic feature in Habick's study is /uw/-fronting, in which the vowel in such words as *chew, hoot, food, shoot* and *glue*, standard [uʊ], occurs with a fronted onset [ʉ] or unrounded [ɨ], and in more extreme cases has a fronted glide as well, [ʉ⁴]. This is an established feature in southern American speech, but Habick's discovery of it in Midland America is not especially surprising because of a long, continuous history of immigration there from the more southerly state of Kentucky.

People of all ages in Farmer City use the fronted onsets some of the time (1991: 205). Nevertheless, the feature is neatly stratified. Parents and grand-parents have the fronted onset about half the time, though the fronting of the off-glide is very infrequent in their speech. Rednecks have the fronted onset most of the time but, like the older people, seldom have the fronted off-glide with it. Burnouts are more advanced: they typically have the fronted onset and occasionally also have the fronted off-glide. Moreover, the regular fronting of /uw/ in their speech exerts a pull-chain effect so that other vowels are also beginning to have wider targets in the vowel space. So, for the Burnouts, the vowels /ʊ/, /ʌ/ and /ow/ occur as fronted variants relatively frequently, but the fronted variants occur infrequently, if at all, in the speech of the Rednecks and older people. The acceleration of /uw/-fronting by the Burnouts is itself a less significant marker of their speech than the overall differences caused by the pull-chain.

As with the suburban Jocks and Burnouts, what is important for our main purpose here is the observation that members of both adolescent networks, however antithetical they may appear, have distinctive markers of the same kind in their speech as compared to the speech of the older people in the community. Their cohesion in this regard is not coincidental. Above and beyond their social differences is their overriding similarity. All of the adolescents are seeking an identity that will mark their separateness from the elders, their former guardians, and so all of them accelerate the use of certain linguistic variants. Linguistic variants already in use in the region are the available markers. At the same time the adolescents need the bonds of peer groups, as compensation for the security of the parental households they are disengaging themselves from. The close-knit peer networks, like the networks discussed in §2.6, powerfully enforce group norms, including the use of linguistic markers.

These are powerful social forces in adolescence – separation from elders and solidarity with peers. Sociolinguistically, they combine to make adoles-cence the focal point for linguistic innovation and change.

4.5   Young Adults in the Talk Market

Adolescence gives way by degrees to adulthood. Under normal circumstances, the early adult years are a period of relative stability after the
vagaries of the teen years. If autonomy has truly been won, then this is a
time to establish the forms it will take, its realizations. The traditional
touchstones are career, marriage, and family. These and the other roles that
young adults take on have in common the assumption of broader responsibilities. Instead of passing examinations in order to get parental permission
for the use of the family car, there are professional certifications and trade
apprenticeships in order to make payments on one's own family car. There
are job applications and probationary periods, learning to follow orders and
learning to give them.

Where adolescents primarily look after themselves, young adults must
assume a share in looking after others. The stakes are high and get higher.
In shucking off their dependency, they not only become independent but
usually add dependents of their own.

Young adults also establish a set of personal preferences in many areas
such as dress, recreations, living conditions, politics, and work ethic. They
may modify these somewhat as they grow older but they usually do not
reverse them or alter them radically. The nuances are almost boundless,
encompassing such things as mahogany furniture or teak, brogues or loaf-
ers, heels or flats, bowling or bridge, tennis club or Rotary, flat or house,
films or television, midtown or suburbs, activist politics or guarded secrecy,
early or late to work, and late or early back home.

The preferences may take some years to crystallize and when they do
they are likely to fall within broad limits appropriate to the individual's
class, education, occupation, and other social factors, but even small variations in numerous attitudes and activities amount to a gestalt different, at
least slightly, from everyone else.

Among the personal preferences is dialect. Some young adults appear to
set their sociolinguistic range according to their ambitions. It is likely to be
completely subconscious, and it will most likely take the form of retrenchment following the adolescent years.

4.5.1   The marché linguistique in Montreal

Systematic studies of the sociolinguistic adjustments in young adulthood
have been carried out on Montreal francophones in an influential survey
(Sankoff and Sankoff 1973) that resulted in several innovations. The studies
took their impetus from the sociological concept of the *marché linguistique*

(Bourdieu and Boltanski 1975), usually translated (not very aptly) as the linguistic market or marketplace. A non-literal but more appropriate translation might be "marketplace dialect".

The concept of the *marché linguistique* begins with the common-sense observation that some people have a greater stake in speaking the "legitimized" dialect, that is, in using standard or prestigious variants, than others. These people are not always identified reliably by their social class or other major social attributes. In fact, it is intuitively clear that market pressures toward standardizing one's speech should cut across class categories and the like. For instance, laborers in a maintenance crew in a factory have less economic motive for standardizing their speech than do laborers who make their livings by servicing private homes, because the latter, unlike the former, must deal daily with the people who hire them. Similarly, there are "professionals of language" such as writers, teachers and lawyers, whose work involves speaking to a much greater degree than other professionals such as engineers, chemists or surgeons, and there are "technicians of language" such as secretaries, announcers and actors whose occupations require linguistic intercourse, unlike laboratory technicians, mechanics and computer programmers (Sankoff et al. 1989).

Market pressures toward standardization differ considerably in different social contexts. Typical examples are the urbanized professions and technicians mentioned above, but King (1992) discovered a more homely case in an Acadian enclave in the isolated Canadian province of Prince Edward Island. King's subjects were Acadian French speakers working to preserve their language in an anglophone district. She found that the individual differences in the subjects' use of Acadian vernacular variables did not correlate with sex, age or class.

The two subjects with the most standard (or least regional) speech were a secretary and a janitor. The secretary's dialect is readily explained in terms of the linguistic marketplace, but King notes that the janitor's legitimized speech is also a response to market pressures in his community. Like the secretary, the janitor is employed in the French-language school, a prestige setting that provides year-round employment in a largely seasonal economy. The janitor is in constant contact with the teachers, who often come from larger French-speaking centers, and with the students, whose French heritage is promulgated as a source of pride. As King says, "The school is the locus of standard French in the region and all who work there, I think, must strive for what they regard as *le bon français*." In these circumstances, the janitor no less than the secretary is expected to provide a linguistic role model for the students.

In the Montreal survey, the major social variables of age, sex and class correlated with the subjects' vernacular use to some extent but often left a wider range of variability than the linguists felt comfortable with. Market pressures were adopted as another kind of categorization that might account for some of that range.

In order to classify the speakers according to market pressures on their speech, Sankoff and Laberge (1978) recruited eight professional and graduate student sociolinguists actively working in the Montreal francophone community to act as judges. They provided each of the judges with profiles of the 120 subjects in the survey and asked them to divide them into groups according to "the relative importance of the legitimized language in the socioeconomic life of the speaker" (1978: 241). The profiles included information about the occupations, with a description of duties, but left age and education unspecified or vague because those variables were going to be used separately. The judges were free to make as many groups as they chose.

The judges sorted the subjects into four to 12 groups. To convert the individual rankings into a composite ranking, Sankoff and Laberge (1978: 242–5) pegged each judge's lowest-ranked group at zero and the highest-ranked group at 1, with their other groups at equal intervals between. Statistical tests of the judges' rankings showed that, in spite of the divergence in number of groups, they were highly consistent for each subject. The linguistic market index for each subject, a number between 0–1, was the average of all eight judges' scores. The linguistic market index scores provided a ranking of subjects against which their use of linguistic variables could be compared.

The primary tests for the saliency of the linguistic marketplace as an independent variable were three grammatical variables. As we have noted several times (especially §2.3.4), grammatical variables typically stratify social groups more sharply than phonological variables. That holds for some grammatical variables in Montreal (for instance, *que*-deletion, §2.3.5), but there are also some grammatical variables there which appear, when correlated with social class, to be distributed gradually rather than sharply. The subjects' participation in the linguistic marketplace potentially provided an inter-class difference that might account for the gradation.

One of the three grammatical variables, auxiliary *avoir* and *être*, is discussed in detail in the following section. The other two are complementizers *ce que/qu'est-ce que* and indefinite *on/ils*.

The complementizer variable contrasts the standard form *ce que* with the vernacular form *qu'est-ce que* at the beginning of headless relative clauses, indirect questions and certain cleft constructions (Sankoff and Laberge 1978: 247). The indefinite pronoun variable contrasts the standard impersonal subject pronoun *on*, meaning (roughly) "some/any people", with the vernacular use of *ils*, literally "they" (Sankoff and Laberge 1978: 248).

When the use of these variables by the Montreal subjects was correlated with their linguistic marketplace indices, the tendency toward more standard use by individuals who used language integrally in their jobs became obvious, as the following section illustrates.

4.5.2 *Auxiliary* avoir *and* être

In standard French, a few verbs take *être* as the auxiliary in compound tenses but most take *avoir*. For instance, the verbs *partir* "to leave" and *arriver* "to arrive" are prescribed as taking *être*, in sentences such as:

> *Jean est parti ce matin.*   *Jean est arrivé ce matin.*
> John left this morning.   John arrived this morning.

The verb forms *est parti* and *est arrivé*, called *passé composé*, consist of the third person singular form of *être* with the past participle of *partir* and *arriver*. Most verbs, including *courir* "to run", take *avoir*, as in this sentence:

> *Jean a couru ce matin.*
> John ran this morning.

The verb form here, *a couru*, consists of the third person singular of *avoir* with the past participle of *courir*.

The distinction between the verbs that take these different auxiliaries is arbitrary and, consequently, French vernaculars often show variability in their use. In the Montreal sample, of the verbs that occurred in the *passé composé* frequently enough to make a valid sample, 16 varied in the selection of auxiliaries (Sankoff and Thibault 1980 [1977]: 312). For instance, *arriver* occurred in 9 percent of all instances (45/426) with *avoir*, and *partir* occurred 36 percent of the time (54/148) with *avoir* (1980 [1977]: 331).

When the use of *avoir* is correlated with social attributes of the subjects, the results are not very revealing. Sankoff and Thibault (1980 [1977]: 340) summarize their findings as follows:

> More highly educated people . . . tend to use less *avoir*. Men seem to use *avoir* more than women. Holding constant "years of schooling", we find a slight tendency for younger speakers to use more *avoir*, but this tendency doesn't seem strong enough to indicate a real change in progress, especially since young people are spending more and more years in school, an experience that encourages *less* use of *avoir*.

The most striking correlate proved to be the linguistic market indices. Table 4.5 shows the relationship by grouping the subjects according to the probability of their using *avoir* instead of standard *être*: **frequent** users of

Table 4.5 Percentage of speakers with similar linguistic marketplace indices who use *avoir* frequently, moderately or infrequently (Sankoff and Thibault 1980: table 15–4, p. 341). Shaded cells show the sub-groups that constitute the plurality in each category.

	Linguistic marketplace indices			
avoir	0–0.25	0.26–0.50	0.51–0.75	0.76–1.0
Frequent	51	22	17	6
Moderate	28	44	23	11
Infrequent	21	33	60	83

avoir have probabilities in the range 0.68–1.00, **moderate** users in the range 0.34–0.67, and **infrequent** users in the range 0.33–0. When these groups are subdivided according to their linguistic market indices (as shown in the column headings), the relationship is marked by a steady decline of the **frequent** users across the top row and a steady increase of the **infrequent** users across the bottom row. The significance of the correlation is also evident by noting which sub-group forms the largest constituency in each of the marketplace groups (shown in table 4.5 by the shaded cells). By any measure, the proportions offer impressive support for the hypothesis that market pressures can have a standardizing influence on an individual's speech.

4.5.3 Playing the talk market

So far, there have been no developmental studies documenting the stages in which some young adults adjust their adolescent accents to accommodate the pressures of the marketplace. Such a study would ideally involve tracking a large sample of adolescents from the time of their most peer-dominated years, around 15, through the increasing maturity of their late teens and early twenties, when occupational aspirations normally develop, and then into the mid-twenties or perhaps early thirties, as they settle into the work force and begin to realize their ambitions. The study would require observations of speech in "official" contexts (school and work) and in casual contexts (hang-outs and home) in order to contrast the use of variables. In the sub-set of subjects in whom the market pressures evoke a linguistic response, the reaction might be measurable either as an increase in the range of variable use or as a general increase in standard variants, depending upon whether the individuals restricted their accommodation to the workplace or extended it to all settings.

A study like that one poses numerous challenges. So many, in fact, that a decade or so ago it might have been unthinkable. Since then, methodological developments in sociolinguistics, particularly in handling large corpuses (as in Poplack 1989), make it feasible. When such a study is made, it should reveal numerous subtleties about the social use of language in these crucial, formative periods.

In the meantime, our best evidence for post-adolescent adjustments under marketplace pressures have come about accidentally, from studies that happen to use both age and occupation as independent variables, and, in so doing, distinguish the behavior of subjects in salient occupational groups. One example, involving Glasgow subjects, is discussed below (in §4.6.1.2). The one we will deal with here again draws on the Montreal survey.

Sankoff and several of his associates (1989) reviewed the performances of the Montreal subjects in different age groups with respect to ten different grammatical variables including the three discussed above. Each speaker's scores on all ten variables were then compared to each of the others to produce a measure of similarity. Because there are ten variables, the measures of similarity between subjects are actually ten-dimensional. Highly complex interrelationships like this are made comprehensible by descriptive statistical procedures called multivariate analysis, which give a composite picture of each subject's similarities to and differences from other subjects on multiple variables by showing their proximity or distance from one another. The graphic representation of this composite picture shows the individuals suspended in a multidimensional space in which the position of each one is determined by their covariation with each other one on each of the variables. If we had to construct a model of these relationships by hand, it would require almost endless tinkering with the relative positions of the individuals as each new similarity measurement was introduced. Fortunately, the modeling – known as multidimensional scaling – can be carried out by a computer in seconds.

Figure 4.5 shows the graphic representation of multidimensional scaling of two different age groups in the Montreal sample. The scaling reduces the ten dimensions to two for purely practical reasons. The relative positions of the individuals are thus pictured as two-dimensional. The important dimensions in the diagram are the relative proximity of the individuals to one another and their clustering in the quadrants. The relative proximity indicates how similar individuals are to one another, and the clustering in the quadrants indicates that the relative importance of each variable is similar.

Fortuitously, Sankoff et al. (1989) subdivided the Montreal subjects into age groups. One of their purposes was to compare attitudes expressed by the subjects and they found such large differences between the attitudes of the age groups that they were effectively incomparable. As a result, they

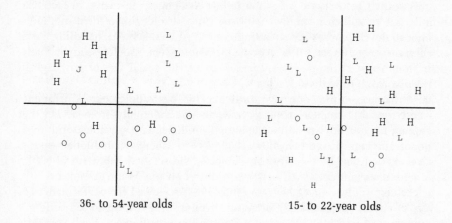

36- to 54-year olds   15- to 22-year olds

Figure 4.5 Multidimensional scaling of Montreal subjects in two age groups based on their use of ten grammatical variables, identified by their marketplace indices: H = high, L = low, and O = nil (Sankoff et al., 1989: figures 4a and 6a, 115, 117)

divided their subjects by age. This age subdivision suits our purposes here perfectly, although it is altogether accidental, because it makes it possible to compare adolescents and adults. In order to show that some people adjust their sociolects after adolescence as their socioeconomic circumstances become fixed, it is necessary to show that adolescents who pursue language-sensitive occupations as young adults tend to standardize their speech.

Figure 4.5 indicates the tendency toward standardization by implication only. Instead of comparing the speech of individuals when they are adolescents with their speech when they are adults, it shows a group of adolescents (the 15- to 22-year-olds on the right) and a group of adults (36- to 54-year-olds on the left) from the same place interviewed by the same fieldworkers at the same time. (In terms that will be discussed in detail in §4.6.2 below, this is an apparent-time comparison rather than a real-time comparison.)

The identification of individuals by their marketplace indices has been superimposed on the scaling diagram by Sankoff et al. (1989: 111); the input to the multivariate analysis includes linguistic information only and does not include marketplace indices or any other social information. The codings differ from the ones used in table 4.5 (above) by merging the top two categories so that "high" (marked H) includes index scores from 0.51 to 1.0, "low" (L) includes 0.11 to 0.5, and "nil" (O) includes 0-0.1. The adolescents earned their marketplace indices not for their own attributes, so to speak, but for their parents' attributes, since the adolescents were students at the time of their interviews and could not be evaluated by their own occupations. There will be some inevitable discrepancies in their scoring, because some adolescents whose parents do not work in language-centered positions will ultimately join the work force in occupations that are language-centered, and vice versa.

Notwithstanding these problems, figure 4.5 is fairly revealing. The essential difference between the age groups is that the older group is relatively orderly but the younger group is helter-skelter. Reading across the scaling diagram for the older group diagonally from top left to bottom right places the marketplace groups roughly in rank order. The subjects with high scores are mainly at the top left, and the second group, the low scorers, are mainly in a band diagonally near the intersection of the axes, with the nil group below them. The two high-index subjects who disrupt the pattern are the wife of a journalist, in the lower-right quadrant, and a police clerk, considerably separated from the others in the lower left quadrant. For the younger group, although the high-index subjects are mainly in the upper right, one or more of them is found in all the quadrants. The low-index and nil-index groups are generally mixed together.

These patterns suggest that the older subjects have resolved their responses to the marketplace linguistically, whereas the younger group have not yet done so. Hence the cohesion of the older pattern and the relative formlessness of the younger.

Admittedly, the sociolinguistic evidence for the linguistic retrenchment following adolescence is less well studied than is adolescent linguistic extremism. Two reasons for this are presumably the protracted time span in which the linguistic adjustments take place, and the subtlety of those adjustments, which appear to be realized as a broader range of variants generally and a preference for standard variants in certain situations. Neither of these factors lends itself readily to study by established methodologies, since the former requires a lengthy survey period and the latter requires a variety of observation sites. Nevertheless, such a study is of critical importance for increasing our understanding of the final formative period in sociolectal development.

4.5.4   *Linguistic stability in middle and old age*

For the stages of life beyond young adulthood, our best evidence indicates that once the features of the sociolect are established in the speech of young adults, under normal circumstances those features remain relatively stable for the rest of their lives. Even when linguistic changes take root in the speech of younger people in the same community, the older people usually remain impervious to it, or nearly so. That is perhaps a linguistic reflex of the conservatism that often accompanies aging, mentioned in §4.1.1, but it is also a function of the slowing of the language-learning capability beyond the critical period, as discussed in §2.9.1.

From middle age onwards, then, people's speech preserves markers, some subtle and some blatant, that indicate where they have been. For most people, these markers include tell-tale signs of the home dialect where they spent their childhood, the fossilized slang of a faded adolescence, and the fine adjustments of maturity. Having worked their way through these formative periods, people apparently reach a point where the range of styles and the inventory of socially significant variants are deemed sufficient, at least by their subconscious minds, for their purposes in the situations they find themselves in.

4.6 Changes in Progress

Variability in language often indicates instability. Occasionally it does not, but instead belongs to a pattern that repeats itself in a community in generation after generation. An example of stable variability was discussed at some length in §3.2, where the variable (ng) provided an example of a linguistic feature in which the parents' frequencies are maintained in the speech of their offspring.

Other variables appear to be stages in the movement from one linguistic state to another. Weinreich, Labov and Herzog (1968: 188), in their third postulate for a theory of language change, say, "Not all variability and heterogeneity in language structure involves change; but all change involves variability and heterogeneity."

Where change is involved, a certain variant will occur in the speech of children though it is absent in the speech of their parents, or, more typically, a variant in the parents' speech will occur in the speech of their children with greater frequency, and in the speech of their grandchildren with even greater frequency. In the community at large, successive generations will show incremental frequencies in the use of the innovative variant. The logical conclusion, as time goes by, will be the categorical use of that new variant and the elimination of older variants.

Historical linguistics abounds with evidence of such changes. Latin words with initial consonant clusters such as *scola* 'school' occur in some Romance languages with a prothetic vowel, as in Spanish *escuela*, Portuguese *escola*, and French *école*, so we know that the intermediary language developed constraints on syllable structure that eventually led to the modern forms. In English, Alexander Pope rhymed *eat*, *meat* and *great* with *state* in the eighteenth century but a little more than a century later Lord Tennyson rhymed *eat* and *meat* with *fleet*, not *state*, though *great*, spelled like *eat* and *meat*, still rhymed with *state*; evidently some of these vowels changed their phonetic values in the interim. In Quichean, a Mayan sub-group, one contemporary language has a rule palatalizing /k/ before uvulars, but in the earliest word-lists of that language only one word, the word for *horse*, has a palatalized /k/ (Campbell 1974); between those two stages, the palatalization evident in *horse* became a general process.

Until the advent of sociolinguistics, historians of language inferred that linguistic changes had taken place by comparing the data at two widely separated historical moments much as we have done in these examples. What happened in the interval between those historic moments was ignored, and considered outside of their purview. Bloomfield (1933: 347), in his influential synthesis of structural linguistics, said, "The process of linguistic change has never been directly observed; . . . such observation, with our present facilities, is inconceivable." It was probably not the facilities so much as the axiom of categoricity (§1.3) that made it inconceivable, for the observation of change in progress integrally involves variability, social correlates, stylistic contexts and quantification. In other words, the observation of change in progress required a variationist view of language.

Following Bloomfield, Hockett (1958: 444–5) offered this elaboration on the inconceivability of observing sound change:

> Only indirect methods could show us sound change in progress. Suppose that over a period of fifty years we made, each month, a thousand accurate acoustic records of clearly identifiable initial /t/s and /d/s, all from the members of a tight-knit community. At the end of the first five years we could compute and draw the curve representing the sixty thousand observations made up to that time: the resulting graph would be a reasonably accurate portrayal of this portion of the community's expectation distribution. After another year, the first year's observations would be dropped, the sixth year's added, and a new curve drawn. Each subsequent year the same operation would be performed. The resulting series of forty-six curves would show whatever drift had taken place.

Hockett has the air of presenting a *reductio ad absurdum* in this passage, but in a couple of respects he actually anticipated the methods that have developed for observing sound change in progress.

The essential method requires repeated observations within a speech community, as Hockett suggests. However, it would not be useful to make these observations about any random feature of the language, certainly not of a feature that appears to be highly stable, as initial /t/s and /d/s are in most English dialects. And the observations need not necessarily be made throughout the community if the locus of the change is restricted to a particular social group. Observations of a feature that may not be changing or of a population that may not be involved in change will not be be fruitful, and proliferating those observations by the thousands is genuinely absurd.

When pilot studies or informal observations indicate a change might be taking place, apprehending it does indeed require numerous observations of the feature believed to be changing in the social stratum where it appears to be taking place. If it is actually a sound change, the observations will fall out coherently, with identifiable innovators and conservatives in the social groups and perhaps with inhibiting and promoting factors in the linguistic context.

The observation will be quantitative, as Hockett surmises. Bloomfield, Hockett and their neogrammarian forebears restricted themselves to observations made at widely separated historical moments in order to compare one structural state with another. The states could then be described qualitatively – two phonemes in the earlier inventory had merged in the later inventory, the instrumental case in the earlier grammar had disappeared and a postposition marked that adjunct in the later grammar, and so on. Such descriptions maintain the axiom of categoricity.

Looking at the interval between the two structural states, of course, inevitably shows features in contention with one another as the new features gradually supplant the old. The situation is dynamic, not static, and the proportions of the variants in the speech of the community alter as time passes. At any moment in that passage of time, the proportions will differ among the innovating group and the conservative group. Describing these situations in qualitative terms would require ignoring the dynamism altogether, for at any moment the most that could be said is that the language admitted two (or more) options. How those options were distributed in the speech of the community, what they signified socially at any moment, how the minor option emerged as the major one – these and other questions require that variability not only be admitted but studied in its own right.

Besides elucidating the mechanisms of historical linguistics – bypassing, as Weinreich, Labov and Herzog (1968: 99) say, "the fruitless paradoxes with which historical linguistics has been struggling for over half a century" – the study of change in progress has proved a boundless source of sociolinguistic hypotheses. On the sociohistorical side, which has implications beyond the scope of this book, see, especially, Weinreich, Labov and Herzog 1968, Labov, Yaeger and Steiner 1972, Wang 1977, Trudgill 1986, Milroy 1992 and Labov 1994.

Numerous examples presented so far in this book are examples of change in progress, explicitly when the generational correlates are stated or, more often, implicitly when they are unstated in favor of class, network, sex, or some other correlates. In the rest of this section, I outline the main types of sociolinguistic changes and provide prototypes for them. The first, age-grading (§4.6.1), is relatively rare, and appears to be a change that is a

marker of a maturational stage. The second, generationally progressive change
(§§4.6.2–3), is constant and largely irreversible.

4.6.1   Age-grading

In a sense, sociolectal adjustments to the linguistic market (as in §4.5) are
age-graded, because they involve changes correlated with a particular time
of life and they are repeated in successive generations. They are not usually
thought of by sociolinguists as age-graded changes, however, perhaps because
they involve only a sub-set of young adults, the ones in occupations that are
somehow language-dependent, and, because they are so diffuse, taking in
several variables and involving fine tuning in the use of variants in particular circumstances.

Age-graded changes are usually thought of as changes in the use of a
variant that recur at a particular age in successive generations. They are,
then, regular and predictable changes that might be thought of as marking
a developmental stage in the individual's life.

Very few changes of this kind have been reported. The two that I will cite
here take place in adolescence. Thus the early variant might be thought of
as a marker of children's speech. Its elimination or reduction in the speech
of individuals normally takes place without conscious effort on their part,
and the linguistic effect of the change is minor, but it is no doubt one of the
dozens of miniscule changes that contributes to the perception of their
maturity in the view of parents, teachers, and other adults.

4.6.1.1   Zee and zed in Southern Ontario   The first example is probably
more interesting socially than linguistically. In southern Ontario, the
southernmost part of Canada and also the most populous, the proximity of
the United States on three sides makes the American presence a constant
factor, and one that Canadians feel compelled to resist in order to keep their
autonomy. Their resistance involves matters both large and small.

One of the small matters is the name of the last letter of the alphabet. "Z"
is called "zed" everywhere in the world, not only in English but also in
French, German, and most other languages, except in the United States,
where it is called "zee." Hence "zee" is an American shibboleth.

In southern Ontario, the pronunciation of "Z" as "zee" is stigmatized, as
might be expected. American immigrants to the region, numbering several
hundred annually, routinely report that their name for "Z" is one of the
first things they change after arriving there, because calling it "zee" unfail-
ingly draws comments from the people they are talking to.

Nevertheless, some children in southern Ontario learn the American
name and use it for several years. Lexical surveys in the region repeatedly

show a higher proportion of young people with "zee" than of older people. In a Toronto survey in 1979, two-thirds of the 12-year-olds completed their recitation of the alphabet with "zee" but only 8 percent of the adults did. In 1991, when those 12-year-olds were 25, another survey showed that 39 percent of 20 to 25-year-olds said "zee". Obviously, a large number of them had changed their pronunciation in the interval, but it is also obvious that even more of them would eventually change, because only 12.5 percent of the people over 30 in that same survey said "zee".

The pattern of declining use of "zee" as people grow older repeats itself in succeeding generations in southern Ontario. Its high frequency in the speech of young people does not persist, as it would if the standard name were changing from "zed" to "zee." Instead of marking a change in progress, the high frequency decreases as the generation grows older. It is therefore an example of an age-graded change.

With the use of "zee" stigmatized, it is perhaps strange that children should learn it at all. Their source is pre-school television shows beamed from the United States, notably one called *Sesame Street*, which was almost universally watched by children in the 1960s when it had no serious rivals – hence the extraordinarily high frequency of "zee" among those 12-year-olds in 1979. *Sesame Street* and its imitators promote the alphabet with zeal, almost as a fetish, thus ensuring that their young viewers hear it early and recite it often. The "zee" pronunciation is reinforced especially by the "Alphabet Song," a piece of doggerel set to music that ends with these lines:

> ell em en oh pee cue, ar ess tee,
> yoo vee double-yoo, eks wye zee.
> Now I know my ey bee sees,
> Next time, won't you sing with me?

The rhyme of "zee" with "tee" is ruined if it is pronounced "zed," a fact that seems so salient that many Ontario nursery school teachers retain it in the song even though they would never use it elsewhere.

Something like the power of rhyme must have been involved in propogating the American pronunciation in southern Ontario in earlier generations, because the zee/zed issue antedates television and even radio. The issue was raised as early as 1846, when a person named Harris complained about it in a letter to a newpaper editor, saying, that "the instructor of youth, who when engaged in teaching the elements of the English language, direct them [the students] to call that letter *ze*, instead of *zed*, are teaching them error" (Chambers 1993: 12).

Even today, newspaper stories regularly spread mild alarm in their southern Ontario readers with stories reporting the high frequency of "zee" among schoolchildren and inferring from that the spectre of American domination. It is a story that can be written over and over again, generation after generation, unless the newpaper readers come to understand the socio-linguistic difference between a change in progress and an age-graded change. Since that does not seem imminent, newspaper editors will no doubt keep on assigning the story to cub reporters any time they face a slow news day.

4.6.1.2 Glottal stops in Glasgow The other example of an age-graded change also involves a stigmatized feature, and also shows youngsters alter-ing their speech as they mature.

In Scotland and Northern England, the use of the glottal stop, [?], as a variant for /t/ is, as Macaulay (1977: 47) says, "the most openly stigmatised feature." Linguistically, the glottal stop variant can occur in any non-initial post-tonic position. That excludes words like *time* and *tide*, where it is initial, and words like *preténd* and *patélla*, where it is pre-tonic, but still includes a large set of words, many of them highly frequent, such as *better, city, dirty, football, hitting,* and *water.*

As a shibboleth of British WC speech, it is scorned by teachers and other authority figures. A vivid illustration occurs in this excerpt from the open-ing of a short story called "Wa'er" by George Rew (1990), set in Dundee, Scotland:

"What is the more usual name for H_2O, Ballantyne?"
I realise that the teacher has spoken my name. I look up to see Mr Houston's thin face peering expectantly at me through his thick round glasses. He is almost smirking with anticipation. Does he think I don't know the answer? Surely not! What has he planned for me, I wonder frantically.
"Wa'er!" I answer confidently, in my distinctive Dundee accent.
Houston's smile grows slightly wider.
"Pardon?"
He puts a hand behind his ear and cocks his head.
"Wa'er!" I say again, thinking perhaps I had mumbled the first time. . . . [After several repetitions and growing confusion] I look over and see Caroline Paterson leaning toward me. . . .
"James, it's water!" she whispers, and suddenly I understand I am not speaking correctly, at least not in the opinion of Mr Houston. He is mocking my Dundee accent.

As the story unfolds, the student defies the teacher's efforts to "correct" his speech, and in the ensuing confrontation is, to his surprise, supported by the headmaster.

In the next issue of *The Scots Magazine*, where the story appeared, a letter to the editor complained about the author's "casual canonisation of the glottal stop" and deplored his "thin tale which appears to celebrate the triumph of ignorance and insolence in a (typical?) Scottish classroom."

Macaulay found this same attitude in his Glasgow sociolinguistic survey. "Of all features of Glasgow speech the most notorious is the glottal stop," he says (1977: 45), "and it was the feature most frequently singled out by teachers as characteristic of a Glasgow accent." He also found a high level of linguistic insecurity. One of his subjects says, "The first time I heard standard English was at school . . . We didn't expect people to speak as we did after we heard the school teachers. We knew there was some other language. . . . You did grow up with a sense that what you were speaking was regarded as inferior" (1977: 107).

The strength of the attitudes inveighing against certain variants including the glottal stop, on the one hand, and the pressures favoring standardization, on the other, create a considerable tension over dialect and accent. Macaulay's documentation of it in Glasgow makes a striking contribution to the sociolinguistic literature.

In this critical climate, perhaps it is not as surprising as it otherwise would be to see the results plotted graphically in figure 4.6. The figure plots the index scores for the use of the glottal stop variant in three age groups – 10, 15 and adults – in three occupational groups. Transliterating Macaulay's occupational groups into more familiar class labels would split them into MC and WC, with I (managers) as the MC and both IIa (clerks) and IIb (trades workers) as WC.

In the light of the previous discussion of the *marché linguistique* (§4.5), Macaulay's separation of his WC subjects into IIa and IIb has added interest here, because it essentially divides them by occupational groups that make use of language (IIa) and those that do not (IIb). The pattern shown by the middle group in figure 4.6 is partly explained by that fact. The adults in IIb score much lower than the younger people of the same class. They tend to avoid the glottal stop variant, almost to the same degree as the adults in the MC. The large gap between them and the WC trades workers in IIb, people who might be their neighbors, is presumably the result of market pressures to standardize their accents.

For our immediate purposes, figure 4.6 provides a striking example of age-grading in the MC group. The WC groups show fairly predictable patterns. The IIb group (trades workers) have very high frequencies of the stigmatized variant at all ages, around 80 percent. In the IIa group, the two younger age groups are also very similar, both to one another and to their age-mates in the other WC group. When we turn to the MC, the low scores of the adults show the expected behavior, and the 15-year-olds, also as expected, cluster with them. The 10-year-olds, however, appear to be anomalies, far removed not only from their parents but also from their slightly older siblings. Under ordinary circumstances, we should expect the 10-year-olds to form a cluster with the others in their class, between 10–20 percent. They do not do so, and in fact are slightly closer in the frequency of their use of the stigmatized variant to their age-mates in the lower classes.

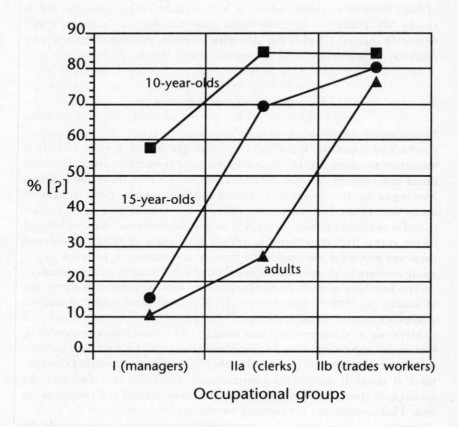

Figure 4.6 Percentage of variable (ʔ) in three age groups in three occupational groups in Glasgow (based on Macaulay 1977: table 16, 47)

What happens, by inference, is that between the ages of 10 and 15, MC Glaswegians learn to control the use of the WC shibboleth in their speech. They do so, as we have seen, under the impetus of considerable pressure from their elders. The social function of stigmatization is to enforce norms of behavior deemed appropriate to class and other social characteristics, and in Glasgow it works very effectively on the MC youth. Although the norm-enforcement mechanisms cannot prevent the class-insensitive youngsters from learning to use the glottal stop variant, they can prevent its perpetuation into adolescence.

In the speech community, glottal stop thus becomes not only a characteristic feature of WC speech, where it persists, but also, incidentally, a feature of MC children's speech, where it is age-graded. The contempt for it among MC arbiters is probably more acute because they associate it not only with manual laborers but also with children, two social groups with relatively little prestige in all the industrialized nations.

4.6.2   Real time and apparent time

In discussing Glasgow age-grading immediately above, we drew certain conclusions about the social significance of the glottal stop variant. It is important to realize that those conclusions came from inferences rather than direct observations. We did not literally observe MC Glaswegian children learning to use the variant up to age 10 and then observe them bringing it under control as adolescents to the point where, around the age of 20, their use of it stabilized so that, according to our observations, they maintained its use at that frequency throughout their adult years. Instead, we observed three age groups at the same time, and by comparing the behavior of the groups inferred the temporal chain of events that must have happened.

The first kind of study, whereby linguists make a series of observations of similar populations over many years is a "real-time" study. Real-time studies are relatively rare in the social sciences for obvious reasons. In order to carry out a real-time study that would yield information comparable to that in, say, the Glasgow study cited above, researchers would have to begin making observations on 10-year-old subjects and continue making observations at intervals until those subjects were about 40. It would take the researchers thirty-odd years from the time they started the project to its end. That is obviously far too long to wait for the results.

In some projects, where the time frame is shorter, real-time studies are more practical and often indispensable. In an earlier section on dialect acquisition (§4.3.1), I described some developmental studies in which the same individuals were observed over several months or, in one case, a few years – a span, that is to say, of real time.

More often, as in the Glasgow study and dozens of other studies cited in this book, subjects of different ages are interviewed at the same time and the differences in their behavior, subject to whatever checks are available and with appropriate precautions, are inferred to be temporal analogues. When different age groups are observed simultaneously and the observations are extrapolated as temporal, the result is an "apparent-time" study.

Apparent-time studies have the inestimable advantage of making information about temporal developments available in a shorter time than the developments themselves take. The inferences are generally reliable as we will see in §4.6.3. Because they are not arrived at by direct observation, however, those inferences depend upon the validity of a particular hypothesis, namely, that the linguistic usage of a certain age group will remain essentially the same for the people in that group as they grow older.

An obvious problem for the apparent-time hypothesis is age-grading, in which the frequency of some linguistic variable at one age does not stay the same but is instead altered or "corrected" at a later age. Since age-grading is relatively rare and is realized in a distinctive, identifiable pattern, it does not refute the hypothesis but is a codicil on it.

For reasons discussed in §4.5.4 above, linguistic differences between well-chosen samples of, say, 42-year-olds and 62-year-olds in a community will, under ordinary circumstances, be perpetuated over the course of time. In other words, twenty years later the speech of 62-year-olds in that community will be largely the same as it was when they were 42-year-olds at the time of the original study.

Real-time studies are rarer not only because they pose numerous practical problems but also because, in the relatively short history of sociolinguistics, there have been few opportunities to return to a community in order to make a comparative study using the same methods. Before sociolinguistics, the dialectologist Hermann (1929) revisited Charmey, Switzerland, to test Gauchat's inferences (1905; see §2.6.3 above), but that was a rare and auspicious event.

In §4.6.3 I review some studies where sociolinguists have returned to the site of an earlier survey in order to compare their apparent-time predictions with real-time developments. In the next two sub-sections, I describe a prototypical study made in real time and one made in apparent time.

4.6.2.1 Real-time changes in Tsuruoka   The National Language Institute in Tokyo conducted dialect surveys in the northern city of Tsuruoka at twenty-year intervals in 1950, 1971 and 1991 under the direction of Kiyoshi Egawa (Yoneda 1993). The method was kept the same each time: the fieldworkers interviewed subjects individually for 40 minutes guided by a questionnaire that ensured comparable data from all of them. In 1950, the subjects comprised a random sample of 577 citizens from the municipal register, and in the next two surveys they were made up of panel samples of 107 (1971) and 314 (1991) individuals interviewed before and new random samples of 457 and 405 people.

The time period perfectly suited a real-time study of change because Tsuruoka was relatively isolated in 1950 and then became much more accessible with the rapid industrialization and commercialization that took root around that time. With the provision of high-speed transportation lines came not only geographical mobility but also occupational and class mobility, affecting a social transformation not unlike that in the new world societies discussed in §2.5.

These massive social changes in the 40-year period from 1951 to 1991

Table 4.6 Regional variants in Tsuruoka dialect and the standard dialect as examples of general phonological processes and, in the bottom row, pitch accent differences (from Yoneda 1993: 3–4)

Process	Regional	Standard	Gloss
labialization	ɸjakμ	hjakμ	*one hundred*
palatalization	ʃenaga	senaka	*back*
voicing	hadʒɨ	hatʃi	*bee*
nasalization	õbɨ	obi	*belt*
centralization	sɨmɨ	sμ mi	*chinese ink*
vowel shift	ɨgɨ	iki	*breath*
pitch accent	ne̞go (LH)	ne̞ko (HL)	*cat*
	ka̞ras ɨ (LHL)	ka̞rasμ (HLL)	*crow*

brought about numerous linguistic replacements of Tsuruoka regionalisms in favor of standard forms. The Tsuruoka accent was distinguished from the Tokyo standard by a number of general phonological processes. Table 4.6 names some of these processes in the left column and illustrates them with examples of the standard and regional variants of one of the lexical items elicited in the survey (from Yoneda 1993: 3–4). Some of the items chosen illustrate more than one of the processes, such as *õbɨ* "bell", an example not only of nasalization in the first vowel but also of centralization in the second vowel. The examples of pitch accent differences in the bottom row of table 4.6 are somewhat different from the others in that they are prosodic rather than segmental. The parenthetical designations indicate high (H) and low (L) pitches in the pitch accent contours that characterize Japanese. These are not rule-governed but lexemic in the language.

The real-time surveys track the increasing standardization of the Tsuruoka dialect in very dramatic fashion. Figure 4.7 summarizes the general findings by combining the overall indices of segmental (4.7a) and accentual (4.7b) standard forms for six age groups across the twenty-year intervals. Looking first at the segmental results, in 1991 the subjects under 35, that is, in the three youngest age groups, almost categorically use standard variants. Clearly, those standard variants are the norm for Tsuruokans of all ages in 1991. Two decades earlier, they were already very well entrenched, though categorical only for the very youngest subjects. Within the forty-year period of these studies, standardization increased most strikingly from 1950 to 1971, as indicated by the size of the gap between the subjects in these two surveys.

There is also ancillary evidence from Figure 4.7a for the acceleration of

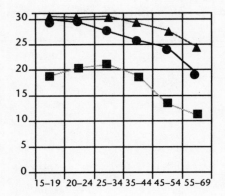

Figure 4.7a   Phonetic indices by age (maximum is 31)

standardization in this period. If you look at the 35–44 year-olds in the 1950 survey, you can infer that they maintained their usage of standard and regional variants as they grew older. They are represented in the 1971 survey, of course, as 55–69 year-olds, and their score (19.5/31) indicates very similar proportions to what it indicated in the earlier survey (18.9/31). That was not true for the people younger than they were in 1950. By 1971, those subjects had all increased their use of standard variants as compared to their use when they were under 35 in the earlier survey. Standardization presumably became firmly established as the community norm in this interval.

Figure 4.7b makes an interesting comparison with Figure 4.7a. The most obvious observation is that the increasing standardization is almost as evident in changes in pitch accent as it is in segmental phonology. That is, the tendency is for the younger subjects to have more standard responses than the older subjects as shown by the downward slope of the lines in the graph. Equally obvious when the two graphs are placed side by side is the observation that pitch accent changes lag behind segmental changes. In 1950, pitch accent had barely begun to standardize: it was not noticeably correlated with age as indicated graphically by its relatively flat line close to the abscissa. At the same time, segmental phonology was quite advanced and clearly age-related. In 1971, the age relation of pitch accent standardization emerged clearly, although its progress was relatively slow, taking in only two-fifths of the elicited instances for the most advanced age group, the 20 to 24-year-olds. Twenty years later, in 1991, the correlation with age is more obvious, with everyone under 35 using standard pitch accent about 60 percent of the time, but no age group approaches categoricity, as the under-45s do in segmental phonology.

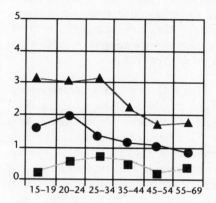

Figure 4.7b Pitch accent indices by age (maximum is 5)
Increasing standardization in Tsuruoka, Japan, as shown in surveys conducted in
1950 (■), 1971 (●), and 1991 (▲) (Yoneda 1993: from figures 15 and 17, 7–8)

The comparison shows that, even in a dialect undergoing cataclysmic changes, the rates of change can differ for different linguistic domains. The practical effect of this difference in Tsuruoka is that the younger Tsuruokans in 1991 may no longer be identifiable to people from other parts of Japan by their phonetics but are still easily identifiable by their prosody. If the current trends continue, they will certainly be less easy to identify prosodically by the year 2011, when the next survey takes place, and may be impossible to identify prosodically after that, in 2031.

It is worth pausing here to note that this example of prosodic dialect differences is one of the very few in this book or, for that matter, in the sociolinguistic literature. Prosody is not as well understood as many other levels of linguistic structure and consequently is not as well studied; the paucity of sociolinguistic studies is merely a reflection of a more general state of affairs in linguistics. However, the Tsuruoka example probably represents the most typical sociolinguistic situation in the sense that, whenever segmental and prosodic elements are involved in change, prosodic elements are likely to lag behind segmental ones. The reason for this is that prosodic features have primacy in the acquisition schedule: because of that, they are reinforced constantly and deeply imprinted. They are acquired very early, as shown by the fact that infants recognize adult prosodic patterns at two or three months and can mimic them as early as six months (Crystal 1979: 38). These developments precede comparable developments in segmental phonology by several months and they precede comparable developments in grammar by even longer. (It is because they are so deeply imprinted that adult learners of second languages often retain the prosodic patterns of their native language in the the new language, as when Scandinavians learn English.) Prosodic patterns are apparently difficult to dislodge even in situations of cataclysmic dialect change.

4.6.2.2 An apparent-time change in Milwaukee   When I compared the Tsuruoka 35- to 44-year-olds in 1950 and the 55- to 69-year-olds in 1971, I was, in effect, comparing the behavior of the same people twenty years apart. Some of the individuals in the 55–69 age group were literally the same individuals that had been interviewed as 35- to 49-year-olds in the earlier survey. Others were different individuals but randomly sampled from the same population base and thus collectively (and statistically) comprised of matching individuals. The comparison was thus a real-time one.

Elsewhere in the discussion of the Tsuruoka data, I contrasted the under-35s with the over-35s in the 1991 survey, and extrapolated the results of that comparison into the future, on the assumption that the differences would be perpetuated as those subjects grew older. That comparison was an apparent-time one, and was only possible on the assumption of the correctness of the apparent-time hypothesis.

If you look back through the examples cited in the previous chapters from the perspective presented in this section, you will become aware that several inferences have been based tacitly on the apparent-time hypothesis. Its validity is deeply engrained in sociolinguistics.

One further example will be presented here because it neatly encapsulates several useful sociolinguistic points including one of the main points of this section, the generational progress of change.

In Milwaukee, as in other parts of the American Midwest, /æ/ often becomes raised and tense when it precedes either a /g/, in words like *flag*, *wagon*, and *aggravate*, or a nasal, in words like *anger* and *hang*. Zeller (1993) plotted this change by measuring the first formants (F1) of several tokens of /æ/ in these environments in the speech of subjects of different ages. Figure 4.8 illustrates the phonetics of two generations of Milwaukeans with respect to the changing vowel. As it happens, the subjects shown in the figure are members of Zeller's family. The top bar is her brother, PZ, the middle one her father, JZ, and the bottom one her mother, DZ.

The height of the first formant varies inversely with the height of the tongue, so that lower the F1 the higher the vowel. PZ typically has F1 at 400–500 Hz, and his father, JZ, typically has F1 at 500–600 Hz. They exemplify the sound change in progress in neat, predictable ways. The son's vowel is typically higher than his father's by about 100 Hz, and is therefore typically higher, closer to [e], the mid front unrounded vowel. The father's is typically lower, closer to [æ], the low front unrounded vowel. Zeller

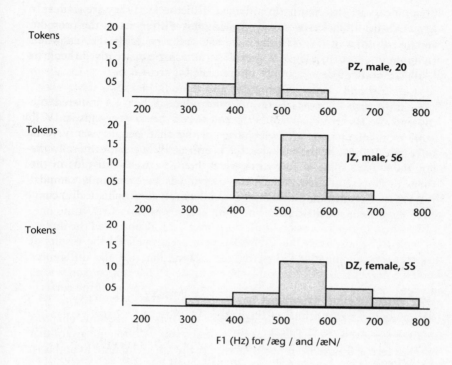

Figure 4.8 First formant (F1) of the stressed vowel in words such as *flag, wagon, aggregate* (/aeg/) and *anger, hang* (/æN/) by three Milwaukeans (based on Zeller 1993: figures 6 and 7)

shows that the generational difference between the father and son is representative of the community as a whole.

When we look at DZ, however, her F1 is not quite so neat or predictable. The plurality of her vowels have the F1 at 500–600 Hz, like her husband, but her range also encompasses her son's range. Although she clearly lines up linguistically as belonging to the same generation as her husband, she has some instances of very raised vowels in this context, like her son's, as well. Her median F1 is the same as her husband's but the standard deviation of her F1 is greater. This difference makes a graphic illustration of an important point in the preceding chapter, the fact that women command a greater range of linguistic variation than do men (§3.4.2).

For our purposes here, however, the significance of figure 4.8 lies in the difference between PZ on the one hand and both JZ and DZ on the other. A glance at the shifted median in PZ's production of /æ/ makes a concrete illustration of the phonetic difference between two generations of Milwaukeans. As I have already noted, this difference occurs not only among members of the Z family but much more generally throughout the community. As such, it is taken as evidence of a linguistic change in progress.

Its status as evidence is only inferential. Figure 4.8 does not explicitly measure a sound change in progress, and it would not even if we were to augment it with F1 measures of hundreds of subjects. What it does explicitly measure is a difference in the speech of two different age groups at the same moment in time. In order of generalize that fact into an historical inference, it must be the case that the people of PZ's generation will maintain the median value of /æ/ throughout their lifetimes so that by the time they are the age of their parents that vowel will have a different standard realization. Simply put, for the historical inferences to be valid, the apparent-time hypothesis must be valid.

4.6.3   Testing the apparent-time hypothesis

The apparent-time hypothesis has proven a highly productive tenet in sociolinguistics and historical linguistics. Only recently have we begun to accumulate evidence that tests it directly (Bailey, Wikle, Tillery and Sand 1991, Cedergren 1988, Thibault and Daveluy 1989, Trudgill 1988, Yaeger-Dror 1989). That evidence shows, crucially, that it is basically sound. It also reminds us, if a reminder should be necessary, that it is only an hypothesis. It holds perfectly only when the linguistic and social circumstances under which the measurements were made are immutable, and of course the complexities of language and society do not stay fixed for long.

In the following two sub-sections, I describe one situation where the change did not continue directly as the apparent-time data suggested (§4.6.3.1), and another where the change did progress as predicted (§4.6.3.2). These two examples, one from Trudgill's work in Norwich and the other from Cedergren's work in Panama, were originally salient applications – classics of the sociolinguistic literature – of the apparent-time hypothesis.

4.6.3.1   Slower progress at higher frequencies: (e) in Norwich   In Trudgill's Norwich survey, for which the interviews were conducted in 1968, the variable (e) provided the clearest example of a variable undergoing change (1974: 87, 104–5). The variable occurs as realizations of the phoneme /ɛ/ before /l/, as in *tell*, *bell*, *well* and *healthy*. The standard variant in England, as in most other standard accents, is [ɛ], but in Norwich in 1968 Trudgill found a noticeable centralization of the vowel, to [ɜ], and for the most innovative speakers, especially the LWC, backing to [ʌ].

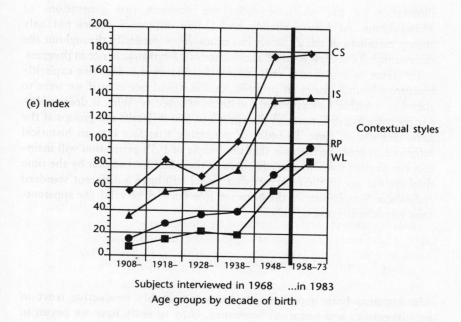

Figure 4.9 Norwich (e) by age groups and style, in apparent time (left of heavy line) and real time (based on Trudgill 1988: figure 6, 47)

The class stratification for variable (e) proved notably fractious, with the WC groups reversed, but when the figures were recalculated for age groups (regardless of social class) they became coherent, with subjects under 40 showing considerably more vowel backing than those over 40.

The major portion of figure 4.9, including all but the segment to the right of the heavy line, shows the 1968 results for the youngest groups in four stylistic contexts. (Trudgill's results also include two groups older than the ones shown here but they are not involved in the change; see Trudgill 1988: 36, 45.) The maximum index score on the ordinate is 200, a score which would indicate invariable use of [ʌ]; the minimum score, 0, along the abscissa, would indicate invariable use of [ɛ], the standard variant. Distance above the abscissa indicates, as usual, degrees of non-standardness, with scores around 100 having a preponderance of central [ɜ] and above that some further backed [ʌ] variants as well.

The 1968 results typify the pattern for a change in progress. The oldest subjects have lower scores than the younger subjects, so that the slope of the lines on the graph is generally upward. For all subjects there is a fair amount of style-shifting, indicating that in monitored speech the innovative variants were avoided as far as possible. The style-shifting is most pronounced for the younger groups, those born in 1938–47 and 1948–57: the gap between their reading passage styles and interview styles is considerable, and for the latter group, the youngest subjects in the 1968 survey, it is about 60 index points. Subconsciously, the new variants were evidently the source of some self-consciousness in the community as they were becoming established.

In 1983, Trudgill returned to Norwich in order to follow up his original survey after an interval of fifteen years. Instead of re-interviewing a cross section of age groups, he chose to collect data from subjects who had attained the ages of 10–25 since the first survey, in effect extending the coverage of the original survey by adding a new sample of the youngest age groups. This methodological choice makes a limited test of the apparent-time hypothesis because it looks only at the extent to which the next generation perpetuates the trends observable in the community at the time of the previous survey. It does not test it by checking the extent to which the subjects have maintained their positions in the real-time interval, that is, the extent to which, say, 55-year-olds maintain the same dialect variants they used as 40-year-olds in the original survey, which is the crux of the hypothesis.

Trudgill's 1983 sample of Norwich young people turned up some mild surprises, notably the rapid spread of labio-dental [ʋ] for alveopalatal [ɹ] in their speech, a feature that was almost nonexistent in Norwich at the time of the first survey but was well entrenched by the time of the second, as indeed it is throughout southeastern England (1988: 40). But by and large, Trudgill's real-time findings followed the trends he observed earlier: for instance, the relic form [ɐ] in *bird*, *turkey*, and similar words had completely disappeared, and the long monophthong [eː] in words like *gate* and *face*, vestigial in the earlier survey, was more vestigial now, heard only in the speech of people over 80 and variably even there.

The new results for the variable (e) shed light on the apparent-time hypothesis in a couple of interesting ways. Looking at the results on the right in figure 4.9, one observation is that the change appears to have been arrested. In the least formal styles, interview style and casual style, the line between the two youngest groups – one from the 1968 survey and other from the new survey – has flattened. The steep slope leading up to the 1948-57 group is not sustained by similar increases by the youngest subjects. A second observation is that the more formal styles do sustain the change in the old terms: the steep slope of the older age groups is matched by the youngest subjects.

Trudgill (1988: 46) notes that "this halting of centralisation was not predictable from the 1968 data" but "there is a clear and interesting explanation" for it. In informal speech, he notes, /ɛ/ has merged with /ʌ/ completely, so that words like *hell* and *hull* are homophones. They are still kept separate in more formal styles, however, so that the merger of /ɛ/ with

/ʌ/ before /l/ is incomplete. Mergers are, he notes, "stylistically gradual" types of change. He then adds, "Exactly *why* the phonological merger means the halting of a phonetic change in progress is not entirely clear" (1988: 46).

Evidence that mergers are gradual changes was presented most influentially by Labov, Yaeger and Steiner (1972: 229–54), when they demonstrated that five reported vowel mergers in current dialect studies were actually incomplete. Auditory reports judged vowels to be the same in, for instance, *source* and *sauce* in New York and *loin* and *line* in Essex, but acoustic measurements revealed that the vowels remained subtly distinct in their range of realizations. Those subtle distinctions are sufficient, apparently, to form the basis for the unmerging of reportedly merged vowels, as in the classic case of the *line/loin* pairs in standard English, which appeared to merge in the eighteenth century and then unmerge in the nineteenth (Nunberg 1980).

Trudgill's real-time data suggests another means by which apparent mergers can retain their distinctness. The merger can be complete in informal styles but far from complete in formal styles. For speakers who make the stylistic distinction, the phonemes keep their status although their allophones may overlap. Casual observations may lead an observer to believe that the merger is complete if they are made of informal speech. Systematic observations of the whole stylistic repertoire will be required to show it is incomplete.

The reason the merger has halted in the informal styles does not really seem puzzling. There is now abundant evidence that sound changes start slowly until about 20 percent of the affected tokens have undergone the change, and then progress rapidly through the next 60 percent of the tokens, and then slow down again in the last stages. This pattern is called the S-curve model, first observed by Wang and Cheng (1970) and since confirmed in numerous studies (enumerated in Chambers 1992: 693–95). Indeed, the top two lines of figure 4.9, representing the Norwich responses in the two informal styles, make handsome S-like forms. The top curve of the S, representing the tailing-off of a change as it approaches categoricity, discussed at length by Wang (1969), appears to have had its inception right around the time Trudgill was recording his youngest speakers in 1968. In their informal speech, /ɛ/ was realized as [ʌ] in more than 80 percent of all instances, and consequently the change was about to slow down.

Although Trudgill says that its slowing down was not predictable from his Norwich dialect data, it was perhaps predictable from more general principles of language change. Or perhaps it is only predictable – actually explicable – in hindsight. In any event, Trudgill's second real-time observation – the perpetuation of the original rate of change in the more formal styles – is also explicable by the S-curve model in a direct and simple way.

Since in these styles the sound change is only in its middle stages, far from categorical, it continues its rapid progress, in fact at about the same rate it was progressing in the earlier survey. It will presumably continue at this rate for a few more decades, until it too approaches categoricity and slows down.

4.6.3.2 *Verifying inferences about change: (CH) in Panama*   The second classic change in progress comes from Cedergren's study of Spanish in Panama City in 1969 (1973) which she later restudied in 1982–4 (1988). The time lapse is thus very similar to Trudgill's, almost 15 years.

The change involves a process known as CH-lenition, which occurs generally in Central American and Caribbean Spanish but only in Panama occurs in the speech of the higher social classes as well as the lower ones. The phoneme /tʃ/ has the standard variant [tʃ], a voiceless palatal affricate, and the non-standard variant [ʃ], a voiceless palatal fricative, regarded as a weakening (or lenition) because of the loss of the stop articulation. In her original survey (1973: 66–79), Cedergren also recorded instances of a third variant, [ʹʃ] an affricate with a reduced stop onset. This variant is apparently what is called a "fudge" (Chambers and Trudgill 1980: 135; also §3.2.1.1 above), a phonetic compromise between the standard and the innovative variants that, in effect, allows users to avoid choosing between them. In the second survey, Cedergren does not mention [ʹʃ] and so it was presumably a transitional feature of no particular social significance.

Several independent variables affected the use of the non-standard variant, with women ahead of men, city-born subjects ahead of rural immigrants, and the middle social classes (UWC, LMC) ahead of other groups. But the most salient independent variable, naturally, was age. Exactly the same relations held in the later survey: age was still the most salient correlate.

On Cedergren's return to Panama, she used a random sample of all age groups and added a new group born in 1967–77, unborn or merely infants at the time of the first survey. Interviewing a full sample the second time constitutes the strongest possible test of the apparent-time hypothesis.

Figure 4.10 plots the CH-lenition results for the two surveys together. The broad similarities are obvious at a glance. Both surveys show a steep rise from the oldest to the younger speakers, indicating greater use of the [ʃ] variant among young Panamanians. In 1969, the lowest score was 15 percent for the oldest group and the highest score was 62 percent for the second youngest group; in 1982–4, the highest and lowest scores were 7 percent and 62 percent. The incline between the low and high scores is similar, and in fact the lines of the graph intertwine.

The results of the two surveys share what appears to be an idiosyncratic or at least unexpected feature. Figure 4.10 shows a peculiar peak for the

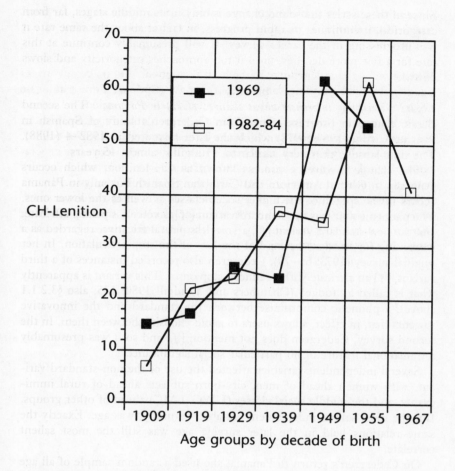

Figure 4.10 Real-time comparison of age groups in two surveys of CH-lenition in Panama City (Cedergren 1988: figure 6, 54)

second-youngest age group in both surveys. The second youngest speakers have a higher percentage of the [ʃ] variant than the youngest subjects. The frequent use of the new variant by the post-adolescent subjects, Cedergren (1988: 53) says, confirms "the social importance of CH-lenition in the linguistic marketplace" (Bourdieu et Boltanski 1975; also see §4.5 above). For the young adults, it should be "interpreted as an indication of their sensitivity to the social importance of the newer variant."

More generally, Cedergren's real-time comparison lends strong support to the apparent-time hypothesis. Comparative studies such as hers and the others that are now available are invaluable because the most fundamental tenets of an empirical discipline require the continual questioning of our assumptions.

When time is the independent variable, it is impossible to make our investigations without adopting some simplifying assumptions. Time cannot be observed directly, as St Augustine said, because our observations are always made of a moment that has passed. Time is perpetually in motion. We can only draw inferences about time's effects by looking at what it leaves behind, and linguistically what it leaves behind – its residue, as it were – are generations of speakers who sometimes share certain norms, variants and styles with one another much more than with the generations that precede and follow them. Sociolinguistics, as numerous examples in this chapter show, is trying to come to grips with the linguistic effects of time by studying them minutely – not millennially – for the first time. Probably no other aspect of the young discipline has proven as fruitful.

5

Adaptive Significance of Language Variation

> *Once the familiar and comfortable idea of the homogeneity of linguistic communities is abandoned, the world appears as an ocean of conflicting attractions, convergence here breeding divergence there, with new centres of attraction developing at all times and threatening to disrupt existing ensembles.*
>
> *André Martinet (1962)*

So far, we have been concerned mainly with discovering the social meanings of linguistic variation. Upon observing variability, we seek its social correlates. What is the purpose of the variation? What do its variants symbolize? These are the central questions of sociolinguistics, and they have been the central questions of this book.

Behind these questions lies another one – an ontogenetic question. Why, we must ask, does linguistic variation exist at all? What is its purpose or function? What is its adaptive significance for human beings?[1]

Linguists have seldom posed this ultimate question, probably because it is hard to see how to go about answering it. Nevertheless, since it underlies much of what we do as sociolinguists, it is important to keep it in mind. Our research into other aspects of linguistic variation ought to shed light on its answer, however dimly. Looked at from the opposite viewpoint, the larger question should inform our specific research questions, guiding, so to speak, the whole research enterprise.

Research pursuits that have no imaginable bearing on the adaptive significance of linguistic variation are probably not worth pursuing.

One sociolinguist who directly broached this topic is Labov, who briefly addressed this question (1972: 323–5): "Is there an adaptive function to linguistic diversity?" The form of his question – as of our variants of it above – resembles the question asked commonly by biologists engaged in the study of animal dialects. Indeed, Labov suggested that the adaptive function of human dialects might be biological and therefore the answer might some day be found in biological research. In §5.3 below, I look at the question biologically and review some findings in animal dialectology. In §5.4, I look at the question socially and search for the reasons that might underlie the endurance of dialect diversity. Finally, I look for the source of diversity in terms of social structure, reviewing some traditional theories in §5.5, and developing a sociolinguistic theory in §5.6. First, however, I consider an answer that antedates sociolinguistics by several centuries (§5.1) and then its converse (§5.2), bringing to bear some current research findings.

5.1   The Babelian Hypothesis

The fact that linguistic variability is universal and ubiquitous suggests strongly that it is fulfilling some essential human need. Yet some thinkers, unswayed by its universality, have concluded that it has no adaptive function whatever – that it is, in fact, counteradaptive, even dysfunctional.

That conclusion comes from what is certainly the best-known discussion of the question of linguistic diversity, and probably the earliest extant one. The myth of Babel from the Old Testament Book of Genesis 11: 1–9, some three millennia old, begins by postulating a time when there was only one language with a single dialect:

> Once upon a time all the world spoke a single language and used the same words. As the people journeyed in the east, they came upon a plain in the land of Shinar and settled there . . . "Come," they said, "let us build our-selves a city and a tower with its top in the heavens, and make a name for ourselves . . ." Then the Lord came down to see the city and tower which the mortals had built, and he said, "Here they are, one people with a single language, and now they have started to do this; henceforward nothing they have in mind to do will be beyond their reach. Come, let us go down there and confuse their speech, so that they will not understand what they say to one another." So the Lord dispersed them from there all over the earth, and they left off building the city. That is why it is called Babel, because the Lord made a babble of the language of all the world.

Thus God imposed linguistic diversity on humankind as a punishment for its hubris. Because the tower reached so high as to challenge God's author-ity, God took away the basis of the people's power, their ability to commu-nicate perfectly with one another.

The Babelian hypothesis about the counteradaptivity of linguistic diversity is strongly supported by sociocultural observations. In Western (or, at least, Judaeo-Christian) cultures, numerous institutions have as their primary or secondary function the curtailing of linguistic diversity in favor of the standard dialect: hence prescriptive dictionaries, school grammars, nationalized authorities such as the Académie française, school bussing, training in the dramatic arts, British "public" schools, and media network hiring practices. International politico-linguistic movements for auxiliary languages such as Esperanto and Basic English have no other rationale but the curtailing of diversity.

Similarly, many mundane events suggest that people have a deeply ingrained attraction to linguistic conformity. The stigmatization of certain dialect features appears to be an overt attempt by communities to stamp out certain variants. School children – and sometimes adults too – have been known to choose sides on the basis of accents, as if people's vowel formants were a determinant of their character. People who move from one dialect region to another often find themselves subjected to ridicule because of their accents and are thus goaded into adapting as far as possible to local norms.

5.1.1   *The evidence of subjective reaction tests*

So compelling is the attraction of standardized speech that speakers of non-standard varieties denigrate their own speech out of deference to the standard variety. Subjective reaction tests have shown this result so frequently that it is no longer surprising in any way but is actually expected. In a classic case, Labov (1966: 405–503) discovered that his New York subjects consistently downgraded accents that were the same as their own. Paradoxically, working-class men of Italian ancestry in New York showed both the highest frequency of stops for (th) – [tʰɪŋ] for *thing*, etc. – and the greatest awareness of it in the speech of others (Labov 1972: 130). Results like these led Labov to talk about "the linguistic self-hatred which marks the average New Yorker" (1966: 480). As in many other things, the New Yorkers provide an extreme example, but they are by no means unique. Similar conclusions about linguistic self-hatred or at least dislike have been reported in Montreal (Lambert 1967), Glasgow (Macaulay 1975), Dublin (Edwards 1979), Newfoundland (Clarke 1984), and numerous other places.

The fact that people taking subjective reaction tests typically downgrade a speaker's competence, character, and career potential solely on the basis of a taped speech sample that includes non-standard features is itself proof that linguistic diversity invokes prejudices and, it follows, underlies some social inequities.

5.1.1.1   Teachers' evaluations of students   In a telling example, British teachers awarded students lower marks when they spoke with a regional accent regardless of the quality of the other samples of their schoolwork. In an experiment by Giles and Powesland (1975: 2–3), student teachers were asked to assess eight hypothetical students on the basis of three types of information: a photograph, a tape-recorded speech sample, and an essay and drawing. The essays and drawings ranged in quality from very good to poor, and the speech samples included standard accents, regional standard accents and regional non-standard accents. The experimenters then controlled the combinations of materials in the dossiers, so that sometimes a certain photograph was bundled with good schoolwork and the non-standard accent, sometimes with middling schoolwork and the standard accent, and so on, in all combinations. It turned out that the best predicter of how the teachers would assess any dossier was the speech sample. If the speech sample was the standard accent the student was graded higher, and if it was non-standard the student was graded lower when the quality of the schoolwork that accompanied it was the same.

5.1.1.2   Employers' evaluations of job candidates   Similarly, people appear to place limits on an individual's career possibilities based on accent. In a typical experiment, subjects were asked to act as "personnel consultants" for a company hiring foremen, industrial mechanics, production assemblers and plant cleaners (Kalin, Rayko and Love 1986). The subjects were asked to rate each of sixteen candidates for each job as they listened to tape-recorded statements by them. This experiment was carried out in Canada, and each of the taped voices had an ethnic accent, either English, German, South Asian or West Indian. The results showed "stable discrimination" favoring the ethnic groups in the order listed for the higher prestige jobs and denigration by favoring them in the reverse order for the lower prestige jobs.

The subjective evaluations appear to be acutely tuned to dialect features. New Yorkers reacted to a small phonetic difference from one speaker by downgrading her potential occupation (Labov 1966: 429–33). The subjects were asked to act as personnel managers and assign the speakers they heard in taped samples to jobs according to a scale that listed occupations ranked by prestige: television personality, executive secretary, receptionist, switchboard operator, salesgirl, and factory worker. Labov selected statements from the reading passage that was part of his survey, some with standard variants and some with mixed variants, often by the same speaker. The listeners did not realize, of course, that the person they were evaluating on the basis of a speech sample was the same speaker they evaluated on the basis of another speech sample later on.

Labov found that the listeners did not significantly downgrade (th) and (dh) variants, so that, for instance, a speaker who in one sample said "[ð]ere's some[θ]ing strange about [d]at . . ." and was also heard in a sample with only standard [ð] and [θ], was ranked the same (factory worker) both times. But subjective reactions to (r) were acute. A speaker was heard once saying "We didn't have the heart to play cards all morning" with all four / r / s pronounced, and then was heard later saying the same sentence with one difference: "cards" pronounced as [kʰɑːdẓ]. Most listeners (62 percent) downgraded her from "television personality" to "receptionist". Significantly, all of the youngest listeners, aged 18–39, downgraded this speaker and all other speakers when they had one r-less variant.

Although subjective reaction tests tend to emphasize the prejudices people might have by forcing them to make decisions about such things as a person's occupation and character from a sample of taped speech, the consistency with which subjects make their decisions indicates that the prejudices have some basis in reality. In so far as they are largely shared by a roomful of listeners, they are not random or arbitrary judgements. The results of experiments like these and many similar ones leave no doubt that dialect differences can impose a priori constraints on social acceptability and occupational mobility.

5.1.2   Dialect as a source of conflict

In virtually all social strata, people find the speech of others an irresistible target for criticism. At the most homely level, it can be a source of domestic conflict. In the novel *The Stone Angel* (1968), Margaret Laurence's main characters, Hagar Shipley and her husband Bram, are both natives of Manawaka, a fictional region of Manitoba in central Canada, but Bram is said to be "common as dirt." At one point (1968: 71), Bram, in all innocence, remarks, "Look, Hagar – this here one is half the price of that there one." Instead of responding to what he said, Hagar responds to the way he said it. She says, "This here. That there. Don't you know anything?" And Bram says, "I talk the way I talk, and I ain't likely to change now."

We seldom stop to consider how unproductive these exchanges are, except perhaps when they occur in an artistic context. Occasionally such criticisms might cause speakers to alter their speech, or try to, but most people, like Bram, will not change. If people who receive criticism would like to change but find themselves incapable of it, the criticisms merely serve to make them self-conscious and insecure.

Globally, numerous conflicts on the front pages of our newspapers are played out by antagonists identified with different languages: Québecois in Canada, Basques in Spain, Serbians, Croatians and Slovenes in the former Yugoslavia, Hindis and Urdus in the Indian subcontinent, Azerbaijanis and

Armenians in Nagorno-Karabakh. Linguistic differences are so intimately associated with political conflict that opposed groups sometimes exaggerate them. Hindis and Urdus speak dialects of the same language and so do Serbs and Croats but both groups insist on their differentness. In an oft-cited example due to Wolff (1959), the Isoko of Nigeria claim they cannot understand the neighboring dialects of the same Urhobo family but their neighbors claim few problems in understanding the Isoko. The most likely explanation for the asymmetrical claims is political rather than linguistic: the Isoko are pushing for greater autonomy in the region, and the intelligibility of their language is a factor in the political debate.

Observations like these, then, seem to provide a solid basis for the Babelian hypothesis that linguistic diversity is counteradaptive. Against that, however, stands the overwhelming fact that linguistic diversity not only endures but actually prevails.

5.2 Global Counteradaptivity and Local Adaptivity

If linguistic diversity were truly (or solely) counteradaptive, why should human beings, the most adaptable of all species, resist so hardily the imposition of standardization? Educational measures have had some success in standardizing writing but much less, almost none, in standardizing speech. Politico-linguistic movements for auxiliary languages have invariably failed. Attempts at annihilating regional dialects (or minority languages) have seldom, perhaps never, succeeded except when accompanied by total assimilation or total destruction of the speakers, that is, except as a concomitant of acculturation or genocide. Regional dialects appear to be no less diverse and no fewer in number in the era of the global village than they were in the eras of the city-state or the market town.

5.2.1 Counteradaptivity and power

If one looks critically at the kinds of situations in which linguistic diversity appears to be counteradaptive, they all turn out to be power relationships. The Urhobo seeking to keep the Isoko in their federation, personnel managers deciding the occupational rank of applicants, teachers evaluating students, children taking a round out of a newcomer, Hagar Shipley lording it over her low-born husband – in all instances the inequality of the participants is a crucial factor in the interaction.

Linguistic prescriptivism is, as Kroch and Small put it, "the ideology by which the guardians of the standard language impose their linguistic norms on people who have perfectly serviceable norms of their own" (1978: 45).

The codification of linguistic norms and their imposition is culturally determined. There is no evidence to suggest that it is natural behavior. Indeed, one of the advances brought about by sociolinguistics is that it is possible to track the changes in children as they get a grasp on the society's norms, as in broad transitions of Canadian youngsters transplanted to the south of England (discussed in §4.3.1 above) and the increasing suppression by MC Glasgow children of the stigmatized glottal variant (in §4.6.1.2 above). The cultural norms are not inherent but are arbitrary, as Sankoff (1976: 5) makes clear in her characterization of the way in which political power transforms the essentially neutral linguistic system to its service:

> . . . social processes seize upon linguistic disparities that are intrinsically sym-
> metric, and upon innocuous linguistic processes constantly operating in any
> language, and systematically manipulate them into a highly structured system
> of speech varieties which mirrors and reinforces social class and power dis-
> tinctions.

Demonstrably, no language or dialect is *inherently* better than any other as a medium for exposition, narration, phatic communion, or any other kind of communication. One of the tacit strategies of the elite is to install their own dialect as the "correct" one. The "constitution" that empowers their dialect takes the form of dictionaries, grammars and usage guides in which their linguistic preferences are promulgated as models of correctness. The "legislation" that puts it into place is its imposition as the norm in state-run systems such as government bureaux, broadcasting and education.

All of this is not necessarily bad. If linguistic similarity enhances political unity, then societies are better off with a linguistic standard, wherever it originates. (Underlying this conditional statement is another one, of course, that political unity is a worthy goal if it enables initiatives for the common good, but sociolinguistics does not seem to have an empirical stake in deciding that.)

If the presupposition that political unity is enhanced by linguistic unity is at least partly true, then linguistic standardization is politically defensible. But in fact it has almost never been challenged in any society, and the reason seems to be the general ignorance that language is a discussable, analyzable object in its own right, separable from society itself and a principal component of it. If common knowledge included an enriched notion of the properties of language and how they function socially, at the level of sophistication comparable to common knowledge of, say, arithmetic or national history, people would be better able to understand the bigotry in their attitudes toward the way other people talk and, of course, to assess the value (or the lack of it) when they are chided for the way they talk.

The perception that a particular dialect carries prestige is simply an adjunct of the fact that its speakers are the ones in power. This is the point of Max Weinreich's famous dictum: "A language is a dialect with its own army and navy." The social stratum with political, economic, social and/or military clout usually sets the standard for dress, manners, education, material possessions, and, of course, speech. No matter how comfortable others may be in their own strata, when they encounter those in power they are likely to betray some self-doubts – shyness, self-consciousness, even, as in the case of the New Yorkers, linguistic self-hatred.

5.2.2   *Adaptivity and community*

Clearly, then, linguistic diversity is counteradaptive only when speakers meet in asymmetrical social situations. To put it in terms that have been used elsewhere in this book, it is counteradaptive only for the mobile elements in society. In modern industrial nations, that includes most adults, but not all of them. More significantly, it includes no children.

The first social milieu of human beings is highly circumscribed. From birth to puberty (and sometimes much longer), all human beings are largely dependent upon families and other intimate connections for nurturing and growth. And it is in this setting, of course, that language develops. Along with grammatical and communicative competence and inseparable from them come linguistic markers of regional bonds and community ties (as we have seen in §4.2.2 above). Those markers are emblematic of the dependency relationship in the first instance and of local allegiance thereafter. Speaking the home dialect has adaptive significance.

The antinomy between local adaptivity and global counteradaptivity is sometimes discernible sociolinguistically. In a few studies, as we have seen, linguists have unearthed individual aberrations from well-defined local speech norms that correlate with differences in the individual's orientation, either embedded in the local community or focused beyond it. In Articlave, Northern Ireland, those individuals whose speech was measurably less regional than their peers were the ones whom everybody recognized as the most ambitious members of the community, with aspirations to "get on in the world" beyond Articlave (Douglas-Cowie 1978; discussed in §2.9.4.2). In Belfast, people who kept dense network ties by working, shopping, and pubbing exclusively within their Belfast working-class parishes exhibited more local (i.e., less standard) speech features than their peers who occasionally ventured outside it (Milroy 1980; discussed in §3.3.2). In Martha's Vineyard, off the Massachusetts coast, use of a highly localized dialect variant correlated with the individuals' allegiance to their home territory: among teenagers, the variant occurred much less frequently in the speech of those who intended to leave the island for education or employment than in those who intended to stay (Labov 1972: 1–42; discussed in §2.7.1).

These studies and most others reported in this book show that linguistic variation is essentially a social phenomenon. It is not essentially biological. In fact, the best evidence of a biological contribution to sociolinguistic competence is in women's greater range of variants when gender roles are undifferentiated (discussed in §3.4.2). But the existence of variability – of accent and dialect as universal attributes – definitely has less to do with biology than with sociology.

The idea that dialect and accent are more deeply rooted in our biological nature was assumed by several seventeenth-century philosophers, as we will see in §5.5.1. The biological basis for linguistic variation might also appear to be supported by the fact that dialects are not uniquely human attributes. Dialects also occur in lower animals. That fact alone might promote the inference – indeed, has occasionally done so – that the function of linguistic variability is rooted in our biological nature. In the strongest interpretation, human linguistic diversity would be the atavistic residue of our evolutionary ascent. As we will see in the next section, when we look at animal vocalizations and their variability from this perspective, dialects primarily serve a social purpose for the lower animals as they do for us.

5.3 Dialects in Lower Animals

Biologists have long been aware of regional differences in the vocalizations of lower animals. They have called these differences "dialects", and we will use this term here without concerning ourselves about the appropriateness of applying the same word to both animal calls and human language. (For a discussion of this issue, see Moulton 1985.)

As the most conspicuously fluent species, birds were the first to draw the attention of biologists. Bird songs are far and away the most carefully studied animal dialects, and they will provide the illustrations in this section.[2] However, it is worth nothing that birds are by no means alone in the animal world in their vocal diversity. The dialects of squirrel monkeys (Winter 1969), Japanese monkeys (Green 1975), gibbons (Marshall and Marshall 1976), apes (Snowdon, Brown and Peterson 1982), tamarins (Hodun, Snowdon and Soini 1981), and elephant seals (LeBoeuf and Peterson 1969), among other species, have also been studied.

Both the study of animal dialects and its putative relationship to human dialectology are venerable. Darwin (1871: 462–3) postulated the connection as follows:

> Nestlings which have learnt the song of a distinct species, as with the canary-birds educated in the Tyrol, teach and transmit their new song to their offspring. The slight natural differences of song in the same species inhabiting different districts may be appositely compared, as Barrington remarks, "to provincial dialects;" and the songs of allied, though distinct species may be compared to the languages of distinct races of man.

The similarities in distributional patterns are indeed intriguing, and, as I shall argue below, so are the similarities in adaptive function.

5.3.1   *Buzzy and Clear white-crowned sparrows*

Looking at the distribution of one dialect grouping, though not directly related to the main point about adaptive function, will help to illustrate what biologists mean by bird song dialects as well as showing some gross similarities with human dialect distribution.

Colonies of white-crowned sparrows in the region of Point Reyes, in northern California, have been so well studied that one zoologist called them the "white rat of the ornithological world" (Baptista 1975). There is, for all that, no serious allegation that white-crowned sparrows differ in any significant way from any other species, or that one would draw any different conclusions by studying the dialects of chaffinches or starlings.

Two adjacent white-crowned sparrow dialects in Port Reyes are called Buzzy and Clear (Baker and Cunningham 1985: 90–1). The salient dialect feature, and the source of the names, occurs in the part of the song called "complex syllables," shown in the labeled sprectrograms of figure 5.1.

The song has four parts: an introduction, a pair of complex syllables, a number of (unpaired) simple syllables, and an ending. Though the songs shown in figure 5.1 clearly differ in the introductions, these differences are not crucial. Both dialect groups permit the same range of variants in the introductions. This is one way in which the sparrow dialects resemble human dialects, which often share the same range of variants as an areal feature. Crucially, in the Buzzy dialect, the complex syllables characteristically have the rapid modulations shown in the spectrogram, called "buzzy vibratos," whereas the Clear dialect characteristically lacks them. Here again there is a resemblance to human dialects because these differences are not categorical but are probabilistic: the buzzy vibratos occur in the songs of about 90 percent of the songbirds (i.e., the males) in the Buzzy region, and the clear syllables occur in the songs of about 90 percent of the songbirds in the Clear region.

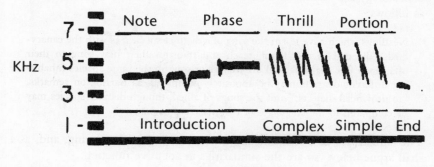

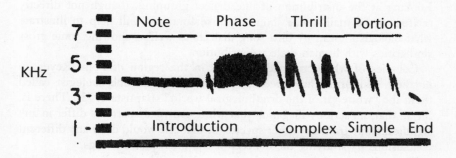

Figure 5.1 Components of a song in Clear dialect (top) and the Buzzy dialect (bottom) of white-crowned sparrows in Marin County, California (based on figures in Cunningham and Baker 1983, and Baker and Cunningham 1985)

The border between the dialect regions is shown in figure 5.2, along with two additional dialect groups, the Drake and the Limantour. The Buzzy, Clear border was established impressionistically before the sound spectrograms were made. Redrawing the line, however, would not make the separation of dialect regions more categorical than it presently is. The reason for this is that the line cuts through what Baker and Cunningham call an "intergrade zone of 'hybrid' song" about 1.5 km wide "in which songs contain complex syllables of the Buzzy dialect and simple syllables of the Clear dialect" (1985: 90–1). This is exactly equivalent to what is called, in the terms used in (human) dialectology, a transition zone with mixed lects

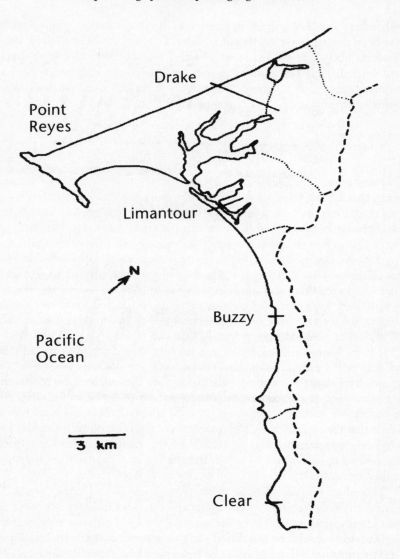

Figure 5.2   Map of Point Reyes area in Marin County, California, showing location of four dialect groups of white-crowned sparrows: Drake, Limantour, Buzzy, and Clear (from Baker and Cunningham 1985: 91)

(Chambers and Trudgill 1980: chapter 8). A similar dialect continuum has also been described for chaffinches (Slater, Clements and Goodfellow 1984). It seems likely that the existence of transition zones between both human and bird dialects has nothing to do with linguistic similarities between human beings and songbirds but follows from universal patterns in the spatial distribution of non-discrete entities of all kinds.

5.3.2   The theory of genetic adaptation

Turning now to the adaptive significance of songbird dialects, it is useful to recall that Labov, in raising the question about the "adaptive function [of] linguistic diversity" cited at the beginning of this chapter, was necessarily inconclusive but expressed the hope that bird song research might some day point the way to an answer. More than twenty years later, the findings of the biologists suggest that Labov's optimism was not justified. Biologists are no closer now to deciding the adaptive significance of bird song dialects than they were then, and future research is unlikely to narrow the range of possibilities, even if it might eliminate some and introduce others. Nevertheless, the weight of the evidence seems quite clearly to go against any kind of biological function.

If there were a biological function for bird song dialects, it would entail what is called genetic adaptation (Baker and Cunningham 1985: 97). This theory hypothesizes that bird song dialects are used as a means of identifying members of the communal cohort for purposes of inbreeding, thus speeding the natural selection of physical adaptations to the local habitat. Birds that thrive in a particular environment are likely to be those that have physical characteristics well suited to the local conditions. Bird song dialects are posited to be a means by which females can select mates from the region rather than interlopers, who may not be as well adapted.

This theory makes certain predictions: each dialect group should be genetically differentiated, their habitat should differ from that of other dialect groups, females should prefer mates of the local dialect group, and bird song dialects should be imprinted early to prevent mimicry by interlopers.

The problem is that the evidence for genetic adaptation is equivocal. The genetic differentiation of dialect groups, when it is found, is never complete but always partial (Baker 1974), and can in any case be explained simply as an accident of socialization (Baker and Marler 1980). Female preference for mates of the same dialect group was evident in a laboratory experiment (Baker 1983) in which a stimulated Buzzy female responded more strongly to a recording of a Buzzy song than to a Clear song, and more weakly yet to two songs from more distant habitats. Again, this result "can be equally well interpreted as a preference for a familiar song" (Jenkins 1985), that is, as a consequence of social conditioning. In other words, birds that flock together inevitably share the same gene pool and develop a feeling for the local song.

A somewhat stronger case might be made for the earliness of dialect learning and its apparent impermeability once learned. For white-crowned sparrows the critical period for learning the bird song dialect is the first 50 days, and adult males transported to different dialect areas do not alter their song (Baker and Cunningham 1985: 87–8). These facts seem to invite the inference that dialect learning has biological significance, but, again, the facts have been called into question. Petrinovitch and Patterson (1981) caged a 50-day-old male with an adult male of a different sub-species with a different song and found that in response to repeated attacks by the adult the juvenile learned the adult's song. This relatively late acquisition of the sub-species dialect can be seen as a natural response to the unnaturally intense social pressure exerted by the adult.

So, under unusual social circumstances, neither the earliness of learning nor its impermeability seem to hold. Typically, birds spend their lives within their natal populations, where early and unalterable song learning can be the norm.

5.3.3   The theory of social adaptation

All of these observations about bird song dialects are consistent with the effects of socialization, without the need for invoking biological functions. So, of course, are all of the observations about human dialects.

For humans, any postulated theory of dialects as genetic adaptation mechanisms seems implausible. Gene flow and allele fixation can be ruled out as simply irrelevant. Mating is not determined linguistically for humans, although in communities with extremely dense networks some stigma is attached to a member who takes a spouse from "outside." Territoriality along dialectal lines sometimes occurs among humans, with speech-based antagonisms detectable at several social levels, but it probably becomes a fighting matter only between the most insular groups, if at all.

One large difference is that most humans, unlike birds, do not spend their lives within their natal populations. Human social groups range along a continuum between the polar extremities of global mobility and local insularity. Sociolinguistically, the effects of high mobility include multilingualism, code-switching, diglossia, accommodation, style-switching – none of which has a counterpart in the communication systems of lower animals.

One of the consequences of high mobility is that people with linguistic systems acquired among their natal populations encounter different systems. These encounters carry an element of risk. They can lead to isolation, misunderstanding, embarrassment, harrassment or ostracism. If they do, then an observer might be justified in claiming that linguistic diversity is counteradaptive, even dysfunctional. It appears to be the price we must pay for the security of beginning our lives in a circumscribed dialect area with regional bonds and community ties.

Evidently it is a price we are willing to pay. As yet, no political theorist has devised a social system that would "liberate" people by removing them as infants from their natal communities. Just as songbirds carry with them the linguistic markers of their origins from an early age, so most humans carry their linguistic markers from puberty onwards.

5.4   The Persistence of the Non-standard

If regional and social accents cause their bearers discomfort or grief, why do they continue to exist? If New Yorkers and Montrealers disparage the way they sound when they speak, why don't they speak differently?

Although it is impossible for most people to transform their accents completely, it is not hard for them to use standard variants alongside non-standard ones, especially in more careful styles. In the course of two or three generations, if the pressures against speaking non-standard accents were painful enough, there would be a massive shift in the direction of the standard.

There is of course an observable tendency toward the standard, though it probably cannot be called a massive shift. In fact, as we have seen, it is typically restricted socially to the speech of the upper working class and the lower middle class, and it is more noticeable in the speech of women than of men. At the same time, as we have also seen, there are always shifts away from the standard happening as well, and new variants developing in non-standard accents.

5.4.1   Covert prestige

If there are social pressures that promote standard dialects, there must also be counter-pressures favoring the local, the informal and the vernacular in speech. But if so, those counter-pressures must be tacit rather than conscious, because they are not easy to identify. The forces favoring the standard are crystal clear: middle-class parents talk about "good" language, school teachers correct the usage of students, letters to the editor deplore slips away from prescribed usage. We are as aware of the social acceptability of standard speech as we are of good manners, to the point that interviewees

sometimes apologize to interviewers for the way they talk and people sometimes blush if someone finds a spelling mistake in something they have
written.

By contrast, the social pressures that maintain the non-standard have no
identifiable lobbyists. No one complains publicly about hypercorrectness in
newspaper articles, or about the uniformity of accents by broadcasters, or
about the tyranny of our spelling conventions.

"Why don't all people speak in the way they obviously believe they
should?" Labov (1972: 249) asks, and then he offers this answer:

> Careful consideration of this difficult problem has led us to posit the exist-
> ence of an opposing set of covert norms, which attribute positive values to the
> vernacular. In most formal situations in urban areas, such as an interview or
> a psycholinguistic test, these norms are extremely difficult to elicit. Middle-
> class values are so dominant in these contexts that most subjects cannot
> perceive any opposing values, no matter how strongly they may influence
> behavior in other situations.

An indication of these tacit values can be seen in this comment by one of
Labov's New York informants (1966: 494), a middle-aged man who was
born outside the city and moved there as a youngster:

> To me, I t'ink I got de New York speech. At one time I had good speech, and
> vocabulary too, when I first came from Massachusetts. But I lost it. When I
> first came here, to New York, they used to say, "You speak like a fairy – like
> they do in Massachusetts." When I kept going back to Massachusetts, they
> said, "Gee, you got the New York lingo."

Even though this man overtly contrasts his "New York speech" with "good
speech," it seems quite clear that he takes pride in his accent, though
covertly. His real values are revealed in his recollection that his New York
peer group considered his Massachusetts accent effeminate when he arrived
there, and in his feeling – real or imagined – that his former neighbors in
Massachusetts were very impressed by his new accent.

The tacit value is known as covert prestige, the term Trudgill (1972,
1983: 169–85) gave it when he provided the first objective evidence for it.
The concept has its origin in Labov's discussion (1966: 499–501) of the
"negative prestige" of New York City speech, though at the time Labov
considered "the exact description of the covert values" that gave it that
negative prestige a task for future research.

In his Norwich survey, Trudgill administered a self-evaluation test to
half his subjects. The individuals listened to phonetic variants of words and
then were asked to indicate which one they themselves regularly used. For
instance, variable (er) in Norwich, in words like *ear*, *near*, and *idea*, occurs
with the standard variant [ɪə] and with the regional variant [ɛ:]. When

Table 5.1 Percentage of informants over- and under-reporting (er) (from Trudgill 1983: 176)

	Total	Male	Female
Over-report	43	22	68
Under-report	33	50	14
Accurate	23	28	18

Table 5.2 Percentage of informants over- and under-reporting (ō) (from Trudgill 1983: 176)

	Total	Male	Female
Over-report	18	12	25
Under-report	36	54	18
Accurate	45	34	57

subjects were asked whether they actually said [nɪə] or [nɛ:] for "near", the results showed some striking discrepancies, as indicated in table 5.1.

There is a tendency in tests such as this for subjects to report their behavior inaccurately, as Labov established in his pioneering work in self-evaluation testing (1966: 455–81). Trudgill's Norwich subjects were very inaccurate in their ability to hear themselves with respect to (er). Only 23 percent of them reported accurately, as shown in the lower left cell of table 5.1. The other cells in the third row show that more men (28 percent) than women (18 percent) report their behavior accurately for this variable. However, more significantly, the direction in which the subjects err tends to be different for men than for women. Men are much more likely to under-report their behavior (as 50 percent do in this case) and women are more likely to over-report (68 percent in this case). This means that 50 percent of the men claimed to use the non-standard variant when in fact they most frequently used the standard variant, and that 68 percent of the women claimed to use the standard variant when in fact they used the non-standard variant.

Trudgill got similar results for the other three variables tested in the same way. Table 5.2 shows the results for (ō), the vowel in words such as *road, nose* and *moan* which occurs either as the standard nucleus [ou] or as the highly distinctive Norfolk [u:] or [ʊ]. Notice that for this variable the women are more accurate self-reporters than the men, suggesting that accuracy is not predictable and is therefore probably not socially significant. Here again, however, the discrepancy occurs between men and women with respect to over-reporting and under-reporting, as indeed it does in all four of Trudgill's test variables: 54 percent of the men claim the non-standard variant when they actually use the standard one, and 25 percent of the women claim they use the standard variant when they actually use the non-standard one.

Trudgill's results provide interesting evidence for the values that comprise covert prestige. We assume, as a lemma, Labov's explanation for the discrepancies between self-reports and actual usage, namely, that when people think they are reporting their own usage, they are actually reporting their "norm of correctness" (1966: 455). In other words, as Labov (1966: 480) also said, "most of the respondents seemed to perceive their own speech in terms of the norms at which they were aiming rather than the sound actually produced."

In these terms, most women in Trudgill's test report themselves using the standard variant. They therefore hold as their norm of correctness standard speech, a conclusion that is consistent with the tendency discussed in chapter 3 for women to use more standard features than men of the same social group. Their linguistic norms are thus the consciously promulgated social standards.

For the men, by contrast, the tendency to under-report their actual usage leads by the same argument to the conclusion that many men subconsciously favor non-standard speech forms. This is partly explained by the fact that some men associate non-standard speech, especially WC speech, with masculinity and ruggedness. As Trudgill (1983: 177) says:

> the norm at which a large number of Norwich males are aiming is non-standard WC speech. This favourable attitude is never overtly expressed, but the responses to these [self-evaluation] tests show that statements about "bad speech" are for public consumption only. Privately and subconsciously, a large number of male speakers are more concerned with acquiring prestige of the covert sort and with signalling group solidarity than with acquiring social status, as this is more usually defined.

Trudgill also considers, briefly, why these results arose so clearly in the Norwich survey but not – or at least not so clearly – in the New York survey or other American studies. A possible answer, he says, might be the sharper stratification in England between classes, particularly the fact that there is relatively less "embourgeoisement" of the working class.

5.4.2   *Status and solidarity*

Having identified covert prestige as a psycholinguistic factor, the question now remains as to why regional and working-class varieties of speech should be the ones to which covert prestige is attached. The reason is apparently deducible from a highly robust result from subjective evaluation tests.

In numerous tests conducted in diverse linguistic situations, subjects have repeatedly discriminated between standard and non-standard varieties on two dimensions. One dimension, called "status-stressing" (Ryan 1979: 151), includes qualities having to do with intelligence, education, ambition, wealth, success and achievement, and subjects typically assign highest evaluations for these qualities to standard speakers. The other dimension, "solidarity-stressing," includes qualities such as kindness, likability, friendliness, goodness, and trust, and subjects assign highest evaluations for these qualities to regional or other non-standard speakers.

5.4.2.1 Jewish and MC accents in Montreal This distinction has shown up repeatedly in the results of subjective reaction tests. In one of the very first, Anisfield, Bogo and Lambert (1962) elicited reactions to taped texts read in matched guises in MC Montreal English and in Jewish-accented English. All subjects rated the MC guises more highly with regard to status-stressing traits such as leadership and self-confidence. Subjects who were themselves Jewish concurred on those judgements but rated the Jewish guises more highly for sense of humor, entertainingness and kindliness, the solidarity-stressing traits.

In a variation on the test design, Edwards and Jakobsen (1987) elicited evaluations for a set of four regional accents without any standard accent among them. The evaluators included speakers of all four accents being judged, and the purpose of the experiment was to discover both how they would assign status-stressing ratings in the absence of a dominant standard accent and how they would allot solidarity-stressing ratings in the presence of several regional accents.

Put simply, the subjects made no significant distinctions among the accents on traits having to do with integrity and attractiveness, but they significantly favored the most local of the accents on traits having to do with social status and educational success. That is, they conferred solidarity on all the regional accents but gave the edge for local success to those who were linguistically identifiable as local progeny. They too assigned prestige covertly to the speakers of low-status varieties by attributing positive human qualities to them.

5.4.2.2 High and low accents in Guangzhou Covert prestige appears to be associated with working-class speech varieties in all urbanized, industrialized societies. Kalmar, Zhong and Xiao (1987) reported "a textbook case of attitudes to a high and low dialect . . . in a bidialectal . . . community" in Guangzhou (Canton), a sprawling industrial city in the People's Republic of China. Even though the social conditions there are very different from most places where subjective evaluation tests have been carried out, the results are consistent with tests carried out in Western cities. The experimenters based their test on recordings by two speakers in two different guises: Putonghua, literally "general speech", is the national standard based on Mandarin Chinese, and Cantonized Putonghua is a heavily accented regional variety.

The listeners were both native Cantonese and non-natives working in Canton. In their evaluations of the taped accents, all agreed that the Putonghua speakers would be more likely to hold white collar jobs, to be the offspring of white collar workers, to find new jobs if they lost theirs, to occupy positions requiring interpersonal skills, and to be more ambitious for social advancement. The Cantonese listeners judged – though the non-Cantonese listeners did not necessarily agree – that the Cantonese-accented speakers would be preferred to approach for help, to supervise their work, and to consult about personal problems.

The authors note that, "despite the relatively small size of the sample, many of the results were statistically significant, indicating the remarkable strength of the attitudes we measured" (1987: 502). Again we see that the standard dialect overtly receives social approbation while the regional variety evokes an undefined but nonetheless real kind of intimacy or comfort.

The persistence of non-standard varieties appears, then, to be a direct consequence of the deep-seated feelings, conscious or not, their speakers have for them. Ryan (1979: 147–8) says:

> although regional, ethnic, and lower-class individuals have limited access to opportunities for acquiring the prestige variety compared to members of the high status groups, much of the failure of these individuals to profit from whatever opportunities are available is due to counteracting pressures favouring their native speech styles. Most importantly, a certain amount of language loyalty is natural in every language user because of the inescapable emotional involvement with one's mother tongue *as one learned it in childhood*.

In other words, the local accent goes right to the heart. The Newfoundland dialectologist Harold Paddock put it more simply in explaining his feelings for his accent to a newspaper reporter (Cox 1992). "When I'm in an airplane and I hear that it has lost an engine," Paddock said, "I'll pray in my own dialect. I figure it's the only language God understands."

5.5   Traditional Theories of the Sources of Diversity

Almost three thousand years ago, the myth of Babel attempted to establish divine retribution as the cause of linguistic diversity, as we have seen. After that, there was a hiatus of several centuries when there appears to have been little or no theorizing about linguistic diversity at all. One reason for this is undoubtedly the intellectual domination of the Greeks for almost a millennium. The Greeks established inquiries into rhetoric and poetics, and categorized grammatical elements such as *onoma* 'noun' or 'name', *rhēma* 'predicate' or 'saying', and *logos* 'sentence' or 'argument' (Dinneen 1967: 72–113), but they did not inquire into linguistic variability of any kind.[3] In fact, the Greek classical literature makes virtually no mention of any language other than Greek, or of any dialects or accents.

The most famous classical discussion of language, Plato's *Cratylus*, centers around a debate about relative merits of *nomos*, the notion that words have meanings only because people agree on them, as opposed to *physis*, the notion that words are inherently and naturally related to the things they name. Socrates supports *physis*, and in its defense proposes several etymologies – patently ridiculous ones in hindsight – intended to demonstrate the necessary connection between certain objects and their names.

If Plato had wondered about linguistic diversity, he would presumably have had to conclude, based on the doctrine of *physis*, that it could not exist.[4] Since Plato believed that words have to have the meaning they have, it follows that they can have no other meaning and moreover that no other word can possibly have that meaning. This seems an inauspicious basis for theorizing, since the most mundane detail about natural language would seem to refute it, and mercifully Plato did not consider it. Theories of linguistic diversity came into their own many centuries later.

5.5.1 Variation and climates

Eighteenth century philosophers believed that language was God-given, as the authors of the myth of Babel had also believed. This belief was simply taken for granted in most philosophical treatises. Locke (1690: 101) attributed to God a sociolinguistic purpose in bestowing it on humankind. "God, having designed man for a sociable creature," Locke said in *An Essay Concerning Human Understanding*, "made him not only with an inclination, and under a necessity to have fellowship with those of his kind, but furnished him also with language, which was to be the great instrument and common tie of society."

God's beneficence thus accounted for the origin of language. It also tended to eliminate speculation about it in general.

As a natural, organic entity, language was not unlike a plant, and its diversity was thought to have the same source as the diversity of vegetation. Just as vegetable life took on distinctly different appearances according to the climate and soil that nourished it, so languages were distinctly different in different physical environments.

One expression of this viewpoint, a famous passage by Herder (1764; quoted by Brown 1967: 74), looked at linguistic diversity through the haze of the Romantic *Sturm und Drang*, and arrived at this bathetic conception:

> When the children of dust undertook that structure that menaced the clouds – the Tower of Babel – , then the pleasure-cup of confusion was poured out over them, their families and dialects were transplanted in divers regions of the earth; and there came into being a thousand languages according to the climate and the customs of a thousand nations. If the oriental burns here under a hot zenith, then his bellowing mouth also streams forth a fervid and impassioned language. There the Greek flourishes in the most voluptuous and mildest climate; his body is, as Pindar expresses it, suffused with grace, his organs of speech are fine, and among them, therefore, originated that fine Attic speech. The Romans had a more vigorous language. The martial Germans spoke still more stoutly; the sprightly Gaul invents a salutory and softer speech; the Spaniard imparts to his a solemn appearance, even though it be only by mere sounds; the slothful African stammers brokenly and droopingly . . . Thus transformed itself this plant – human speech – according to the soil that nourished it and the celestial air that drenched it: it became a Proteus among the nations.

To readers with linguistic training, Herder's errors are obvious. We know that climate does not affect speech organs, as Herder, accepting the theory of a man named Johann Winckelmann (Brown 1967: 72–3), believed it did. We recognize Herder's fallacy – a common one to this day – in conferring to languages traits that more appropriately belong to cultures or literatures but are completely irrelevant to language, such as the purported "grace" of classical Greek and "vigor" of Latin. And we see his description of Oriental and African languages, which we now know to be typologically diverse and structurally complex, as sheer ignorance.

5.5.2   Variation and contact

A later theory of linguistic diversity, propounded by philologists starting in the late nineteenth century and perhaps most fully delineated by Jespersen, maintains that diversity is mainly the product of lack of social contact. Although this idea may seem obvious to us, a truism perhaps, the philologists had inherited the idea of climatically controlled physiological differences as determinants and had to divest themselves of it before they could look closely at language. Jespersen begins (1946: 35–6) with a mild rebuff of Herder and his contemporaries, saying, "The most important cause of a language splitting into dialects is not purely physical, but want of communication for whatever reason." And somewhat more broadly (1946: 40): "Linguistic unity depends always on intercourse, on a community of life, whereby the chief roughness of different dialects are [*sic*] smoothed down."

He recognizes two "opposing tendencies" in language, one favoring diversification and the other favoring unification. He disputes what he sees as the majority opinion among philologists that "the natural process of evolution is steadily in the direction of splitting and cleavage, so that out of unity arises variety." He says (1946: 38):

> With what might be called a fatalistic belief, they [the philologists] put forward this side of the question without seeing that there are forces working in exactly the opposite direction, and completely overlooking the fact that these unifying forces have in historical times been really stronger than the differentiating forces, that they are so particularly at present, and certainly will be so in the future.

Among the unifying forces, Jespersen discusses the growth of national standard languages (39–44), written as opposed to oral literary traditions (44–48), national theatre companies (48–9), the agglomeration of people from various districts in military service and universities (54–7), and urbanization (57–64). The standard dialect will naturally be, he believes, "an upper-class language," because "the upper class travels more and mixes more with people of similar standing from other parts of the country" (54).

Jespersen claims that all these factors have had a "colossal influence" in promoting linguistic unity, and he predicts "the future will see greater and greater unifications in all languages which are spoken essentially in the same way by millions of speakers" (64).

5.5.3 The prevalence of diversity

The ensuing half century has not borne out Jespersen's prediction. Dialects are not demonstrably fewer in number. Although it is obviously true that the proportion of rural accents has diminished with increasing urbanization, it is just as obviously not true that in the cities standardization has leveled the diversity. Instead it appears that proximity, even though it brings with it increased contact, does not promote homogenization in asymmetrical social situations, as between service workers and their higher-class clients, teachers and their lower-class students, and the like. Labov (1984) shows that in the most segregated black communities in Philadelphia the "dialect is drifting further away" from other dialects despite four to eight hours daily exposure to standard English on television and in schools. Most casual contacts in urban settings are scarcely more personal than the contact between a television character and a viewer, and consequently have no more impact on dialects.

Against those impersonal encounters, there appears to be a natural tendency for people to cling to the linguistic markers that imbue their most personal encounters. We come full circle, then, to the role of covert prestige in maintaining dialect diversity. The notion underlying covert prestige was not completely unknown to Jespersen. He mentions people who, "even though they belong to the best educated classes, feel a certain pride in retaining traces of their native district, and with a certain coquetry flaunt before our eyes some of the most noticeable features of its dialect" (1946: 66). But he appears to have underestimated its strength as a countervailing force.

It is not clear, in any case, whether Jespersen really offered his view as a linguistic theory or as a political ideal. Certainly there are many points where his rhetoric seems more appropriate to politics than to philology, as when he says (1946: 72): "If we think out logically and bravely what is for the good of society, our view of language will lead us to the conclusion that it is our duty to work in the direction which natural evolution has already taken, i.e. towards the diffusion of the common language at the cost of local dialects."

Essentially he is reasserting the Babelian hypothesis. The only linguistic claim he makes is that "natural evolution" tends to favor standardization, a point which, as we have seen, seems dubious.

Another flaw in his theory is the claim that standardization will favor upper-class speech. In industrialized Western societies it favors middle middle-class speech. And his postulated cause of dialect unification, contact among speakers, seems a simplification. Judging by the individuals whose speech undergoes some notable degree of standardization, the social prerequisite is not merely contact but at least two and perhaps all three kinds of mobility: geographical, social and occupational (as discussed in §2.4).

Among highly mobile individuals in any of these three senses, a large number of social contacts is likely, but it is not the contacts themselves that matter but their quality – the proportion of those contacts that are meetings among equals. Jespersen's prediction of standard-dialect diffusion would surely come true in a society that unequivocally promoted high mobility for all its citizens. The converse is also true, as we concluded earlier: non-standard accents and other forms of linguistic diversity would be counterproductive in a society with a great deal of mobility.

5.6   A Sociolinguistic Theory of the Sources of Diversity

Social, occupational and geographical mobility are never perfectly realized in industrialized societies or any others. All societies encompass social and occupational inequalities of various kinds – white collar vs. blue collar, rich vs. poor, insiders and outsiders, haves and have-nots, Them and Us. The

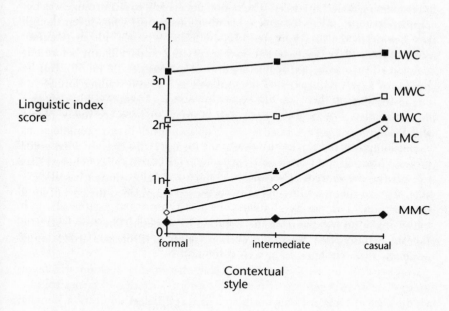

Figure 5.3 Typical pattern of social stratification, with the border-line social groups showing the broadest linguistic repertoire

preservation of these distinctions, apparently in perpetuity, even when public policy purports to eliminate them by universal access to education, training and employment, may not be entirely accidental, or the result of innate inequalities. They may be, to use Kroch's term which will be important in the rest of the discussion in this chapter, ideological. To see this, we must review the loci of linguistic diversity in the social structure.

5.6.1 Linguistic diversity and social strata

Trudgill (1974: 62) first observed that the greatest amount of style-shifting normally occurs among members of the UWC and the LMC, that is, among the social groups at the borderline of the principal class division in industrialized societies.[5] This observation has now been confirmed countless times and is one of the best established results of sociolinguistic research. (For a comprehensive examination, see Labov 1980.)

Figure 5.3 shows a stylized representation of the prototypical stratification of a linguistic variable. The LMC and the UWC have the widest stylistic repertoire. They are transitional in the sense that they approach the norms of social groups both above and below them. In the diagram, the LMC and UWC score less than $1n$ in the formal style as does the MMC, but they score more than $1n$ in the casual style as do the WC groups. Such a pattern is not at all surprising: as the most mobile individuals in the community, the LMC and UWC naturally find themselves in reciprocal contact with people on both sides of them in the social hierarchy. They are quite literally intermediaries, bridging the social gap between the more entrenched MC and WC groups.

Sociolinguists have naturally shown the most interest in these transitional groups. After all, they are where the action is. For our purposes in seeking to discover the sources of sociolinguistic diversity, however, we must consider instead the more linguistically stable groups at the top and bottom of the diagram. The norms of their behavior, represented graphically as in figure 5.3, form parallel lines that cannot converge. They presumably hold the key to any laws we might discover about setting and perpetuating linguistic differentiation in speech communities.

5.6.2   *Two tenets about standard dialects*

In our search for a set of linguistic principles and constraints that will provide a unified view of the social stratification of language, I am going to take as a point of departure two tenets from Kroch (1978). Although neither one can be adopted in its original form, each of them opens up issues that must be decided in an integrated theory of sociolinguistic variation.

The first tenet is that the standard dialect differs from other dialects in the community by resisting certain natural tendencies in the grammar and phonology. This is an extension of Kroch's notion (1978: 18) that the standard dialect inhibits "many of the low-level, variable processes of phonetic conditioning that characterize spoken language and that underlie regular phonological change" whereas other dialects do not.

The second tenet is that the root of these dialectal differences is ideological, not linguistic. In the sphere of language, it is not the content of nonstandard dialects that arouses criticism but their form. The arbiters of "good" language are less concerned about breakdowns in meaning or comprehensibility than they are about deviations from an imposed form. Taking umbrage at someone's use of *ain't* for *isn't*, to take a simple example, has no linguistic basis when the interchangeability of their meanings is known to everyone, but it has an ideological basis insofar as the usage marks a class distinction in the community. Drawing attention to the usage reinforces the class distinction, and that – rather than any linguistic purpose – is presumably the purpose of doing so. (The main discussion of this tenet is in §5.8.)

Whether or not these two tenets are necessary conditions for sociolinguistic diversity is impossible to determine in the present state of our knowledge; there may well be other factors that contribute, as Labov (1980) points out. But these two appear to be sufficient conditions, at least with certain refinements, and I have found their plausibility enhanced, not limited, by attempts to expand them beyond Kroch's terms. For example, Kroch discussed the first tenet about the suppression of natural processes solely as it applied to phonetics. As the main illustration below I apply it to English morphology with obvious and, I think, convincing results.

5.6.2.1 *Naturalness and economy*

Kroch's discussion of the suppression of natural tendencies by speakers of the standard dialect suffers from his identifying those tendencies with "ease of articulation," sometimes called economy or the principle of least effort. It is easy to agree with his contention that "non-prestige dialects tend to be articulatorily more economical than the prestige dialect" (1978: 20). But it is obviously not true that economy is the sole, or even the guiding, principle. Labov (1972: 249) earlier pointed out that "there is no foundation for the notion that stigmatized vernacular forms are easier to pronounce."

This is an important point for linguists to recognize and publicize because the most voluble critics of non-standard speech often rationalize their prejudices by contending that the speech they despise is "sloppy" or "lazy" or "slovenly". The relevance of those terms to ease of articulation is obvious.

In fact, although some natural processes in language are governed by ease of articulation, some others are not. Labov notes that the vowel shifts in progress in many American working-class vernaculars involve tensing and thus actually increase the muscular effort as compared to standard speech. One celebrated example among many others is the raising and tensing of /æ/ in the northern cities shift (Labov, Yaeger and Steiner 1972, Labov 1991). The sound which is typically realized as low front unrounded [æ] in standard pronunciations of *Ann, bad, bag, bash*, and so on, occurs in cities like Buffalo, Rochester and Chicago as [ɛə] or [ɪə]; Labov notes that speakers of standard dialects sometimes mistake the name *Ann* for *Ian* when they hear it spoken in northern cities vernacular. The comparative complexity of the non-standard nucleus is patent.

Faced with Labov's argument against ease of articulation, Kroch (1978: 20) claims that the evidence is "irrelevant" because the tendency toward ease of articulation "manifests itself primarily in the consonant system." But even here it is an occasional concomitant rather than the rule. To take a straightforward counter-example, the most pervasive consonantal variable in English is the replacement of standard [ŋ] by [n] in participial forms like *walking, running* and *jogging*. The non-standard reflex is often held up to ridicule by prescriptivists on the grounds that "leaving off the g" is mere sloth. Linguistically, of course, the prescriptivists' allegation is ridiculous, because the variation has nothing to do with 'g' or with deletion. The variation between the velar nasal stop and the alveolar nasal stop is not construable in terms of articulatory economy by any objective criterion.

5.6.2.2   Medial /t/ Further complicating the situation is the inherent vagueness of the notion of economy. If we look, for instance, at various dialect reflexes of post-tonic prevocalic /t/, we get a fair indication of the difficulty of determining ease of articulation. In standard British accents, /t/ in words like *pity, putting, propensity, forty, plenty*, and the like, occurs as alveolar, fortis [t]. In Trinidadian English and many other Caribbean varieties, in these environments, it occurs as aspirated [tʰ]. Here is a clear counter-example inasmuch as the prestige standard in Trinidad is RP, with non-aspirated [t], which would not be characterized as less economical than [tʰ] by any phonetic criterion. In Canadian English post-tonic /t/ is usually voiced to [d], a lenition and arguably an "easier" articulation. In some American varieties it is not only voiced but flapped, as [ɾ], which is a lenition with respect to voicing but involves an additional articulatory gesture, flapping, and probably is not more economical. In many Southern England vernaculars including Norwich (Trudgill 1974: 80–3), it occurs variably as [t], [tʔ], or [ʔ]: the glottal stop eliminates the alveolar closure but replaces it, in effect, with glottal closure which is probably not by any criterion articulatorily easier, and the coarticulated glottalized alveolar is obviously more complicated articulatorily. Finally, in Wales and much of northern England, working-class vernaculars have [ts] for /t/, an affrication which, by assibilating the stop release, is palpably a complication.

These reflexes form a kind of phonetic continuum along which it is impossible to determine unequivocally the point at which ease of articulation begins. Wherever that point might be, the distribution of articulatory economy does not follow Kroch's putative tendency.

Table 5.3 attempts to consolidate these phonetic features into a measure for ease of articulation. The features in the leftmost column indicate lack of ease by positive integers, so that +**voiceless**, for instance, is more fortis than -**voiceless**. The glottalic feature **constricted glottis** is defined as non-vibrating closure of the vocal cords, as differentiated from voicing, which is vibrating closure. By definition, **constricted glottis** is less tense than voicing, but it is nevertheless more tense – or less economical, in the terms we are interested in – than unconstricted glottis (Lombardi 1991).[6] **Delayed release** refers to the tenseness of the articulatory gesture in the release of the stop closure. **Additional gesture** is a heuristic category that merely saves making separate rows for each of three relevant features,

Table 5.3 Measurements of ease of articulation for seven dialectal reflexes of post-tonic prevocalic /t/

	d	ɾ	t	tʰ	ʔ	tʔ	ts
Voiceless	−	−	+	+	+	+	+
Constricted glottis	−	−	−	−	+	+	−
Delayed release	−	−	−	−	−	−	+
Additional gesture	−	+	−	+	−	+	+
Economy metric	0	1	1	2	2	3	3

namely, (1) the apical tap that distinguishes [ɾ] from [d], (2) the coarticulation that distinguishes [tʔ] from all the other phones in the list, and (3) the assibilation in the release of [ts] that distinguishes it from the non-assibilated release of [tʰ]. By adding the plusses in each column we derive a handy, if crude, measure of the ease of articulation: the lower the number, the greater relative ease of articulation.

Clearly, the results do not support Kroch's contention that non-prestige dialects tend to be more economical. On the contrary, the phones found in standard dialects, [t], [d], and [ɾ], measure zero or 1 and are actually *more* economical than the non-standard phones, [tʰ], [ʔ], [tʔ] and [ts], which measure 2 or 3.

5.6.2.3 *Economy as a general linguistic force*

Finally, even when ease of articulation can be incontrovertibly identified as a motivating factor in a linguistic process, it applies as often to standard dialects as to non-standard ones. In other words, it appears to be a general linguistic factor involved in linguistic change and variability of all kinds rather than a differentiating characteristic of certain social dialects. This is not surprising in view of the fact that ease of articulation is partly a physiological demand. As Lindblom (1990: 425) says, discussing variation phonetically without regard for its social implications, "Unconstrained, a motor system tends to default to a low-cost form of behavior."

5.6.2.4 *Morpheme-final consonant clusters*

The variable (CC̲), morpheme-final consonant cluster simplification, provides a well-studied example that also makes an instructive illustration of the generality of the principle of ease of articulation. The phonetic motivation for the rule is the reduction of consonant clusters, a highly natural process because it simplifies articulatory gestures in the stream of speech. What we will discover is that all social groups default to a low-cost form of behavior by reducing the articulatory gestures but that the constraints consistently differ.

In standard MC vernaculars virtually everywhere in the English-speaking world, (C$\underline{C}$) is tightly constrained both linguistically and stylistically. It applies only when the morpheme-final cluster precedes another consonant across the word boundary, so that *first base* can be pronounced *firs' base*, and *second base* can be pronounced *secon' base*. It can also apply before semi-vowels across the word boundary – *firs' one, secon' one* – but much less frequently. Moreover, it does not apply freely in these linguistic environments but is restricted socially to relatively casual situations, with deletions before semi-vowels permitted only in highly colloquial situations, and deletions before consonants perhaps permitted in more careful styles after obstruents (as in *firs' base*) than after sonorants (as in *secon' base*). Quite specifically, then, in MC speech (C$\underline{C}$) has as its motive the simplification of triconsonantal clusters (i.e., C$\underline{C}$#C → C$\emptyset$#C) particularly in styles where allegro speech makes complex articulatory gestures inconvenient.

5.6.2.5 Standard and non-standard (C$\underline{C}$)

When we look at vernaculars in social groups below the MC, (C$\underline{C}$) occurs with a different set of linguistic and stylistic constraints. In BEV (Guy 1980) and rural northern England (Chambers 1982), to take two widely separated dialects, cluster simplification can occur not only before consonants and semi-vowels across a word boundary but also before vowels (*firs' out, secon' out*), and before pauses (*firs', secon'*). Furthermore, these deletions can occur in most or all stylistic registers.

In the most segregated BEV dialects and in the most isolated rural northern England dialects (the Isle of Man) final cluster simplification approaches categoricity, suggesting that morphemes have been relexified with no final clusters. Evidence for this is found in plurals such as *tesses* for (standard) *tests*, which appears to have been formed on underlying *tes'* (not *test*), and derived forms such as *win'y* for (standard) *windy*, which appears to have the derivational suffix added to underlying *win'* (not *wind*).

Note that these forms could only have evolved from a system where the constraints on (C$\underline{C}$) were more general than for MC speech. Unlike MC speech, (C$\underline{C}$) in non-standard and regional vernaculars has as its motive the simplification of biconsonantal clusters (C$\underline{C}$#V → C$\emptyset$#V and C$\underline{C}$## → C$\emptyset$##), as well as triconsonantal.

It is presumably the naturalness underlying both the MC vernacular and the non-standard vernacular that accounts for the wide distribution of (C$\underline{C}$). Speakers of urban MC English in, say, Toronto and Toledo did not directly influence one another and yet, with respect to (C$\underline{C}$), they carry similar, perhaps even identical, constraints. The vernacular English spoken in inner city Detroit and rural Durham had no influence whatever on one another and yet they share the same set of contraints for (C̲C̲). In contrasting the MC constraints with the vernacular constraints, it is clear that their domains differ, with one set based on triconsonantal clusters and the other on biconsonantal clusters. Both are natural – and both are interpretable in terms of articulatory ease.

5.6.3   Naturalness beyond phonetics

There is, then, no compelling reason for invoking economy as an explanatory principle for social dialects. Moreover, once it is abandoned, we find we can construct a postulate not inconsistent with Kroch's general contention but demonstrably more general.

All the examples so far have shown that the prestige dialect differs from other social dialects by permitting fewer natural phonetic processes and by placing more constraints on them where they are permitted. Further, once freed from the putative articulatory constraint, the postulate can be generalized beyond phonetics.[7] We can now broaden it to include natural processes at any linguistic level. The generality of the revised postulate will be illustrated in the next section with an example from English morphology.

5.6.3.1   *The principle of conjugation regularization in English*   There is a centuries-old tendency in English to level past tense and past participle forms. This analogical leveling appears to be a natural process inasmuch as its goal is to regularize a sub-system of the grammar that historically consisted of several sub-sub-systems with numerous highly marked exceptions. As Pinker and Prince (1988) have shown, these properties of the verbal system in modern English carry a high cognitive cost because they rely on memory and idiosyncratic retrieval rather than rule-governed or inferrable generalizations. The modern system, though still fairly complex, represents a considerable regularization from Old English. It is a reasonable inference that the tendency toward conjugation regularization, which has been detectable for all thirteen centuries of recorded history, originated because of the cognitive overload. As such, it is a highly natural process.

The mechanism for conjugation regularization in English is this simple principle: make the past tense and past participle forms the same (Chambers and Trudgill 1991).

Although Modern English still includes a few dozen verbs in which the past tense and the past participle are not the same, scores of verbs have been re-formed according to this principle in the last millennium. Table 5.4 lists six verbs in their Old English (OE) forms (from Morris 1903: 232, 234, 239, 243) alongside the Modern English (MnE) counterparts. These are just a smattering of the verbs that were strong verbs in the earliest documents

Table 5.4 Six Old English strong verbs alongside their direct descendants in Modern English illustrating the generalization of the weak inflectional forms to make the past tense and past participle forms the same

OE	Past Tense	Past Participle	MnE	Past Tense	Past Participle
cráwe	créow	cráwen	to crow	crowed	crowed
helpe	healp (sg) { } hulpon (pl)	holpen	to help	helped	helped
melte	mealt (sg) { } multon (pl)	molten	to melt	melted	melted
rówe	réow	rowen	to row	rowed	rowed
scafe	scóf	scafen	to shave	shaved	shaved
súce	séac (sg) { } sucon (pl)	socen	to suck	sucked	sucked

and have become weak verbs with the passage of time. Though the verbal forms may appear to differ in numerous ways – by virtue of the fact that I have chosen the OE verbs from four different conjugations – the essential difference is that the OE past tenses and past participles have different stems (sometimes a different one for both singular and plural in the past tense) and different endings whereas the contemporary forms have the same stem and the same (orthographic <-ed>) ending.

Although the usual strategy for making the two forms the same is to generalize the weak past tense form as the past participle, as in the MnE examples in table 5.4, this is not the only strategy. In many cases the verbs have undergone ad hoc changes such that the past tense and past participle forms are irregular – that is, they are not weak forms – but they nevertheless end up the same. Table 5.5 shows four more OE verbs (Morris 1903: 234, 237, 239) alongside their MnE descendants. For *sit* and *stand*, the analogical leveling has taken place by generalizing the past tense form as the past participle, just as it does in the weak form already discussed. Thus the past tense forms, as in *They sat or stood in the searing heat*, become the past participle forms, as in *They have sat or stood as long as they could endure*, and the historical past participles, *seaten* and *standen*, have disappeared. But it is not always the past tense form that generalizes, as the other two examples in Table 5.5 show. For *bind* and *fight*, it is the past participle form – after the

Table 5.5 Four Old English strong verbs alongside their direct descendants in Modern English illustrating the ad hoc generalization of irregular inflectional forms to make past tense and past participle forms the same

OE	Past Tense	Past Participle	MnE	Past Tense	Past Participle
binde	band (sg) { bundon (pl) }	bunden	to bind	bound	bound
feohte	feaht (sg) { fuhton (pl) }	fohten	to fight	fought	fought
sitte	sæt	seten	to sit	sat	sat
stande	stód	standen	to stand	stood	stood

loss of its inflectional ending – that generalized to replace both the past singular and past plural form.

Examples like these show that the governing principle in this ancient change has not been the elimination of the past participle in favor of the past tense, as some philologists and others claim, but simply making the two forms the same, regardless of provenance of the form that endures.

For about 60 verbs in MnE, the principle of conjugation regularization has not applied and as a result the past tense and past participle forms are still distinguished. These tend to be highly frequent and early acquired verbs like *go–went–gone, eat–ate–eaten, sing–sang–sung*, the copula *be–was/were–been*, and auxiliaries *have–has–had* and *do–did–done*. Evidently the irregularities of these verbs get imprinted so early that they resist the pressures of conjugation regularization.

After more than a thousand years of change, one might assume that the most susceptible verbs would have been leveled and only the most resistant would remain, but in fact the change is continuing at a pace that does not seem any different from the rate of change since the fourteenth century.[8] At the moment, the change is evident in standard dialects in the variability of past participle forms in such verbs as *mow, prove* and *saw*, all of which have weak past tense forms (*mowed, proved, sawed*) and historically had strong past participle forms (*mown, proven, sawn*). Very conservative speakers and some very old speakers still use the strong forms. But the strong past participle forms have receded to the point where it would take a hidebound purist to find anything objectionable in a sentence like *Sally has mowed the lawn, sawed down the tree, and proved the four-color hypothesis all in one morning.*

5.6.3.2 Standard and non-standard conjugation regularization Crucially for our purposes here, the standard dialect lags well behind many non-standard dialects in the process of conjugation regularization. Indeed, the progress in this regard seems to form a continuum in which the dialects most distant from the standard are the most advanced.

Traditional dialects, defined by Wells (1982: 4; also Trudgill and Chambers 1991: 2–3) as geographically peripheral, isolated dialects, have leveled some verbs which are, in standard dialects, not only not leveled but in fact retain highly differentiated paradigms. For instance, the verb *draw* in standard English has a vowel change in the past tense *drew* and an *-n* suffix in the past participle *drawn*; in traditional dialects, *draw* not only occurs with just one form but also weakens that form so that both past tense and past participle are *drawed*. Similarly, the verb *know*, distinguished in the standard dialect as *knew* and *known*, occurs with the single weak form *knowed* for both inflectional forms. *Write*, with standard *wrote* and *written*, in many traditional dialects does not weaken but has the single form *writ*, as in *John writ the shopping list for me*, and *John has writ a letter to his father*.

Traditional dialects include a number of other leveled forms which are also common in non-standard mainstream dialects, especially in the urban working class. Many of these are markers of WC speech in widely scattered areas of the English-speaking world. Among the most ubiquitous are the following:

> We seen it in the papers.
> He done it before we had a chance to stop him.
> She come too late for breakfast.

In these three verbs, it is the traditional (and standard) past participle form that generalizes to become the past tense, a venerable form of the change as we noted in connection with figure 5.3, but perhaps more common now than ever before. Other variants generalize the past tense, as in *They've took the teacher to the hospital*, *They've went and changed the road signs on us*, and *They've drank the worst wine first*. The latter form – *drank* for standard *drunk* – now occurs fairly widely in MC speech in North America (and perhaps elsewhere) and seems well advanced along the venerable pathway from the non-standard into the standard, as an increasingly tolerable variant that will eventually become the accepted form.

Verb conjugations are cogent markers of English social dialects (and probably of social dialects in all languages). As table 5.6 shows, the more conjugation regularization a dialect allows, the less standard it is. The standard dialect thus differs from urban WC dialects and traditional dialects in the extent to which it suppresses or inhibits the regularization of verb conjugations. It draws the line much lower than the others.

Table 5.6   Conjugation regularizations as markers of social dialects

Traditional dialects	He's drawed pure poison from outa that well.
	We've knowed for a long time.
	He writ/He's writ to his family every week. . . .
Mainstream non-standard	We seen it in the papers.
	He done it before we had a chance to stop him.
	She come too late for breakfast.
	They've took the teacher to the hospital.
	They've went and changed the road signs on us.
	They've drank the best wine already.
Standard	Sally has proved/proven the four-color hypothesis.
	They've already mowed/mown the lawn.
	By then, they had sawed/sawn down the old oak.

Although conjugation regularization is a grammatical process, it is exactly parallel to the restriction in standard accents of (C<u>C</u>) to triconsonantal clusters in casual speech where other dialects allow it freely with biconsonantal clusters in several styles as well (as in §5.6.2.5). Though parallel, they are not identical. As we will see in the next section, one represents a qualitative difference and the other a quantitative difference.

5.6.4   Two constraints on variation in standard dialects

In all the examples we have looked at, both in this section and throughout the book, the difference between standard dialects and non-standard ones follows two apparently universal constraints.

First, when standard speech differs *qualitatively* from other varieties, it is always the case that those other varieties have variants where the standard allows no variation. So, for instance, WC speakers in most parts of the English-speaking world can say either *They've went about as far as they can go* or *They've gone about as far as they can go*. For MC speakers, the first variant is not possible – it does not exist in their dialect – and consequently they have no variants at all. Qualitative differences of this kind, as we have seen several times in this book (especially §2.3), usually involve grammatical variables. Other well-known examples include the form *ain't* as a variant for *isn't* or *hasn't, yous* [jəz] for *you* as second person plural, and *hisself, theirselves* as reflexive pronouns.

All these variants occur widely both in traditional dialects and in WC dialects but not in any standard dialect. The converse of this constraint also appears to hold: there is no variant in standard dialects that does not also occur in traditional and WC dialects.

Second, when standard speech differs *quantitatively* from other varieties, then it is always the case that the standard dialect either imposes more constraints on the linguistic processes or retains higher frequency of the traditional or historical forms or both. For instance, both (ng) and (CC) occur in standard accents as well as WC and traditional accents, but in standard accents (ng) is restricted to non-formal styles and (CC) is restricted both in style and in linguistic environment (as discussed in §5.6.2.4).

Again, the converse of this constraint holds: when standard and non-standard dialects do have the same variants, the non-standard dialects are never more restricted in their use than the standard.

5.7   Vernacular Roots

The way in which qualitative and quantitative linguistic variables are embedded in social dialects appears to be universal. Another universal that is becoming established after more than thirty years of empirical research is that certain variables appear to be primitives of vernacular dialects in the sense that they recur ubiquitously all over the world.[9] Two of them, (CC) and conjugation regularization, were discussed in some detail in the preceding section. Some others have, as might be expected, come up repeatedly in this book as they also have in sociolinguistic research from the very beginning. Five variables that appear to be vernacular primitives are listed here with an indication of their global distribution:

- (ng), probably the most-studied variable in sociolinguistics, documented in New York (Labov 1966), Norwich (Trudgill 1974; §3.2.2 above), Sydney (Horvath 1985; §3.2.3 above), several British cities (Houston 1991), and many other places around the world.
- (CC), also a well-studied variable (as in §5.6.2.4 above), called "final stop deletion" in studies in Philadelphia (Guy 1980) and in Carbonear, Newfoundland (Paddock 1981: 32–3), "word-final consonant clusters" in inner city Detroit (Wolfram 1969), and (CC) in rural northern England (Chambers 1982).
- default singulars, illustrated in sentences like *Bob and I* was *the last ones*, where *was*, not *were*, occurs with plural subject, called "invariant *was*"

in Harlem (Labov, Cohen, Robins and Lewis 1968) and in Anniston, Alabama (Feagin 1979), and "subject/verb nonconcord" in Appalachia (Wolfram and Christian 1976); the term "default singulars" is used of comparable constructions in Acadian French (King 1993).
- conjugation regularization (as in §5.6.3.1 above), called "levelling of irregular verb forms" in Appalachia (Wolfram and Christian 1976), "non-standard past tense and -ed participle forms" in inner city Sydney (Eisikovits 1991), and conjugation regularization in Chambers and Trudgill (1991).
- multiple negation, called "negative concord" in Harlem (Labov 1972) and Anniston (Feagin 1979) and "multiple negation" in inner city Detroit (Wolfram 1969, §3.3.1.3 above) and most other places where it has been studied.

This is by no means a complete list. Final obstruent devoicing (Stampe 1969) and verbal adjectives (Bickerton 1981: 68–9), typically realized by copula deletion (Labov 1969; §3.3.1.4 above), are also likely candidates, one phonological and the other grammatical. Once sociolinguists and dialectologists start looking at recurrent variables as primitives in vernacular dialects, I believe they will find many of them, and I also believe that the many variables will ultimately resolve into four or five very general phonological and grammatical processes, especially when we identify them cross-linguistically rather than in English alone (as in §5.7.5 below).

5.7.1 Diffusionist and structural explanations

How does it happen that the vernacular of rural Appalachia shares these features with vernaculars spoken in big cities like New York, Philadelphia, and Detroit? What, except for these vernacular features, does inner city Sydney have in common with Anniston and Norwich, medium-sized cities on different continents? Why does Carbonear, Newfoundland, have features in common with rural Northern England, working-class Britain, and inner city neighborhoods in Detroit and Harlem?

It seems to me that the possible answers to these questions must fall into one of two categories. Either these vernaculars have these common features because they were carried there by people from outside who spoke that way, or they have them because all vernaculars abide by the same linguistic laws. The first explanation is external and diffusional. The second is internal and structural.

The diffusionist position has the virtue of externalizing the explanation in the sense that it is couched in terms of historical movements, migrations, contact, social intercourse, trade routes, and invasions. It precludes any need for mentalist explanations, for bioprograms or collective unconscious or innate properties of the language faculty or of the mind.

5.7.2   *Problems with the diffusionist position*

It seems to me that that avoidance of mentalism more than any positive attribute is what has allowed the diffusionist position to survive. It is not supported by the historical record. There is no attested contact among, say, Newfoundland fishermen and Yorkshire farmers, or Harlem African Americans and inner-Sydney Italians, or any of these with the folk from Appalachia.

The settlers in these places came from different places, and there is no well-defined group that mediated among them, circulating from one group to the other and interacting with them as peers, the only social relationship that makes a linguistic difference. In fact, the social groups involved – rural farmers and semi-skilled laborers – are the least mobile strata of every population. They do not travel far, and they tend to maintain a style of life similar to their parents. They are the very people who are least susceptible to the influence of outsiders.

Against this, diffusionists might claim that the ubiquitous features were there in the beginning – that they existed in the Heimat dialects that were exported globally. But if that were so, we would still have to face the fact that these features prevailed where numerous others disappeared. Why have these survived? Any claim that they were there in the beginning and have remained there for centuries seems, again, like an argument in favor of their privileged position.

More damaging still for the diffusionist case is the highly unnatural way the diffusion of these vernacular variables would have to happen. Morpheme-final consonant-cluster reduction, for example, is exactly the same in rural Yorkshire as in inner city Philadelphia, and (ng) is exactly the same in Norwich as in Anniston. That is, they have the same set of variants, the same set of linguistic and stylistic constraints, and they are embedded socially (by class, age, etc.) in the same way. This is not the normal pattern for linguistic features that diffused in the remote past. Normally, we find further independent developments of the transplanted features. So, to take a classic example (Campbell 1974), in the Quichean (Mayan) languages a rule palatalizing /k/ diffused from west to east, but in one sub-group the palatalization occurred in syllables before uvulars, in another before uvulars and velar fricatives, in another before all uvulars and velars, and in another only in the word for *horse* and thus not rule-governed at all.

That looks like a real diffusion, with phonological differences in contiguous regions. The invariant variability of (ng), (C̲C̲) and the other vernacular features does not look much like it.

Besides, these widespread vernacular variables are not restricted to non-standard dialects. They also occur universally in creole languages (Taylor 1971, Bickerton 1981: 43–135).[10] The recognition of similar features in creoles and non-standard vernaculars has not been construed as a problem by the diffusionists. To them, it indicated that the grammar heard by the slaves and servants was non-standard – that the masters and the bosses spoke non-standard dialects. If there was any doubt about that, then the diffusionists speculated that the masters, whatever their dialects, would in any case have used a simplified grammar – foreigner talk or baby talk – when addressing the slaves.

What does cause problems for diffusionist theories of creole spread, of course, is its breadth. Creole languages, with their remarkable similarities, girdle the globe, usually centered on seaports, often in the area of the tropics. That is perceived to be extensive enough to cast doubts upon the diffusionist explanation, and hence the rise of the polygenetic alternative (for a summary, see Romaine 1988: 71–114). Yet consider how much more extensive is the spread of non-standard vernaculars with their repertoire of common variables, as we have seen from Sydney to Carbonear and Harlem, from Norwich to Anniston and Detroit. By comparison, creoles are relatively restricted and, it follows, if their geographical distribution casts doubts upon the diffusionist explanation then the non-standard vernaculars cast that many more.

Finally, these widespread vernacular variables also occur in child language. As Fasold (1990: 288) says, "a number of the distinctive features called for by the mature grammars of non-standard lects are the same as features that turn up during the acquisition of standard lects by children." Children's lects often include these features even when their parents' dialect does not include them. Here, surely, any appeal to a diffusionist explanation would be absurd. Most children lead highly circumscribed lives – more circumscribed than the rural farmers and the semi-skilled laborers whose vernaculars share so many features with theirs.

The diffusionist explanation, under close scrutiny, is simply implausible.

So we are stuck with the structural explanation. This too has its problems, but it seems to me that the problems are on an entirely different level. It is not that the structural explanations lack credibility. What they lack is generality. We have never given much thought to the ubiquity of vernacular features or what might underlie it. Perhaps diffusion, a convenient assumption, deflected attention from it. As long as it was unexamined, it could serve as a stop-gap, a rationalization for much more than it really covered.

The few linguists who sought internalized, structure-based principles have met with limited success. Yet the most plausible explanation for the global distribution of vernacular variables appears to lie here.

5.7.3   The internal–structural position

In our search for a set of linguistic principles and constraints that will provide an explanation for the structural similarities of vernaculars, a reasonable starting-point is the observation that the standard dialect typically differs from other dialects in the community by being more restricted or more tightly constrained in its grammar and phonology in the sense discussed in §5.6.4 above. Those features that recur in vernaculars around the world have certain inherent privileges, and the standard dialects are characterized partly by resisting them.

A closely related notion gained currency a few years ago in child language acquisition. Stampe (1969: 443) proposed that child language develops partly by suppressing certain aspects of "an innate system of phonological processes, revised in certain ways by linguistic experience." For example, one of the putative processes of the innate system is that "obstruents become voiceless irrespective of their context, because their oral constriction impedes the air-flow required by voicing." The acquisition of an adult phonology requires children to learn to suppress this process depending upon the accent being acquired, either completely in an accent where voiced obstruents occur in all contexts, or partly in an accent where they occur in all contexts except, say, word-finally.

In a further development of the same theory, Braine (1974: 287) claimed that "the mature [phonological] system retains all those aspects of the primitive articulatory tendencies that children have not had to overcome in the course of mastering the pronunciation of their native language."

Though Stampe and Braine developed their theory at a time when language variability was just gaining acceptance as a research area and and its systematic properties were still being discovered, both of them accidentally provided for linguistic variability. Braine noted that "one frequent way" in which children free themselves from the primitive tendencies is by making the rule "probabilistic rather than obligatory: it then simply records a tendency to a certain kind of error" (1974: 286). In sociolinguistics, we now know that probabilistic tendencies are not necessarily "errors", when the home dialects include variable features.

Stampe (1969: 449) also provided for variability of a restricted kind with an incipient sociolinguistic observation. He said:

> The conservative influence of the standard exerts itself by rejecting most of the innovations of children. Innovations are only gradually admitted, often just conditionally at first. Thus it is that phonetic changes often begin as optional rather than obligatory pronunciations. The conservatism of the standard forces the innovator to suppress a process at least in his formal speech.

[For example,] beside the dialects which have admitted obligatory devoicing, there are many others, more conservative, which still admit it only in relaxed speech.

Sociolinguistic research obviously had not influenced their thinking in any way. So Stampe provides for stylistic variability and Braine for graded (or correctable) variability, but at the time neither of them could conceive of stable variability where the probabilistic tendencies repeat themselves in generation after generation, as characteristic of the dialect. Once that is admitted – that is, once the axiom of categoricity is suspended – their observations provide hints of one of the sources of linguistic variability.

Extrapolating the theory further into the social stratification of language, we should expect features of the "innate system" or the "primitive tendencies" to be richly represented in vernaculars everywhere. The standard accent will be the one that places the most stringent constraints on these features, and the vernaculars will differ from it by degrees in an acrolect-to-basilect hierarchy.

Something very similar to this was put forward in a sociolinguistic context by Kroch (1978: 18) when he maintained that the standard dialect inhibits "many of the low-level, variable processes of phonetic conditioning that characterize spoken language and that underlie regular phonological change" whereas other dialects do not.

5.7.4 Primitive and learned features

One of the implications of this theory for sociodialectology is that dialect features must have two sources: one based on primitive tendencies, as Braine (1974: 285) calls them, and the other specific to the dialect or language, in Braine's terms "learned."

Once such a distinction is made, it becomes clear that there is independent empirical evidence for it in dialectology. The most striking example in my own research came to light as an apparent counter-example to one of the principles governing dialect acquisition. Several studies of the speech of people who move from one dialect area to another show that they are more proficient at eliminating rules of the old dialect than they are at acquiring rules of the new dialect (Chambers 1992: 695). This principle appeared to be very secure for most of the available evidence, but then a couple of counter-examples emerged.

In fact, the principle remains secure as long as it is applied to learned processes. It is the primitive processes that appear to be counter-examples to it, as the following two examples show.

5.7.4.1   Obstruent devoicing in second-language learning   One apparent counter-example comes from the related field of second-language acquisition. English speakers learning German master the final obstruent devoicing rule very quickly, but German speakers learning English usually eliminate the same rule with only sporadic success, so much so that devoiced finals are major stereotypes of German-accented English.

This appears to contradict the dialect acquisition principle directly, because the English speakers acquire the rule with much greater success than the German speakers eliminate it.

The explanation lies in the fact that obstruent devoicing is a primitive process. English speakers acquiring German do not need to learn it because it is already in their linguistic competence. All they need to do is release it – unsuppress it, as it were. The German speakers learning English, however, must learn to suppress it.

The primitive status of obstruent devoicing is evidenced by the fact that infants invariably have it in their speech regardless of its status in the adult phonology (Stampe 1969: 447, Braine 1974: 272–3). In addition, foreign-language learners often acquire final obstruent devoicing even when it is not a rule of either L1 or L2 – an astounding fact by any objective criterion. As Odlin (1989: 121–2) says, "the devoicing rule has an existence somewhat independent of both native and target languages." The reason for that, we now know, is that it is not a "devoicing rule" that must be acquired but rather a primitive process that must be suppressed in some accents.

5.7.4.2   Devoicing and voicing medial /t/   A second apparent counter-example to the dialect acquisition principle comes from what appeared at first to be a transatlantic contradiction. Evidence for the principle rested partly on observations of the good progress of my Canadian subjects in England in altering their Canadian English pronunciation of post-tonic prevocalic /t/ in words like *pretty*, *putting* and *party*. In Canadian English these medial /t/s are realized as voiced [d], but the southern England English accent they are learning has voiceless [t]. They make the change fairly successfully, and my original claim was that their success is partly attributable to the fact that they are eliminating a rule of their native Canadian English accents (Chambers 1992: 695–7).

By itself, this explanation looks acceptable, but it is compromised by an observation made in the converse situation. Trudgill (1986: 19–20) noticed that English people transplanted to North America accomplished the opposite process, the voicing of medial /t/, rapidly and completely.

It cannot work both ways. If Canadians in England are fairly successful because they are eliminating a rule, then English people accommodating their accents to North America should be relatively unsuccessful because they are acquiring one. But they are not unsuccessful – in fact they are, according to Trudgill's impressions, almost completely successful, apparently even more successful than the Canadians are at eliminating it.

The resolution of this contradiction comes from the fact that intervocalic voicing of obstruents is a primitive process. It occurs in child language regardless of the adult accents that are their models. As a primitive process, it requires suppression in accents that constrain it.

The English people are not acquiring a rule when they voice medial /t/. To explain the Canadians' success in the opposite direction, there are two other dialect acquisition principles involved – it is a simple process, and it is orthographically transparent (as summarized by Chambers 1992: 701–2) – so that is not a problem. But the problem of explaining the English success, so troublesome when it was considered that they were acquiring a rule, disappears when it is seen not as a learned feature but as a primitive one.

The distinction between primitive and learned features, though it needs to be supported by further research, may have broad implications for dialect studies. Imperfect learning of dialect features, as seen in the speech of interlopers (§2.9.1 above), can presumably only happen with learned, not primitive, features. Geolinguistic transitions with mixed and fudged lects (Chambers and Trudgill 1980: 125–45) may be characteristic of learned, not primitive, features, whereas sociolectal gradations from basilect to acrolect (Bickerton 1975: 60–163) may be characteristic of primitive, not learned, features. Sound changes by lexical diffusion (Wang 1977) may occur with learned, not primitive, processes, whereas regular sound changes (Hockett 1965) may occur with primitive processes; indeed, Labov's discussion of these two kinds of linguistic change (1981) practically invites reinterpretation along these lines.

Considerable work needs to be undertaken before implications such as these can be stated with complete confidence. In particular, the empirical basis for distinguishing primitive and learned processes must be firmly established. If it can be established, it seems to me it could lead to a fundamental reformation of dialectology.

5.7.5 Sociolinguistic implications

If the ubiquity of variables such as (CC) and conjugation regularization really resides in the fact that they are somehow privileged or primitive linguistic processes, then they cannot be English-specific. Presumably they belong to the language faculty in the most general sense. As such, they must have counterparts in the vernaculars of other languages.

No one has yet deliberately searched for cross-linguistic generalizations at this level. Sociolinguistic research has just reached the point where we can confidently make cross-dialect generalizations, allowing us to conclude, for instance, that variable (C̲C̲) is the same in Sydney as it is in Philadelphia. Cross-language generalizations make a logical next step.

In the last thirty years of sociolinguistic research, we have come to understand how variables function in vernacular and standard dialects. It may be possible now to go beyond that and ask why. Why do certain variables recur in dialects all around the world? Why is it these particular variables, not others, that persist? Why are they constrained in almost exactly the same ways in different, widely separated communities? Why are they embedded so similarly in the social strata?

This vast, virtually unexplored area lies at the very root of our discipline. There exists a cluster of linguistic variables, both phonological and grammatical, with certain privileges of occurrence in child language, creoles, traditional and mainstream vernaculars. They are visible partly by their suppression in the standard dialect. Whether these can be reconciled in an integrated, coherent theory remains to be seen, but it is a necessary pursuit, it seems to me, because it lies at the very foundation of linguistic variation.

5.8   Linguistic Variation and Social Identity

The underlying cause of sociolinguistic differences, largely beneath consciousness, is the human instinct to establish and maintain social identity. In case after case, that has been the common motive: from the distinct accents of the three old hunting bands in Sheshatshiu to the homogenization in the new settlement (§2.5.1), from the territoriality of the men in Ballymaccarett to the urbanity of the women (§3.3.2), from the markers of adolescence (§4.4) to the accommodation of young adults (§4.5) – these and numerous other cases show the profound need for people to show they belong somewhere, and to define themselves, sometimes narrowly and sometimes generally.

It is not enough to mark our territory as belonging to us by name tags, mailboxes, fences, hedges, and walls. We must also mark ourselves as belonging to the territory, and one of the most convincing markers is by speaking like the people who live there.

Kroch (1978: 18) sees the need for maintaining social identity as fundamentally antagonistic. In his view,

> Dominant social groups tend to mark themselves off symbolically as distinct from the groups they dominate and to interpret their symbols of distinctiveness as evidence of superior moral and intellectual qualities. This tendency shows itself not only in speech style but also in such other areas of social symbolism as dress, body carriage, and food. In all these areas dominant

groups mark themselves off by introducing elaborated styles and by borrowing from external pressure groups.

Speech is thus a tool, perhaps a weapon, with which the higher class can maintain the gap between itself and the rest of society.

Our experience of social situations makes us aware that this is only partly true. To the extent that educational systems enshrine standard speech in order to exclude non-standard speakers it is true, but if they instruct non-standard speakers in order to improve their ability to function in the society it is false.

It is also overly simple. The linguistic markers of adolescence, as we have seen in §4.4, are motivated partly by the need of young people to differentiate themselves from adults. At the most extreme, the adolescents must diverge if the adults appear to be converging with them. This is an obviously antagonistic stance, but the underlying social motive is not to appear morally or intellectually superior, as in Kroch's view, but to extricate themselves progressively from familial dependence in order to take on adult roles.

If linguistic differentiation is imposed by the higher class to mark their position at the top of the hierarchy, we should expect to find that it is sustained by the higher class. We now have clear evidence that it is by no means one-sided. The other classes play key roles in sustaining linguistic differentiation, albeit covertly, as we have seen (in §5.4.1).

The history of linguistic standardization undeniably involves classism and conservatism, as Kroch implies.

A dialect becomes the standard one because its speakers have power of various kinds – economic, military, political, spiritual. The styles and customs of the powerful group are almost always emulated, no less by the underclasses who were conquered by them than by those who were rescued from their oppressors by them. Generally their manners, values, attitudes, dress, cuisine, and recreations are adopted as the norm. Their dialect, inseparable from the other cultural trappings associated with them, also becomes the norm. Thus the history of linguistic standardization begins with the unequal distribution of power and has the same source as does class differentiation.

The perpetuation of the linguistic standard requires codification. The accumulation of dictionaries, grammars, usage guides, spellers, orthoepies, and readers forms an educational base for preparing future generations of standard bearers. It also forms a bedrock of authorized language in the event of linguistic challenges. Enshrining the standard dialect in print inhibits change as far as possible, although that is never very far. Because change is irrepressible, orthographies become ever more inaccurate reflections of speech, dictionaries become repositories of archaisms, and usage guides become edicts of ritualized grammar. Deviations from the codified norms are vilified as barbarisms. As the most faithful reflection of the codified language, the standard dialect preserves some features that have disappeared from other dialects if they had them in the first place.

Objective observers see the wrong-headedness of this historical chain of events at several points. For one thing, people in power do not always, or perhaps often, deserve our approbation. For another, the codification of language does not make it valid in perpetuity, or at all. Obviously, neither linguistic classism nor linguistic conservatism is functional in any way. They exist, indeed they exist hardily, largely as unexamined and unconscious social impulses. To eradicate them, we do not need revolution, as if they were political dictates, but education, including, among other lessons, empirical studies of the social significance of linguistic variation.

Against this background, several of the points that have come up in this chapter should make more sense than they did before.

Processes of change do not invariably percolate from the higher echelons to the lower. Often, as in the case of leveled past participles such as *sat* for *seaten* and perhaps soon *drank* for *drunk*, the movement is in the other direction, from non-standard into standard. The reason is that the non-standard often has powerful primitive processes on its side which the standard dialect, in its conservatism, has repressed.

The standard dialect is not linguistically superior, but it is presented as if it were. As the language of the powerful and the privileged, it has articulate forces on its side. Against this, the other social dialects seldom find influential advocates. Their silence has apparently been construed as meaningful, as a signal of the general acquiescence to the standard, so much so that arbiters of taste sometimes wonder aloud why non-standard dialects continue to exist. Sociolinguists have discovered, deeply embedded in the linguistic attitudes of several societies, that covert prestige clung to those varieties with no less tenacity than overt prestige attaches itself to the standard.

Jespersen's notion that non-standard varieties must inevitably diminish with the rise of nationalism and other kinds of centralization has proven false, and now we can see why. All social strata, not just the empowered stratum, feel the need to assert their linguistic identity. The fact that the most powerful stratum controls the most powerful tools – educational materials, for instance, and the other codifications – is not enough to overwhelm the need.

Finally, the more deeply we inquire into the social meaning of language, the more clearly we see how arbitrary are the values that are commonly attached to it. There can be no doubt that linguistic variation can be counteradaptive, as the Babelian hypothesis maintains. Stereotypes, we have seen, can be triggered by the presence of one stigmatized variant in 40 seconds of speech.

Prejudices based on dialect are as insidious as prejudices based on skin color, religion, or any other insubstantial attribute, and they have the same result. They unfairly limit self-fulfilment. They do so partly by restricting an individual's occupational and social mobility. Paradoxically, the only social force that can eliminate sharp dialect differences in a community is mobility. Limiting the social and occupational possibilities of people with non-standard accents guarantees that their accents will endure. The stigmatization of accents and dialects, even in fairly benevolent societies, preserves social asymmetries.

The anti-social linguistic forces are not necessarily – perhaps not usually – Machiavellian. They operate beneath consciousness, and sometimes they are misconceived as well-intentioned. The mother who isolates her children from their neighbors lest they start to sound like them, the teacher whose idolatry of prescriptive norms causes students to tremble as they write, the supervisor who dismisses a worker's suggestion because of the way it was stated, the manager who declares that the voice at the switchboard will reflect ignominiously on the whole corporation – these and dozens of other situations occur daily.

None of them has anything to do with substance. All of them instil and perpetuate embarrassment, insecurity, and alienation. They may not be sinister but they are certainly ignorant, in some cases to the point of culpability.

To combat this ignorance, we now have, in addition to common sense, a wealth of empirical evidence about the social significance of linguistic variation. It has to be admitted that common sense has made very few inroads into the linguistic prejudices and inequities that have been enmeshed in the social fabric since the beginning of the historical record. Perhaps we can do better by spreading the lessons of sociolinguistics. In some thirty years, no time at all, we have devised methods of isolating, as far as possible, the role of language in numerous social situations.

No one ever doubted that language played a crucial role in social situations, but until very recently no one could say exactly how it worked or why. We have begun to understand how – and occasionally why – and we have developed methods and means that help us to isolate its essential components.

The challenges of seeing language clearly in social situations in which it is just one strand of a fractal web may never be perfectly met, but we have made a start, and it is an auspicious one.

Notes

Notes to Chapter 1

1   In what follows, I use only the portion of the data from Labov (1966a) needed to make the point and I recalculate his percentages to bring them into conformity with graphing conventions that became established subsequently (as reviewed in §1.2.7 below).

2   Labov (1966) represents this variable as (eh) but subsequently it is usually represented as (æh), as in Eckert 1988 and Labov 1991. It is called *short a*, and has been called that at least since Ferguson 1972.

3   As Hockett (1955: 17) said, speaking for the Bloomfieldians: "In general . . . if we find continuous-scale contrasts in the vicinity of what we are sure is language, we exclude them from language."

4   David Sankoff (1988), in an article on linguistic epistemology (albeit somewhat disguised by both its title and its context), proposes that linguistics has three basic branches rather than the two discussed here. The branch that includes sociolinguistics he calls "descriptive interpretive." Chomskyan theoretical linguistics he calls "introspective–generative." The third he calls "experimental–evaluative" (142–3) and it involves "controlled experimentation, laboratory conditions, questionnaire survey methods, proficiency testing and a conceptual apparatus . . . developed for the prediction and control of natural processes." This would include experimental psycholinguistics, experimental phonetics, second-language testing, language planning, and the like.

5   Chomsky (1965: 15) specifically contrasts descriptivism with his own framework, criticizing "the descriptivist limitation-in-principle to classification and organization of data, to 'extracting patterns' from a corpus of observed speech, to describing 'speech structures' or 'habit structures', insofar as these may exist."

6   The term "metaphysics" may have unwelcome connotations outside of philosophy. Pirsig (1991) says: "Metaphysics is like a restaurant where they give you a 30,000 page menu and no food."

7   It is somewhat unfair for me to choose generativist ephemera only from Chomsky's publications here. It will be obvious to all linguists that a list such as this would

proliferate voluminously by looking farther, with, say, the flip transformation (R. Lakoff 1968: 38–42), the left-branching constraint (Ross 1967: chapter 4), the φ-voicing rule (Chambers 1971), and approximately one ephemeral proposal per article in *Linguistic Inquiry* since its inception in 1970.

8 For a description of sociolinguistic tools for managing and analyzing data, ingeniously applied, see Poplack (1989).

Notes to Chapter 2

1 Some lower-class variables become a cachet in higher-class dialects. Trudgill (1972) notes that they sometimes take on "covert prestige," especially in the speech of men, for whom lower-class speech carries connotations of masculinity. Covert prestige is discussed in detail in §5.4.1. In a well-known literary example, in *My Fair Lady*, the 1956 musical comedy by Lerner and Lowe (but not in *Pygmalion*, the 1920 play by Shaw on which it is based), when the horse the heroine is backing falls behind in the home stretch at the Ascot races, she forgets herself and shouts, "Come on, Dover, move your bloomin' arse!" After a moment of unease, in which it is feared she may have exposed her low origins, the other ladies gleefully take up the cry in urging on their own horses.

2 Displaying the individuals in rank order as in figure 2.2 gives the appearance of greater similarities between the two age groups than actually exist. Kerswill and Williams (1992: 84) show a positive but weak correlation coefficient of 0.176 for the mother–daughter indices.

3 Enshrinement of social and occupational mobility in a political constitution would seem to be one means of guaranteeing individual self-fulfilment, in so far as that is ever possible. In an ideal system, it would ensure that individuals could develop their talents freely and use them to the best of their abilities and ambitions. In a fully mobile society, merit would be valued over heredity, synecure, nepotism, and other qualities, in determining privileges and the responsibilities that go with them. Yet mobility is never explicitly invoked in political platforms or constitutional reforms.

4 "Cependant il importe de constater qu'à Charmey, où toutes les conditions sont plutôt favorables à l'unité, la diversité est beaucoup plus forte que je ne me le serais imaginé après une courte visite."

5 Table 2.8 simplifies Cheshire's correlations. The figure shown for secondary participants conflates the frequencies for two intermediate groups in the original (1982: table 44, 104). Cheshire's four groups are merged into three here.

6 By way of explaining the curious fact that the 18- to 25-year-olds score slightly higher than the next oldest group, the 26- to 39-year-olds, Edwards (1992: 104) suggests that the younger group have more contact with the oldest group and therefore speak more like them. But this kind of age-grading, whereby the young adults change their speech to sound less like both younger and older groups is unknown. Another possible explanation might lie in the fact that Edwards had trouble locating males in the youngest group, 18–25, willing to be interviewed (1992: 99) but no trouble locating 26- to 39-year-olds. It may be

that the more compliant sample of 26- to 39-year-olds was generally made up of less insular individuals.

Notes to Chapter 3

1   Susan Ehrlich made a crucial contribution to my understanding of gender-based variability in a seminar in 1980, and Sarah Cummins started me thinking about sex-based variability with an off-hand comment in 1992. Because of Manfred Görlach's encouragement, §§3.1, 3.3 and 3.4 of this chapter appeared separately as Chambers 1992a, in a slightly different form.

2   Labov then adds (1990: 206): "In the majority of linguistic changes, women use a higher frequency of the incoming forms than men." It seems to me that these statements may amount to the same thing, since the "majority of linguistic changes" are changes in the direction of standard speech. However, Labov does not identify the "incoming forms" in language change with standard forms, and hence claims that "the two distinct patterns of behavior are difficult to reconcile with one another." Attempting to reconcile them becomes his major theme.

3   As a result of this phonotactic constraint, English has syllables such as /sɪŋ/ 'sing' but not */siŋ/ *'seeng', /tʌŋ/ 'tongue' but not */tuŋ/ *'toong', /lɛŋθ/ 'length' but not */leɪŋθ/ *'layngth', and so on. See Ladefoged 1982: 81–2.

4   The [ɪŋk] variant is probably part of a general process described by Knowles (1978: 85–6) whereby [ŋ] occurs solely as an allophone of /n/ before velar stops. Thus *sing* [sɪŋg] has a final stop, and *singer* [sɪŋgə] rhymes with *finger* [fɪŋgə]. But Knowles does not discuss the devoicing of final /g/ in non-standard English and Australian *something* and the other words in the same lexical set.

5   Variable (ɛ) has other variants in other environments in Belfast. For details, see Milroy and Milroy (1978: 29–32). Figure 3.7 takes into consideration only the variants in monosyllables with final stops.

6   Curiously, Deuchar (1988: 29) claims that, while status consciousness and solidarity are "factors external to the process of communication," her notion of face-saving is "basic to the way language is used for communicative purposes," that is, "internal to language use." This putative distinction is by no means clear. Face appears to be a social impingement upon communication no less than, and presumably related to, status and solidarity relationships.

7   Hoyenga and Hoyenga (1979: 238) report what appears to be a striking example of male bias in the Scholastic Aptitude Test. Beginning in the 1950s, they say, the content of the verbal portion of the test was altered by including more items on areas of primarily male interest. The stated purpose of the examination board was to achieve "a better balance of scores between the sexes." They did nothing, however, to "balance" the mathematical portion, where there was a demonstrable male advantage. The changes in the verbal test evidently succeeded: the 1985 SAT scores show a very slight male advantage (Ramist and Arbeiter 1985; also Hyde and Linn 1988: 63).

8 The robustness of the female verbal advantage is shown by the fact that it shows up even in deleterious conditions. Hyde and Linn (1988) analyzed results of several studies of verbal abilities but restricted their sample to those studies using "normal" North American subjects, and they employed a statistical method, "meta-analysis," that admittedly requires gross statistical significance in the constituent studies to yield any effect at all (1988: 54). The advantage still showed in their results though it was, not surprisingly, smaller (+0.11 SD) than in more inclusive analyses by Maccoby and Jacklin (1974) and Hyde (1981).

9 Lakoff lists traits reminiscent of the ones Edwards mentioned in 1903 "among the misogynist stereotypes in our culture" (1975: 73). It is perhaps disquieting, in those terms, to note that the traits persisted for at least 72 years, and were identified in cultures far removed from one another at the time. On the use of intensive words, Lakoff (1975: 12–13) describes women's propensity for adjectives such as *adorable, charming, lovely, sweet,* and *divine.* On intonational differences, she discusses the fact that, as she puts it, "women speak in italics" (1975: 56). On politeness, she notes discrepancies such as this: "Not only are women more polite, but men are supposed to be more polite around women than they are with each other" (1975: 75). Lakoff's goal, unlike Edwards's, goes beyond recording these as facts. She (1975: 52) says, "My hope is that women will . . . realize that using this language, having it used of them, and thus being placed implicitly in this role, is degrading in that it is constraining."

10 "Literary Arabic" is the term used by Abu-Haidar (1989). Ferguson (1959a) and Haeri (1987) call it "Classical Arabic," and Abd-el-Jawad (1981, 1987) calls it "Written Modern Standard Arabic."

11 So far, this pattern has been found only in Arabic-speaking countries. Some generalizations have included Modern Persian as spoken in Teheran as well, citing Modaressi-Tehrani (1978). But Modaressi-Tehrani (1978: 73) clearly states that "any correlation of sex with linguistic variations should be considered more suggestive than definitive." Inspection of his results indicates that that is certainly true. Most variables show no gender variation at all (for instance, consonant deletion, 130), and those for which gender differences are specifically noted, as for prenasal vowel raising (103), are almost certainly not statistically significant.

Notes to Chapter 4

1 The improved life expectancies began in the eighteenth century with advances in medicine and sanitation. Hishinuma (1976) estimates that life expectancies remained unchanged at 25–30 years all the way from the Bronze Age (3500–1400 BC) to the eighteenth century. Peller (1947) similarly estimates that mortality rates were the same in classical Rome as in seventeenth-century Europe.

2 Anointing people as political leaders solely because they are the oldest individuals in the society is a grave mistake, even if some societies have done it for millennia. Apart from the obvious objection that age alone cannot equip individuals for leadership, it violates the basic principle (stated at the beginning of

chapter 2) that in a just society privileges must be distributed arbitrarily. In the Western industrial nations, the social problem is not with empowering old people but with marginalizing them. "Ageism" is a relatively new movement intended to combat the prejudice of treating "the elderly as a deprived problem group based on the factor of age alone" (Miller 1987: 152).

3   The sociolinguistics of aging has not yet been comprehensively studied. Despite its title, *Language, Society and the Elderly* (Coupland, Coupland and Giles 1991) deals with what is called "the interactional, relational and constitutive perspective" (p. 25), as when we are told, for instance, that a young woman "thematized television watching" (p. 48) but what she actually did was chat with an older woman about a television show. The book includes chapters on "intergenerational goal consonance" (chapter 7, i.e., getting older people to confide in you by confiding in them), "strategic analysis" for "age disclosure" (chapter 6, i.e., getting older subjects to tell you their age), and "the social constructivist approach" to "formulating age" (chapter 3, meaning uncertain).

4   I was introduced to Langer's theory by Professor Ruth Gruhn of the University of Alberta.

5   Most of the slang terms in this section come from observations collected by students in my undergraduate courses at the University of Toronto. For discussions of slang as sociolinguistic use, see Chapman (1986), Eble (1985) and Munro (1989).

Notes to Chapter 5

1   Several of the points made in §§5.1–5.3 originate in Chambers (1985).

2   This section relies heavily on a review article by Baker and Cunningham (1985) and the peer commentaries attached to it.

3   The dominance of the tradition of categoricity (discussed in §1.3) probably has its roots in the venerable intellectual domination of the ancient Greeks.

4   The neo-Platonist Chomsky explicitly espouses a version of this position, as we have seen (§1.3). For Chomsky, linguistic variation exists but language must be abstracted from the variability in order to study it in its ideal form.

5   The principal class division holds beyond Western nations. In the People's Republic of China, according to Xu (1992), the equivalent major division separates ganbus and workers, where ganbus (usually translated as "cadres") are white collar workers ranging in status from clerks to managers.

6   I am grateful to Peter Avery and Keren Rice for discussing these features with me and particularly for drawing my attention to the glottalic features.

7   Kroch (1978: 17fn) explicitly restricts his discussion to phonetics: "There may be important parallels between variation and change at the phonological and other levels; but claims about the one certainly cannot be extended to the others in a direct and automatic way."

8   Determining the rate of change with complete exactitude is of course impossible. However, Baugh (1957: 194–8) provides a useful approximation based on the histories of 333 OE strong verbs. He notes that 12 had developed weak forms by the twelfth century, lists another 12 that began to change in the

thirteenth century, 32 in the fourteenth century when "the movement was at its height", and "about a dozen" in the fifteenth century. He then claims that there have only been about a dozen more since the fifteenth century, and adds that "more than half of the Old English strong verbs have disappeared completely from the standard language" (1957: 195). Both these estimates seem very conservative and are presumably the result of the narrowness of his starting-point of 333 verbs and also his use of strong-to-weak as the criterion rather than the principle of conjugation regularization.

9 The ideas in this section originated in a keynote address at New Ways of Analyzing Variation (NWAV) 22 at the University of Ottawa in October 1993. I have benefited from the comments, both positive and negative, of that audience, especially from Walter Cichocki, William Labov, Shana Poplack, John Rickford, Gillian Sankoff, and Walt Wolfram.

10 Multiple negation is listed among creole grammatical universals but according to Gillian Sankoff (personal communication) "there is no trace of it in Tok Pisin."

References

Abd-el-Jawad, Hassan R. 1981. *Lexical and Phonological Variation in Spoken Arabic in Amman*. PhD dissertation. Department of Linguistics, University of Pennsylvania.

Abd-el-Jawad, Hassan R. 1987. Cross-dialectal variation in Arabic: competing prestigious forms. *Language in Society* 16: 359–68.

Abraham, Ralph H., and Christopher D. Shaw 1992. *Dynamics: The Geometry of Behavior*. Redwood City, CA: Addison-Wesley.

Abu-Haidar, Farida 1989. Are Iraqi women more prestige conscious than men? Sex differentiation in Baghdadi Arabic. *Language in Society* 18: 471–81.

Andersen, Elaine Slosberg 1990. *Speaking with Style: The Sociolinguistic Skills of Children*. London and New York: Routledge.

Anisfield, Moshe, N. Bogo and Wallace Lambert 1962. Evaluational reactions to accented English speech. *Journal of Abnormal Social Psychology* 65: 223–31.

Bailey, Guy, Tom Wikle, Jan Tillery and Lori Sand 1991. The apparent time construct. *Language Variation and Change* 3: 241–64.

Baker, Myron Charles 1974. Genetic structure of two populations of white-crowned sparrows with different song dialects. *Condor* 76: 351–6.

Baker, Myron Charles 1983. The behavioral response of female Nuttall's white-crowned sparrows to male song of natal and alien dialects. *Behavioral Ecology and Sociobiology* 12: 309–15.

Baker, Myron Charles, and Michael A. Cunningham 1985. The biology of birdsong dialects. *The Behavioral and Brain Sciences* 8: 85–100.

Baker, Myron Charles, and P. Marler 1980. Behavioral adaptations that constrain the gene pool in vertebrates. *Evolution of Social Behavior: Hypotheses and Empirical Tests*, ed. H. Markl. Verlag Chemie.

Bakir, Murtadha 1986. Sex differences in the approximation to Standard Arabic: a case study. *Anthropological Linguistics* 28: 3–9.

Balliett, Whitney 1986. *American Musicians: Fifty-Six Portraits in Jazz*. New York: Oxford University Press.

Baptista, L. F. 1975. Song dialects and demes in sedentary populations of the white-crowned sparrow. *University of California Publications in Zoology* 105: 1–52.

Basilius, Harold 1952. Neo-Humboldtian ethno-linguistics. *Word* 8: 95–105.

Baugh, Albert C. 1957. *A History of the English Language*, 2nd edn. New York: Appleton-Century-Crofts.

Bell, Allan 1984. Language style as audience design. *Language in Society* 13: 145–204.

Bernard, J. R. 1981. Australian pronunciation. *The Macquarie Dictionary*. Sydney: Macquarie Library. 18–28.

Bickerton, Derek 1973. Quantitative versus dynamic paradigms: the case of Montreal *que*. *New Ways of Analyzing Variation in English*, ed. Charles-James N. Bailey and Roger W. Shuy. Washington, DC: Georgetown University Press. 23–43.

Bickerton, Derek 1975. *Dynamics of a Creole System*. Cambridge University Press.

Bickerton, Derek 1981. *Roots of Language*. Ann Arbor: Karoma.

Blishen, Bernard R. 1971. A socio-economic index for occupations in Canada. *Canadian Society: Sociological Perspectives*, ed. Bernard R. Blishen, Frank E. Jones, Kaspar D. Naegele and John Porter. Toronto: Macmillan. 495–507.

Bloomfield, Leonard 1933. *Language*. New York: Holt, Rinehart and Winston.

Bogart, Leo 1950–51. The spread of news on a local event: a case history. *Public Opinion Quarterly* (Winter): 769–72.

Boissevain, Jeremy, and J. Clyde Mitchell, eds. 1973. *Network Analysis: Studies in Human Interaction*. The Hague: Mouton.

Bolinger, Dwight L. 1961. *Generality, Gradience, and the All-or-None*. 's-Gravenhage: Mouton.

Bolinger, Dwight L. 1980. *Language, the Loaded Weapon: The Use and Abuse of Language Today*. London and New York: Longman.

Bott, Elizabeth 1957. *Family and Social Network: Roles, Norms and External Relationships in Ordinary Urban Families*. London: Tavistock Publications.

Bourdieu, Pierre, et Luc Boltanski 1975. Le fétichisme de la langue. *Actes de la recherche en sciences sociales* 4 (juillet): 2–32.

Braine, Martin D. S. 1974. On what might constitute learnable phonology. *Language* 50: 270–99.

Briscoe, Anne M. 1978. Hormones and gender. *Genes and Gender I*, ed. Ethel Torbach and Betty Rosoff. New York: Gordian Press. 31–50.

Brown, Penelope, and Steven Levinson 1978. Universals in language usage: politeness phenomena. *Questions and Politeness*, ed. E. Goody. Cambridge: Cambridge University Press. 56–289.

Brown, Roger Langham 1967. *Wilhelm von Humboldt's Conception of Linguistic Relativity*. The Hague, Paris: Mouton.

Calvert, Peter 1982. *The Concept of Class: An Historical Introduction*. London: Hutchinson.

Cameron, Deborah 1988. Introduction. *Women in Their Speech Communities: New Perspectives on Language and Sex*, ed. Deborah Cameron and Jennifer Coates. London and New York: Longman. 3–12.

Cameron, Deborah, ed. 1990. *The Feminist Critique of Language: A Reader*. London and New York: Routledge.

Cameron, Deborah, and Jennifer Coates 1988. Some problems in the sociolinguistic explanation of sex differences. *Women in Their Speech Communities: New Perspectives on Language and Sex*, ed. Deborah Cameron and Jennifer Coates. London and New York: Longman. 13–26.

Campbell, Lyle 1974. Quichean palatalized velars. *International Journal of American Linguistics* 40: 132–4.

Canniff, William 1869. *The Settlement of Upper Canada.* Toronto: Dudley and Burns.

Cedergren, Henrietta 1973. *The Interplay of Social and Linguistic Factors in Panama.* PhD dissertation. Cornell University.

Cedergren, Henrietta 1987. The spread of language change: verifying inferences of linguistic diffusion. *Language Spread and Language Policy: Issues, Implications, and Case Studies*, ed. Peter H. Lowenberg. Georgetown University Round Table on Languages and Linguistics 1987. Washington, DC: Georgetown University Press. 45–60.

Cedergren, Henrietta, and David Sankoff 1974. Variable rules: performance as a statistical reflection of competence. *Language* 50: 333–55.

Chambers, J. K. 1971. A phonological argument for the derivation of the φ-subclass. *Papers in Linguistics* 4: 433–46.

Chambers, J. K. 1973. Canadian Raising. *Canadian Journal of Linguistics* 18: 113–35.

Chambers, J. K. 1980. Linguistic variation and Chomsky's 'homogeneous speech community'. *Papers from the Fourth Annual Meeting of the Atlantic Provinces Linguistics Association*, ed. Murray Kinloch and A. B. House. Fredericton: University of New Brunswick. 1–32.

Chambers, J. K. 1981. The Americanization of Canadian Raising. *Parasession on Language and Behavior, Chicago Linguistic Society* 17: 20–35.

Chambers, J. K. 1982. Geolinguistics of a variable rule. *Discussion Papers in Geolinguistics* 5: 1–17.

Chambers, J. K. 1984. Group and individual participation in a sound change in progress. *Papers from the Fifth International Conference on Methods in Dialectology*, ed. Henry J. Warkentyne. Victoria, British Columbia: Department of Linguistics, University of Victoria. 119–36.

Chambers, J. K. 1985. Social adaptiveness in human and songbird dialects. *The Behavioral and Brain Sciences* 8: 102–4.

Chambers, J. K. 1989. Canadian Raising: blocking, fronting, etc. *American Speech* 64: 75–88.

Chambers, J. K. 1991. Canada. *English Around the World: Sociolinguistic Perspectives*, ed. Jenny Cheshire. Cambridge: Cambridge University Press. 89–107.

Chambers, J. K. 1991a. 'Lawless and vulgar innovations': Victorian views of Canadian English. *Focus on Canada*, ed. Sandra Clarke. Amsterdam, Philadelphia: John Benjamins. 1–26.

Chambers, J. K. 1992. Dialect acquisition. *Language* 68: 673–705.

Chambers, J. K. 1992a. Linguistic correlates of gender and sex. *English World-Wide* 13: 173–218.

Chambers, J. K., and Margaret Hardwick 1986. Comparative sociolinguistics of a sound change in Canadian English. *English World-Wide* 7: 21–46.

Chambers, J. K., and Peter Trudgill 1980. *Dialectology.* Cambridge University Press.

Chambers, J. K., and Peter Trudgill 1991. Non-finite verb forms in English dialects. *Dialects of English: Studies in Grammatical Variation*, ed. Peter Trudgill and J. K. Chambers. London and New York: Longman. 215–17.

Chapman, Robert L. 1986. Preface, *New Dictionary of American Slang*. New York: Harper and Row. vii–xv.

Chao, Yuen Ren 1968. *Language and Symbolic Systems*. Cambridge: Cambridge University Press.

Cheshire, Jenny 1982. *Variation in an English Dialect: A Sociolinguistic Study*. Cambridge: Cambridge University Press.

Chomsky, Noam 1957. *Syntactic Structures*. The Hague: Mouton.

Chomsky, Noam 1965. *Aspects of the Theory of Syntax*. Cambridge, MA: MIT Press.

Chomsky, Noam 1973. Conditions on transformations. *A Festschrift for Morris Halle*, ed. Stephen R. Anderson and Paul Kiparsky. New York: Holt, Rinehart and Winston. 232–86.

Chomsky, Noam 1980. *Rules and Representations*. New York: Columbia University Press.

Chomsky, Noam 1988. *Language and Problems of Knowledge: The Managua Lectures*. Cambridge, MA, and London: MIT Press.

Chomsky, Noam, and Howard Lasnik 1977. Filters and control. *Linguistic Inquiry* 8: 425–504.

Cicero 1891. *On Oratory and Orators; with His Letters to Quintus and Brutus [De Oratore]*, trans. or ed. J. S. Watson. London: George Bell and Sons.

Cichocki, Wladyslaw 1986. *Linguistic Applications of Dual Scaling in Variation Studies*. PhD thesis. Department of Linguistics, University of Toronto.

Clarke, Sandra 1984. Role of linguistic feature types in dialect stereotyping. *Papers from the Eighth Annual Meeting of the Atlantic Provinces Linguistic Association*. Halifax: Dalhousie University. 19–32.

Clarke, Sandra 1987. Dialect mixing and linguistic variation in a non-overtly stratified society. *Variation in Language: NWAV-XV at Stanford*, ed. Keith M. Denning, Sharon Inkelas, Faye McNair-Knox and John R. Rickford. Department of Linguistics, Stanford University. 74–85.

Clarke, Sandra 1988. Linguistic variation in the non-stratified context. *Methods in Dialectology*, ed. Alan R. Thomas. Clevedon, Philadelphia: Multilingual Matters. 684–99.

Coates, Jennifer 1986. *Women, Men and Language*. London: Longman.

Coupland, Nikolas, Justine Coupland and Howard Giles 1991. *Language, Society and the Elderly: Discourse, Identity and Ageing*. Oxford: Basil Blackwell.

Cox, Damien 1992. Newfoundlanders have their own way of talking. *The Globe and Mail* [Toronto]. 18 February, p. A6.

Crystal, David 1979. Prosodic development. *Language Acquisition: Studies in First Language Development*, ed. Paul Fletcher and Michael Garman. Cambridge: Cambridge University Press. 33–48.

Cunningham, Michael A., and Myron Charles Baker 1983. Vocal learning in white-crowned sparrows: sensitive phase and song dialects. *Behavioral Ecology and Sociobiology* 13: 259–69.

Currie, Haver C. 1952. A projection of socio-linguistics: the relationship of speech to social status. *The Southern Speech Journal* 18: 28–37. Reprinted in *A Various Language: Perspectives on American Dialects*, ed. Juanita V. Williamson and Virginia M. Burke. New York: Holt, Rinehart and Winston. 1971. 39–47.

Darwin, Charles 1871. *The Origin of the Species and The Descent of Man* [single vol.]. New York: The Modern Library. [1962].

Davis, Lawrence M. 1990. *Statistics in Dialectology*. Tuscaloosa: University of Alabama Press.

Denno, Deborah W. 1982. Sex differences in cognition: a review and critique of the longitudinal evidence. *Adolescence* 17: 779–88.

Deuchar, Margaret 1988. A pragmatic account of women's use of standard speech. *Women in Their Speech Communities: New Perspectives on Language and Sex*, ed. Jennifer Coates and Deborah Cameron. London and New York: Longman. 27–32.

Dinneen, Francis P. 1967. *An Introduction to General Linguistics*. New York: Holt, Rinehart and Winston.

Douglas-Cowie, Ellen 1978. Linguistic code-switching in a Northern Irish village: Social interaction and social ambition. *Sociolinguistic Patterns in British English*, ed. Peter Trudgill. London: Edward Arnold. 37–51.

Eble, Connie C. 1985. Slang and cultural knowledge. *The Twelfth LACUS Forum*, ed. Mary C. Marino and Luis A. Pérez. Lake Bluff, Illinois: Hornbeam Books. 385–90.

Eckert, Penelope 1988. Adolescent social structure and the spread of linguistic change. *Language in Society* 17:183–207.

Eckert, Penelope 1989. *Jocks and Burnouts: Social Categories and Identity in the High School*. New York and London: Teachers College Press.

Eckert, Penelope 1989a. The whole woman: sex and gender differences in variation. *Language Variation and Change* 1: 245–67.

Edwards, John R. 1979. Judgements and confidence in reactions to disadvantaged speech. *Language and Social Psychology*, ed. Howard Giles and Robert St Clair. Oxford: Basil Blackwell. 22–44.

Edwards, John, and Mary Anne Jakobsen 1987. Standard and regional speech: distinctions and similarities. *Language in Society* 16: 369–80.

Edwards, Walter F. 1992. Sociolinguistic behavior in a Detroit inner-city black neighborhood. *Language in Society* 21: 93–115.

Eisikovits, Edina 1991. Variation in the lexical verb in Inner-Sydney English. *Dialects of English: Studies in Grammatical Variation*, ed. Peter Trudgill and J. K. Chambers. London and New York: Longman. 120–42.

Ellis, Stanley 1953. Fieldwork for a dialect atlas of England. *Transactions of the Yorkshire Dialect Society* liii: 9–21.

Fasold, Ralph 1990. *The Sociolinguistics of Language*. Oxford: Basil Blackwell.

Fasold, Ralph 1991. The quiet demise of variable rules. *American Speech* 66: 3–21.

Feagin, Crawford 1979. *Variation and Change in Alabama English*. Washington, DC: Georgetown University Press.

Ferguson, Charles A. 1959a. Diglossia. *Word* 15: 325–40.

Ferguson, Charles A. 1959b. The Arabic koiné. *Language* 35: 616–30.

Ferguson, Charles A. 1970. The role of Arabic in Ethiopia: a sociolinguistic perspective. *Languages and Linguistics Monograph Series* 23: 355–68.

Ferguson, Charles A. 1972. Short *a* in Philadelphia English. *Studies in Honor of George L. Trager*, ed. Estellie M. Smith. The Hague and Paris: Mouton. 259–74.

Fischer, John L. 1958. Social influences on the choice of a linguistic variant. *Word* 14: 47–56.

Fishman, Joshua A. 1970. *Sociolinguistics: A Brief Introduction*. Rowley, MA: Newbury House.

Fries, Charles C., and Kenneth L. Pike 1949. Coexistent phonemic systems. *Language* 25: 29–50.

Gal, Susan 1978. Peasant men can't get wives: language change and sex roles in a bilingual community. *Language in Society* 7: 1–16.

Gal, Susan 1979. *Language Shift: Social Determinants of Linguistic Change in Bilingual Austria*. New York: Academic Press.

Ganzeboom, Harry B. G., Ruud Luijkx and Donald J. Tremain 1989. Intergenerational class mobility in comparative perspective. *Research in Social Stratification and Mobility* 8: 3–84.

Gauchat, Louis 1905. L'unité phonétique dans le patois d'une commune. *Festschrift Heinreich Morf: Aus Romanischen Sprachen und Literaturen*. Halle: M. Niemeyer. 175–232.

Gibbs, James L. n.d. Social organizational studies in American anthropology. *Anthropology Series*, ed. Sol Tax. Voice of America Broadcast series. Washington, DC: U.S. Information Service. 90–7.

Giles, Howard, and P. F. Powesland 1975. *Speech Style and Social Evaluation*. London: Academic Press.

Gleason, H. A., Jr. 1961. *An Introduction to Descriptive Linguistics*. Revised ed. New York: Holt, Rinehart and Winston.

Gorski, Roger A. 1987. Sex differences in the rodent brain: their nature and origin. *Masculinity/Femininity: Basic Perspectives*, ed. June M. Reinisch, Leonard A. Rosenblum and Stephanie A. Sanders. New York and Oxford: Oxford University Press. 37–67.

Green, S. 1975. Dialects of Japanese monkeys: vocal learning and cultural transmission of locale specific behavior. *Zeitschrift fur Tierpsychologie* 57: 97–110.

Guy, Gregory 1980. Variation in the group and individual: the case of final stop deletion. *Locating Language in Time and Space*, ed. William Labov. New York: Academic Press. 1–36.

Guy, Gregory 1988. Language and social class. *Linguistics: The Cambridge Survey IV: Language: The Socio-Cultural Context*, ed. Frederick J. Newmeyer. Cambridge University Press. 37–63.

Habick, Timothy 1991. Burnouts versus Rednecks: effects of group membership on the phonemic system. *New Ways of Analyzing Sound Change*, ed. Penelope Eckert. San Diego: Academic Press. 185–212.

Haeri, Niloofar 1987. Male/female differences in speech: an alternative interpretation. *Variation in Language: NWAV-XV at Stanford*, ed. Keith M. Denning, Sharon Inkelas, Faye C. McNair-Knox and John R. Rickford. Stanford, California: Department of Linguistics, Standford University. 173–82.

Haggett, Peter, and Richard J. Chorley 1969. *Network Analysis in Geography*. London: Edward Arnold.

Halpern, Diane F. 1986. *Sex Differences in Cognitive Abilities*. Hillsdale NJ: Erlbaum.

Hardcastle, W. J. 1976. *Physiology of Speech Production: An Introduction for Speech Scientists*. London: Academic Press.

Helfrich, Hede 1979. Age markers in speech. *Social Markers in Speech*, ed. Klaus R. Scherer and Howard Giles. Cambridge: Cambridge University Press. 63–108.

Hermann, M. E. 1929. Lautveränderungen in der Individualsprache einer Mundart. *Nachrichten der Gesellschaft der Wissenschaften zu Göttingen* 11: 195–214.

Hibiya, Junko 1988. *A Quantitative Study of Tokyo Japanese*. PhD. dissertation. Department of Linguistics, University of Pennsylvania.

Hishinuma, Shigekazu 1976. *Historical Review on the Longevity of Human Beings*. Schaumburg, Illinois: Society of Actuaries.

Hockett, Charles F. 1955. *A Manual of Phonology*. Baltimore: Waverly Press.

Hockett, Charles F. 1958. *A Course in Modern Linguistics*. New York: Macmillan.

Hockett, Charles F. 1960. The origin of speech. *Scientific American* (September). 89–96.

Hockett, Charles F. 1965. Sound change. *Language* 41: 185–204.

Hodun, A., C. T. Snowdon and P. Soini 1981. Subspecific variation in the long call of the tamarin. *Zeitschrift fur Tierpsychologie* 57: 97–110.

Holmes, Janet 1992. *An Introduction to Sociolinguistics*. London and New York: Longman.

Horvath, Barbara M. 1985. *Variation in Australian English: The Sociolects of Sydney*. Cambridge: Cambridge University Press.

Horvath, Barbara, and David Sankoff 1987. Delimiting the Sydney speech community. *Language in Society* 16: 179–204.

Houston, Ann 1991. A grammatical continuum for (ING). *Dialects of English: Studies in Grammatical Variation*, ed. Peter Trudgill and J. K. Chambers. London and New York: Longman. 241–57.

Hoyenga, Katherine Blick, and Kermit T. Hoyenga 1979. *The Question of Sex Differences: Psychological, Cultural, and Biological Issues*. Boston and Toronto: Little, Brown and Company.

Hubbell, Alan F. 1950. *The Pronunciation of English in New York City*. New York: Columbia University Press.

Humboldt, Wilhelm von 1836. *Linguistic Variability and Intellectual Development*, trans. George C. Buck and Frithjof A. Raven. Philadelphia: University of Pennsylvania Press. 1972.

Hung, Henrietta, John Davison and J. K. Chambers 1993. Comparative sociolinguistics of (aw)-Fronting. *Focus on Canadian English*, ed. Sandra Clarke. Amsterdam, Philadelphia: John Benjamins. 247–67.

Hustead, Edwin C. 1989. *100 Years of Mortality*. Schaumburg, Illinois: Society of Actuaries.

Hyde, Janet Shibley 1981. How large are cognitive gender differences? a meta-analysis. *American Psychologist* 36: 892–901.

Hyde, Janet Shibley, and Marcia C. Linn 1988. Gender differences in verbal ability: a meta-analysis. *Psychological Bulletin* 104 (July): 53–69.

Ibrahim, Muhammad H. 1986. Standard and prestige language: a problem in Arabic sociolinguistics. *Anthropological Linguistics* 28: 115–26.

James, William. 1911. *Some Problems of Philosophy: A Beginning of an Introduction to Philosophy*. London, New York, Toronto: Longmans, Green and Co.

Jenkins, Peter F. 1985. Song learning, competition, and dialects. *The Behavioral and Brain Sciences* 8: 108.

Jespersen, Otto 1921. *Language: Its Nature, Development and Origin*. New York: W. W. Norton & Company. [1946].

Jespersen, Otto 1946. *Mankind, Nation and Individual from a Linguistic Point of View*. Bloomington: Indiana University Press. [1964].

Johnstone, Barbara 1990. Variation in discourse: Midwestern narrative style. *American Speech* 65: 195–214.

Johnstone, Barbara 1991. Individual style in an American public opinion survey: personal performance and the ideology of referentiality. *Language in Society* 20: 557–76.

Joos, Martin 1942. A phonological dilemma in Canadian English. *Language* 18: 141–4.

Joos, Martin 1950. Description of language design. *Journal of the Acoustical Society of America* 22: 701–8. In Joos 1957, 349–56.

Joos, Martin, ed. 1957. *Readings in Linguistics I: The Development of Descriptive Linguistics in America 1925–56*. Chicago and London: University of Chicago Press.

Kalin, R., D. S. Rayko and N. Love 1986. The perception and evaluation of job candidates with different ethnic accents. *Language: Social Psychological Perspectives*, ed. Howard Giles, W. P. Robinson and Philip M. Smith. Oxford: Pergamon Press.

Kalmar, Ivan, Zhong Yong and Xiao Hong 1987. Language attitudes in Guangzhou, China. *Language in Society* 16: 499–508.

Kerswill, Paul, and Ann Williams 1992. Some principles of dialect contact: evidence from the New Town of Milton Keynes. *Working Papers 1992: Occasional Papers in General and Applied Linguistics*. Department of Linguistic Science, University of Reading. 68–90.

Kimura, Doreen 1983. Sex differences in cerebral organizations for speech and praxic functions. *Canadian Journal of Psychology* 37: 19–35.

Kimura, Doreen 1987. Are men's and women's brains really different? *Canadian Psychology* 28: 133–47.

King, Ruth 1992. *Back* in Canadian French. Paper presented at the annual meeting of the Canadian Linguistic Association, Charlottetown, Prince Edward Island. 24 May.

King, Ruth 1993. Subject-verb agreement in Newfoundland French. Paper presented at NWAV 22, University of Ottawa.

Knowles, Gerry 1978. The nature of phonological variables in Scouse. *Sociolinguistic Patterns in British English*, ed. Peter Trudgill. London: Edward Arnold. 80–90.

Kontra, Miklós 1992. Class over nation – linguistic hierarchies eliminated: the case of Hungary. *Multilingua* 11: 217–21.

Kroch, Anthony 1978. Toward a theory of social dialect variation. *Language in Society* 7: 17–36.

Kroch, Anthony, and Cathy Small 1978. Grammatical ideology and its effect on speech. *Linguistic Variation: Models and Methods*, ed. David Sankoff. New York: Academic Press. 45–69.

Labov, William 1963. The social motivation of a sound change. *Word* 19: 273–309. Reprinted as chapter 1 of Labov (1972): 1–42.

Labov, William 1964. Stages in the acquisition of standard English. *Social Dialects and Language Learning*, ed. Roger Shuy. Champaign, Illinois: National Council of Teachers of English. 77–103.

Labov, William 1966. *The Social Stratification of English in New York City*. Washington, DC: Center for Applied Linguistics.

Labov, William 1966a. The linguistic variable as a structural unit. *Washington Linguistics Review* 3: 4–22.

Labov, William 1966b. The effect of social mobility on linguistic behavior. *Sociological Inquiry* 36: 186–203. Reprinted in *A Various Language: Perspectives on American Dialects*, ed. Juanita V. Williamson & Virginia M. Burke. New York: Holt, Rinehart and Winston. 1971. 640–59.

Labov, William 1969. Contraction, deletion, and inherent variability in the English copula. *Language* 45: 715–62. Revised in Labov 1972b, 65–129.

Labov, William 1970. The study of language in its social context. *Studium Generale* 23: 30–87.

Labov, William 1972. *Sociolinguistic Patterns*. University of Pennsylvania Press.

Labov, William 1972a. *Language in the Inner City: Studies in the Black English Vernacular*. University of Pennsylvania Press.

Labov, William 1975. *What is a Linguistic Fact?* Lisse: Peter De Ridder.

Labov, William 1980. The social origins of sound change. *Locating Language in Time and Space*, ed. William Labov. New York: Academic Press. 251–65.

Labov, William 1981. Resolving the Neogrammarian controversy. *Language* 57: 267–308.

Labov, William 1982. Building on empirical foundations. *Perspectives on Historical Linguistics*, ed. Winfred P. Lehmann and Yakov Malkiel. Amsterdam and Philadelphia: John Benjamins. 79–92.

Labov, William 1983. Language structure and social structure. Paper presented at the Conference on Qualitative and Quantitative Approaches to Social Theory. University of Chicago.

Labov, William 1984. The transmission of linguistic traits across and within communities. Symposium on Language Transmission and Change. Center for Advanced Study in the Behavioral Sciences, Stanford University.

Labov, William 1984a. Field methods of the Project on Linguistic Change and Variation. *Language in Use: Readings in Sociolinguistics*, ed. John Baugh and Joel Sherzer. Englewood Cliffs, NJ: Prentice-Hall. 28–53.

Labov, William 1989. The child as linguistic historian. *Language Variation and Change* 1: 85–97.

Labov, William 1990. The intersection of sex and social class in the course of linguistic change. *Language Variation and Change* 2: 205–54.

Labov, William 1991. The three dialects of English. *New Ways of Analyzing Sound Change*, ed. Penelope Eckert. New York: Academic Press. 1–44.

Labov, William 1994. *Principles of Linguistic Change*. Vol. I: *Internal Factors*. Oxford and Cambridge, MA: Basil Blackwell.

Labov, William, Paul Cohen, Clarence Robins and John Lewis 1968. *A Study of the Non-Standard English of Negro and Puerto Rican Speakers in New York City*. Cooperative Research Report 3288. New York: Columbia University.

Labov, William, Malcah Yaeger and Richard Steiner 1972. *A Quantitative Study of Sound Change in Progress.* Philadelphia, Pa.: The U.S. Regional Survery.

Ladefoged, Peter 1982. *A Course in Phonetics.* 2nd ed. New York: Harcourt Brace Jovanovich.

Laferriere, Martha 1979. Ethnicity in phonological variation and change. *Language* 55: 603–17.

Lakoff, Robin T. 1968. *Abstract Syntax and Latin Complementation.* Cambridge, MA, and London: The MIT Press.

Lakoff, Robin 1975. *Language and Women's Place.* New York: Harper & Row.

Lambert, Wallace 1967. A social psychology of bilingualism. *Journal of Social Issues* 23: 91–108.

Langer, Susanne K. 1942. *Philosophy in a New Key: A Study in the Symbolism of Reason, Rite, and Art.* Cambridge, MA: Harvard University Press.

Lass, Roger 1976 Epilogue: linguistics as metaphysics: on the rationality of non-empirical theories. *English Phonology and Phonological Theory: Synchronic and Diachronic Studies.* Cambridge: Cambridge University Press. 213–20.

Laurence, Margaret 1968. *The Stone Angel.* New York: Alfred A. Knopf.

LeBoeuf, B., and R. S. Peterson 1969. Dialects of elephant seals. *Science* 166: 1654–6.

Lindblom, Björn 1990. Explaining phonetic variation: a sketch of the H & H theory. *Speech Production and Speech Modelling,* ed. W. J. Hardcastle and A. Marchal. The Netherlands: Kluwer Academic. 403–39.

Lippi-Green, Rosina L. 1989. Social network integration and language change in progress in a rural alpine village. *Language in Society* 18: 213–34.

Littlejohn, James 1972. *Social Stratification.* London: George Allen & Unwin.

Locke, John 1690. *An Essay Concerning Human Understanding.* Dolphin Books. New York: Doubleday & Company.

Lombardi, Linda 1991. *Laryngeal Features and Laryngeal Neutralization.* PhD dissertation. University of Massachusetts, Amherst.

Macaulay, R. K. S. 1975. Negative prestige, linguistic insecurity, and linguistic self-hatred. *Lingua* 36: 147–61.

Macaulay, R. K. S. 1976. Social class and language in Glasgow. *Language in Society* 5: 173–88.

Macaulay, R. K. S. 1977. *Language, Social Class, and Education: A Glasgow Study.* Edinburgh: The University Press.

Maccoby, Eleanor Emmons, and Carol Nagy Jacklin 1974. *The Psychology of Sex Differences.* Stanford, CA: Stanford University Press.

Maclaran, Rose 1976. The variable (ʌ): a relic form with social correlates. *Belfast Working Papers on Language and Linguistics* 1: 45–68.

Malmberg, Bertil 1963. *Phonetics.* New York: Dover Books.

Marshall, J. T., and E. R. Marshall 1976. Gibbons and their territorial songs. *Science* 193: 235–7.

Martinet, André 1962. *A Functional View of Language.* Oxford: Oxford University Press.

McCormack, Mary 1985. *The Generation Gap: The View from Both Sides.* London: Constable.

McEwen, Bruce S. 1987. Observations on brain sexual differentiation: a biochemist's view. *Masculinity/ Femininity: Basic Perspectives*, ed. June M. Reinisch, Leonard A. Rosenblum and Stephanie A. Sanders. New York and Oxford: Oxford University Press. 68–79.

Mead, Margaret 1953. National character. *Anthropology To-day*, ed. A. L. Kroeber. Chicago: University of Chicago Press. 642–67.

Mencken, H. L. 1919. *The American Language: An Inquiry into the Development of English in the United States*. New York: Alfred A. Knopf.

Miller, Casey, and Kate Swift 1976. *Words and Women*. Garden City, New York: Anchor Press, Doubleday.

Miller, L. 1987. The professional construction of aging. *Journal of Gerontological Social Work* 10: 141–53.

Milroy, James 1980. Lexical alternation and the history of English: evidence from an urban vernacular. *Papers from the 4th International Conference on Historical Linguistics*, ed. Elizabeth C. Traugott, R. Labrum and S. Shepherd. Amsterdam: John Benjamins B. V. 355–62.

Milroy, James 1992. *Linguistic Variation and Change: On the Historical Sociolinguistics of English*. Oxford: Blackwell.

Milroy, James, and Lesley Milroy 1978. Belfast: change and variation in an urban vernacular. *Sociolinguistic Patterns in British English*, ed. Peter Trudgill. London: Edward Arnold. 19–36.

Milroy, James, and Lesley Milroy 1985. Linguistic change, social network and speaker innovation. *Journal of Linguistics* 21: 339–84.

Milroy, Lesley 1976. Phonological correlates to community structure in Belfast. *Belfast Working Papers on Language and Linguistics* 1: 1–44.

Milroy, Lesley 1980. *Language and Social Networks*. Oxford: Basil Blackwell.

Milroy, Lesley 1987. *Observing and Analysing Natural Language: A Critical Account of Sociolinguistic Method*. Oxford: Basil Blackwell.

Milroy, Lesley, and James Milroy 1992. Social network and social class: toward an integrated sociolinguistic model. *Language in Society* 21: 1–26.

Modaressi-Tehrani, Yahya 1978. *A Sociolinguistic Analysis of Modern Persian*. PhD dissertation. Department of Linguistics, University of Kansas.

Moroney, M. J. 1957. *Facts from Figures*. Harmondsworth: Penguin Books.

Morris, Richard 1903. *Historical Outlines of English Accidence*, revised by L. Kellner and Henry Bradley. London: Macmillan and Co.

Moulton, William G. 1985. Bird-song dialects and human-language dialects. *The Behavioral and Brain Sciences* 8: 110–11.

Munro, Alice 1983. *The Moons of Jupiter*. Harmondsworth: Penguin Books.

Munro, Pamela 1989. *Slang U*. New York: Harmony Books.

Murray, Thomas E. 1985. On solving the dilemma of the Hawthorne effect. *Papers from the Fifth International Conference on Methods in Dialectology*, ed. Henry J. Warkentyne. Victoria, B.C.: Department of Linguistics, University of Victoria. 327–40.

Naro, Anthony J. 1980. Review article of *Models and Methods*, ed. David Sankoff. *Language* 56: 158–70.

Nichols, Patricia C. 1983. Linguistic options and choices for Black women in the rural South. *Language, Gender and Society*, ed. Barrie Thorne, Cheris Kramarae and Nancy Henley. Rowley, MS: Newbury House. 54–68.

Notman, M. T., and C. C. Nadelson 1973 Medicine: a career conflict for women. *American Journal of Psychiatry* 130: 1123–7.

Nunberg, Geoffrey 1980. A falsely reported merger in eighteenth-century English: a study in diachronic variation. *Locating Language in Time and Space*, ed. William Labov. New York: Academic Press. 221–50.

Odlin, Terence 1989. *Language Transfer: Cross-Linguistic Influence in Language Learning*. Cambridge: Cambridge University Press.

Orton, Harold 1962. *Survey of English Dialects: Introduction*. Leeds: E. J. Arnold.

Orton, Harold, and P. M. Tilling, eds. 1969–71. *Survey of English Dialects, The Basic Material*, Vol. III (3 Parts): *The East Midland Counties and East Anglia*. Leeds: E. J. Arnold.

Ounsted, Christoper, and David C. Taylor 1972. The Y chromosome message: a point of view. *Gender Differences: Their Ontogeny and Significance*, ed. Christopher Ounsted and David C. Taylor. Edinburgh and London: Churchill Livingstone. 241–62.

Paddock, Harold 1981. *A Dialect Survey of Carbonear, Newfoundland*. Publication of the American Dialect Society No. 68. University, AL: University of Albabama Press.

Payne, Arvilla C. 1980. Factors controlling the acquisition of the Philadelphia dialect by out-of-state children. *Locating Language in Time and Space*, ed. William Labov. New York: Academic Press. 143–78.

Peller, S. 1947. Studies on mortality since the Renaissance. *Bulletin of the History of Medicine* 21: 51–101.

Petrinovich, L., and T. L. Patterson 1981. The responses of white-crowned sparrows to songs of different dialects and subspecies. *Zeitschrift fur Tierpsychologie* 57: 1–14.

Pinker, Steven, and Alan Prince 1988. On language and connectionism: analysis of a parallel distributed processing model of language acquisition. *Cognition* 28: 73–193.

Pirsig, Robert 1991. *Lila: An Inquiry into Morals*. New York and Toronto: Bantam Books.

Poplack, Shana 1980. 'Sometimes I'll start a sentence in English y termino en español': toward a typology of code-switching. *Linguistics* 18: 581–618.

Poplack, Shana 1981. Bilingualism and the vernacular. *Issues in International Bilingual Education*, ed. B. Hartford, Albert Valdman and C. Foster. New York: Plenum Press. 1-24.

Poplack, Shana 1983. Bilingual competence: linguistic interference or grammatical integrity? *Spanish in the United States Beyond the Southwest*, ed. L. Elías-Olivares. Arlington, Virginia: National Clearinghouse for Bilingual Education. 107–31.

Poplack, Shana 1988. Language status and language accommodation along a linguistic border. *Language Spread and Language Policy: Issues, Implications and Case Studies*, ed. Peter H. Lowenberg. Washington, DC: Georgetown University Press. 90–118.

Poplack, Shana 1989. The care and handling of a megacorpus: the Ottawa-Hull French project. *Language Variation and Change*, ed. Ralph Fasold and Deborah Schiffrin. Amsterdam: John Benjamins. 411–44.

Poplack, Shana, and David Sankoff 1984. Borrowing: the synchrony of integration. *Linguistics* 22: 99–135.

Preston, Dennis R. 1989. *Sociolinguistics and Second Language Acquisition*. Oxford: Basil Blackwell.

Priestley, F. E. L. 1951. Canadian English. *British and American English since 1900*, ed. Eric Partridge and John W. Clark. London: Andrew Dakers. 72-9.

Ramist, L., and S. Arbeiter 1986. *Profiles of College-Bound Seniors 1985*. New York: College Entrance Examinations Board.

Rand, David, and David Sankoff 1990. *GoldVarb: A Variable Rule Application for the Macintosh*. Montréal: Centre de recherches mathématiques, Université de Montréal.

Read, Allen Walker 1933. British recognition of American speech in the eighteenth century. *Dialect Notes* VI. Reprinted in *Perspectives on American English*, ed. J. L. Dillard. The Hague: Mouton. 15–36.

Read, Herbert 1940. The philosophy of anarchism. *Anarchy and Order: Essays in Politics*. Boston: Beacon Press. 1971. 35–58.

Reid, Euan 1978. Social and stylistic variation in the speech of children: some evidence from Edinburgh. *Sociolinguistic Patterns in British English*, ed. Peter Trudgill. London: Edward Arnold. 158–71.

Rescher, Nicholas 1969. *Many-Valued Logic*. New York: McGraw-Hill.

Rew, George 1990. Wa'er. *The Scots Magazine* (February): 497–501.

Rogers, Henry 1991. *Theoretical and Practical Phonetics*. Toronto: Copp Clark Pitman.

Romaine, Suzanne 1978. Postvocalic /r/ in Scottish English: sound change in progress? *Sociolinguistic Patterns in British English*, ed. Peter Trudgill. London: Edward Arnold. 144–56.

Romaine, Suzanne 1980. A critical overview of the methodology of urban British sociolinguistics. *English World-Wide* 1: 163–98.

Romaine, Suzanne 1984. *The Language of Children and Adolescents: The Acquisition of Communicative Competence*. Oxford: Basil Blackwell.

Romaine, Suzanne 1988. *Pidgin and Creole Languages*. London and New York: Longman.

Ross, Elliot 1982. The divided self. *The Sciences* (February): 8–12.

Ross, John Robert 1967. *Constraints on Variables in Syntax*. PhD dissertation. Department of Philosophy and Linguistics, Massachusetts Institute of Technology.

Rousseau, Pascale, and David Sankoff 1978. Advances in variable rule methodology. *Linguistic Variation: Models and Methods*, ed. David Sankoff. New York: Academic Press. 57–69.

Ryan, Ellen Bouchard 1979. Why do low-prestige language varieties persist? *Language and Social Psychology*, ed. Howard Giles and Robert St. Clair. Oxford: Basil Blackwell. 145–57.

Salam, A. M. 1980. Phonological variation in educated spoken Arabic: a study of the uvular and related plosive types. *Bulletin of the School of Oriental and African Studies* XLII: 77–100.

Sankoff, David 1985. Statistics in Linguistics. *Encyclopedia of Statistical Sciences*, Vol. 5. New York: John Wiley & Sons.

Sankoff, David 1988. Sociolinguistics and syntactic variation. *Linguistics: The Cambridge Survey*. Vol. IV: *Language: The Socio-cultural Context*, ed. Frederick J. Newmeyer. Cambridge University Press. 140–61.

Sankoff, David, and Suzanne Laberge 1978. The linguistic market and the statisitical explanation of variability. *Linguistic Variation: Models and Methods*, ed. David Sankoff. New York: Academic Press. 239–50.

Sankoff, David, Henrietta Cedergren, William Kemp, Pierrette Thibault and Diane Vincent 1989. Montreal French: language, class and ideology. *Language Change and Variation*, ed. Ralph Fasold and Deborah Schiffrin. Amsterdam and Philadelphia: John Benjamins. 107–18.

Sankoff, David, and Gillian Sankoff 1973. Sample survey methods and computer assisted analysis in the study of grammatical variation. *Canadian Languages in Their Social Context*, ed. Regna Darnell. Edmonton: Linguistic Research Inc. 7–64.

Sankoff, Gillian 1974. A quantitative paradigm for the study of communicative competence. *Explorations in the Ethnography of Speaking*, ed. R. Bauman and Joel Sherzer. Cambridge University Press. 18–49. Reprinted in *The Social Life of Language*, ed. Gillian Sankoff. University of Pennsylvania Press. 1980. 47–80.

Sankoff, Gillian 1976. Political power and linguistic inequality in Papua New Guinea. *The Social Life of Language*, ed. Gillian Sankoff. University of Pennsylvania Press. 1980. 5–28.

Sankoff, Gillian, and Pierrette Thibault 1980. The alternation between the auxiliaries *avoir* and *être* in Montréal French. [Originally 1977 "L'alternance entre les auxiliaires *avoir* et *être* en français parlé à Montréal", *Langue Française*, 34: 81–108.] *The Social Life of Language*, ed. Gillian Sankoff. University of Pennsylvania Press. 311–45.

Sapir, Edward 1921. *Language: An Introduction to the Study of Speech*. New York: Harcourt, Brace and Company. 1949.

Sapir, Edward 1927. Speech as a personality trait. *American Journal of Sociology* 32: 892–905. *Selected Writings of Edward Sapir in Language, Culture and Personality*, ed. David G. Mandelbaum. Berkeley and Los Angeles: University of California Press, 1968. 533–43.

Sapir, Edward 1929. The status of Linguistics as a science. *Language* 5: 207–14. *Selected Writings of Edward Sapir in Language, Culture and Personality*, ed. David G. Mandelbaum. Berkeley and Los Angeles: University of California Press, 1968. 160–6.

Sapir, Edward 1933. Language. *Encyclopedia of the Social Sciences*. Vol. 9. New York: Macmillan. 155–69. *Selected Writings of Edward Sapir in Language, Culture and Personality*, ed. David G. Mandelbaum. Berkeley and Los Angeles: University of California Press, 1968. 7–32.

Saussure, Ferdinand de 1916. *Course in General Linguistics*, ed. Charles Bally and Albert Sechehaye, trans. Wade Baskin. New York and Toronto: McGraw-Hill. 1966.

Schmidt, Richard W. 1974. *Sociolinguistic Variation in Spoken Arabic in Egypt: A*

Re-Examination of the Concept of Diglossia. PhD dissertation. Department of Linguistics, Brown University.

Schuchardt, Hugo 1972 [1885] On sound laws: against the Neogrammarians. *Schuchardt, the Neogrammarians, and the Transformational Theory of Phonological Change*, ed. Theo Vennemann and Terence Wilbur. Frankfurt: Athenaeum. 39–72.

Shaw, Artie 1952. *The Trouble with Cinderella: An Outline of Identity*. New York: Collier Books.

Sherman, Julia A. 1978. *Sex-Related Cognitive Differences: An Essay on Theory and Evidence*. Springfield, Illinois: Charles C. Thomas.

Shuy, Roger W. 1983. Unexpected by-products of fieldwork. *American Speech* 58: 345–58.

Shuy, Roger W., Walter A. Wolfram, and William K. Riley 1968. *Field Techniques in an Urban Language Study*. Washington, DC: Center for Applied Linguistics.

Slater, P. J. B. 1985. White rats and general theories. *The Behavioral and Brain Sciences* 8: 115–16.

Slater, P. J. B., F. A. Clements and D. J. Goodfellow 1984. Local and regional variants in chaffinch song and the question of dialects. *Behavior* 88: 76–97.

Smith, William 1850. *Dictionary of Greek Biography and Mythology*. 3 vols. London: Taylor, Walton, and Maberly.

Snowdon, C. T., C. H. Brown, and M. R. Peterson, eds. 1982. *Primate Communication*. Cambridge University Press.

Spender, Dale 1980. *Man Made Language*. London: Routledge and Kegan Paul.

Stampe, David 1969. The acquisition of phonetic representation. *Papers from the Fifth Regional Meeting of the Chicago Linguistic Society*: 443–54.

Stewart, Ian 1990. *Does God Play Dice? The Mathematics of Chaos*. Oxford and Cambridge, MA: Basil Blackwell.

Tannen, Deborah 1984. *Conversational Style: Analyzing Talk Among Friends*. Norwood, NJ: Ablex.

Tannen, Deborah 1987. Repetition in conversation: toward a poetics of talk. *Language* 63: 574–605.

Tarone, Elaine 1988. *Variation in Interlanguage*. London: Edward Arnold.

Taylor, David C., and Christopher Ounsted 1972. The nature of gender differences explored through ontogenetic analyses of sex ratios in disease. *Gender Differences: Their Ontogeny and Significance*, ed. Christopher Ounsted and David C. Taylor. Edinburgh and London: Churchill Livingstone. 215–40.

Taylor, Douglas 1971. Grammatical and lexical affinities of creoles. *Pidginization and Creolization of Languages*, ed. Dell Hymes. Cambridge: Cambridge University Press. 293–6.

Taylor, John R. 1989. *Linguistic Categorization: Prototypes in Linguistic Theory*. Oxford: Clarendon Press.

Thibault, Pierrette, et Michelle Daveluy 1989. Quelques traces du passage du temps dans le parler des Montréalais 1971–1984. *Language Variation and Change* 1: 19–46.

Trudgill, Peter 1972. Sex, covert prestige, and linguistic change in the urban British English of Norwich. *Language in Society* 1: 179–96.

Trudgill, Peter 1974. *The Social Differentiation of English in Norwich*. Cambridge: Cambridge University Press.

Trudgill, Peter 1983. *On Dialect: Social and Geographic Factors*. Oxford: Basil Blackwell.

Trudgill, Peter 1983a. *Sociolinguistics: An Introduction to Language and Society*. Revised edition. Harmondsworth: Penguin Books.

Trudgill, Peter 1986. *Dialects in Contact*. Oxford: Basil Blackwell.

Trudgill, Peter 1988. Norwich revisited: recent linguistic changes in an English urban dialect. *English World-Wide* 9: 33–49.

Trudgill, Peter, and J. K. Chambers 1991. *Dialects of English: Studies in Grammatical Variation*. London and New York: Longman.

Turner, Lorenzo D. 1949. *Africanisms in the Gullah Dialect*. Chicago: University of Chicago Press.

Vandenberg, Steven G. 1987. Sex differences in mental retardation and their implications for sex differences in ability. *Maculinity / Femininity: Basic Perspectives*, ed. June M. Reinisch, Leonard A. Rosenblum and Stephanie A. Sanders. New York and Oxford: Oxford University Press. 157–71.

Wang, William S-Y. 1969. Competing changes as a cause of residue. *Language* 45: 9–25.

Wang, William S-Y. 1977. *The Lexicon in Phonological Change*. The Hague: Mouton.

Wang, William S-Y., and Chin-Chuan Cheng 1970. Implementation of phonological change: the Shûang-fêng case. *Chicago Linguistic Society* 6: 552–7.

Wardhaugh, Ronald 1985. *How Conversation Works*. Oxford: Basil Blackwell.

Wardhaugh, Ronald 1992. *An Introduction to Sociolinguistics*. 2nd ed. Oxford: Basil Blackwell.

Weinreich, Uriel 1953. *Languages in Contact: Findings and Problems*. With a Preface by André Martinet. Publications of the Linguistic Circle of New York, No. 1. Reprinted 1963. The Hague: Mouton & Co.

Weinreich, Uriel, William Labov and Marvin I. Herzog 1968. Empirical foundations for a theory of language change. *Directions for Historical Linguistics: A Symposium*, ed. Winfred P. Lehmann and Yakov Malkiel. Austin: University of Texas Press. 95–188.

Wells, J. C. 1982. *Accents of English 1: An Introduction*. Cambridge: Cambridge University Press.

Williams, Glyn 1992. *Sociolinguistics: A Sociological Critique*. London and New York: Routledge.

Winter, P. 1969. Dialects in squirrel monkeys: vocalizations of the Roman arch type. *Folia Primatologica* 10: 216–29.

Wolff, Hans 1959. Intelligibility and inter-ethnic attitudes. *Anthropological Linguistics* 1: 34–41.

Wolfram, Walter A. 1969. *A Sociolinguistic Description of Detroit Negro Speech*. Washington, DC: Center for Applied Linguistics.

Wolfram, Walt 1989. Structural variability in phonological development: final nasals in Vernacular Black English. *Language Change and Variation*, ed. Ralph W. Fasold and Deborah Schiffrin. Amsterdam, Philadelphia: John Benjamins. 301–32.

Wolfram, Walt 1991. The linguistic variable: fact and fantasy. *American Speech* 66: 22–32.

Wolfram, Walt, and Donna Christian 1976. *Appalachian Speech*. Washington: Center for Applied Linguistics.

Wolfram, Walter, and Ralph W. Fasold 1974. *The Study of Social Dialects in American English*. Englewood Cliffs, NJ: Prentice-Hall.

Woods, Howard B. 1979. *A Socio-Dialectal Survey of the English Spoken in Ottawa: A Study of the Sociological and Stylistic Variation in Canadian English*. PhD thesis. Department of Linguistics, University of British Columbia.

Woods, Howard B. 1991. Social differentiation in Ottawa English. *English Around the World: Sociolinguistic Perspectives*, ed. Jenny Cheshire. Cambridge: Cambridge University Press. 134–49.

Xu Daming 1992. *A Sociolinguistic Study of Mandarin Nasal Variation*. PhD thesis. Department of Linguistics, University of Ottawa.

Yaeger-Dror, Malcah 1989. Real time and apparent time change in Montréal French. *York Papers in Linguistics* 13: 141–54.

Yoneda, Masato 1993. Survey of standardization in Tsuruoka City, Japan: Comparison of results from three surveys conducted at twenty-year intervals. Paper presented at Methods VIII: International Conference in Dialectology. University of Victoria, British Columbia.

Zadeh, Lotfi A. 1965. Fuzzy sets. *Information and Control* 8: 338–53.

Zeller, Christine 1993. The investigation of a sound change in progress: /æ/ to /e/ in Midwestern American English. Paper presented at NWAV 22, University of Ottawa.

Index